Ben Jonson

His Dramatic Art

Other Titles in English Literature Series

G.B. Shaw: A Critical Response
Sudhakar Pandey and *Freya Barua*

George Bernard Shaw
Vinod Bala Sharma

Goldsmith and Sentimental Comedy
B.S. Pathania

Fictional Theories and Three English Novels
Asha Kanwar

Virginia Wolf and Anita Desai: A Comparative Study
Asha Kanwar

The Novels of Virginia Woolf
B. Sudipta

The Novels of Graham Greene
P.N. Pandit

Kipling's Vision
Sukeshi Kamra

W.H. Auden: The Commissar and the Yogi
M.K. Raju

W.B. Yeats
Rajeshwari Patel

BEN JONSON

His Dramatic Art

K. VENKATA REDDY

PRESTIGE

Published by
Prestige Books
New Delhi 110 008

1994
ISBN: 81-85218-86-2

Typesetting by
Pivot Computers
Delhi 110 006
Ph. 2918404

Printed at
Mehra Offset Press
Delhi 110 006

CONTENTS

I would bring my Precepts into practice.

Ben Jonson, *Discoveries*, ll. 1756-57

For

Prof. M.V. Rama Sarma, M.A., Ph.D (Wales)

In Gratitude and Affection

My praise is plain and wheresoever professed

Becomes none more than you, who need it least.

PREFACE

Ben Jonson has, in the past, suffered more than any other dramatist of the age from invidious comparison with Shakespeare. In the eighteenth century, his personality was reviled, though his plays were enjoyed and his criticism respected. But, his reputation suffered an almost total eclipse in the nineteenth century, as Jonson had neither the lyricism, the responsiveness to nature, nor the interest in the character that the romantic movement demanded of its idols. The twentieth century, however, has seen the rescue of Jonson from his undeserved obscurity and his introduction to a wider audience. It was Jonson's essay, "Ben Jonson," (*Selected Essays*, Faber, 1932) that provided the framework for growing critical respect, and, what is more, post-Eliot interest in the theme, structure and conscious artistry have done Jonson great service. Since then, a number of critics – J. Palmer (1934), L.C. Knights (1937), W.C. Wheeler (1938), H.W. Baum (1939), A.H. Sackton (1948), Marchette Chute (1953), E.B. Partridge (1958), J.J. Enck (1958), Bamborough (1959), Jonas A. Barish (1960), C.G. Thayer (1963), R.E. Knoll (1964), G.B. Jackson (1968), A.C. Dessen (1971), J.A. Bryant (1971), G. Parfitt (1976), A. Leggatt (1981), Richard Dutton (1983), Anne Barton (1984), Peter Womack (1986), Rosalind Miles (1990), D.H. Craig (1990) and Richard Allen Cave (1991) – have contributed a good deal to Jonson criticism, examining his plays from different modernist viewpoints.

All the same, as C.G. Thayer rightly observes, 'there will be no end to Jonson studies, because the wealth of his genius is inexhaustible.' This statement is only endorsed by the common feeling that no commentary ever exhausts the work of a great creative artist. Although Jonson was wedded to 'the Ancients' he was refreshingly avant-garde, and he remained to the end eclectic and experimental, always willing to try new forms and themes in the restless search for perfection and high status. And, as Richard Dutton (*Ben Jonson*, London: Cambridge University Press, 1983) points out, for all that Jonson's major works are rooted in the concerns of his own age, "they are far more accessible and relevant to modern readers than is often assumed." Besides Anne Barton's brilliant study (*Ben Jonson, Dramatist*, Cambridge: Cambridge University Press, 1984), brings us closer than ever before, to Jonson as a great artist in comedy, describing in detail his experimentation with different comic styles and his changing relationship to other Elizabethan and Jacobean poets.

Yet another recent study of Ben Jonson by Peter Womack (*Ben Jonson*, New York: Basil Blackwell, 1987), in its subtle interweaving of textual analysis, social history, cultural theory and, above all, a magnificent sense of theatre, rescues Jonson simultaneously from the classical humanists and the romantic populists, and delivers us a Jonson who is not only readable, but usable, for our own times. On top of that, the detailed portrait of the growth and development of Jonson as a creative artist unique in his own time and rare in any other, most recently given by Rosalind Miles (*Ben Jonson: His Craft and Art*, London: Routledge, 1990) shows that the more we know, the more there is in Jonson to appreciate critically.

Hence, hope for a rediscovery in the 1990s of Jonson's achievement in drama need not appear misplaced. It is as much out of this belief as out of my own interest in Jonson that I undertook the present study which is consciously confined to Jonson's comedies.

The aim of the present book is to make a close and objective study of Jonson's dramatic theory and practice related to his comedies with a view to showing that Jonson is essentially a dramatic artist. It is hoped that an analysis of the inter-relationship of his dramatic theory and practice would help appreciate his dramatic art better.

No doubt, Jonson's theories and practices of drama have sporadically been touched upon by critics like Baskervill, Gregory Smith, and particularly by Elisabeth Woodbridge and Helena Watts Baum. But then, Baskervill is concerned mainly with the theory of 'humours,' limiting his study of Jonson's early comedies only. Gregory Smith just casually states Jonson's theory of comedy, but does not examine the plays in the light of the theory. Woodbridge has confined herself to character treatment and structural features, and Baum to the didactic and the satiric in Jonson's comedy. Even the most recent critics of Jonson like D.H. Craig (*Ben Jonson: The Critical Heritage,* London: Routledge, 1990) and Richard Allen Cave (*Ben Jonson*, London: Macmillan, 1991), who have offered scholarly, critical perspectives on Jonson's works, have not concerned themselves with his dramatic theory and practice.

Hence the need and justification for yet another book on Jonson which seeks to throw some fresh light on his dramatic art by way of examining his plays in the light of his dramatic theory. As we see Jonson at his work, share his struggle with form and content, with reader and audience, and experience the pattern of his failure and success, he emerges as a much more powerful and vital dramatist than the Jonson of literary and critical tradition.

It is, perhaps, not correct to say that Jonson the dramatic practitioner was cramped by his own theories. For, a consciously practised theory of art need not necessarily spoil a good artist nor damp inspiration, but rather canalize it. Besides, theories are all the more necessary at moments when old traditions break up and when all is in a flux exactly as was the case when Jonson appeared on the scene. Again, the deliberateness with which Jonson wrote is not necessarily uninspired, nor his use of literary tradition necessarily uncreative. The fact that Jonson is a theorist and a critic need not preclude him from being a great artist also.

It is not as though Jonson wrote comedies because he has a definite theory about comedy. His earnest desire to analyse and think about his writing does not make him a desiccated theorist. One should not, however, too readily assume that Jonson's dramatic practice squared rigidly with his critical precepts. For, the mere culling of all the lines from the Prologues, Epilogues, Inductions, and critical inter-act choruses of his plays in which he expresses his dramatic theory, will not give quite an adequate conception of his actual work. This is especially true of his comedies where his artisitic sense sometimes compelled him to depart, as a practitioner, from some of his own principles as a theorist. Jonson, then, is essentially a dramatic artist, and his dramatic theory is only a means to achieve artistic excellence. Once we approach Jonson from this angle, he can be fully appreciated, and we get a proper perspective of his dramatic art.

The book is divided into nine chapters. The first chapter is by way of a general introduction to Jonson the playwright, the emphasis being on the social and literary climate of the 1590s, his reaction to the state and condition of the contemporary drama, his independent attitude to classicism and his intellectual outfit for the self-appointed task of reforming the Elizabethan drama.

The second chapter deals with Jonson's theories of comedy and tragedy, testifying to his endeavour to achieve a harmonious fusion of the classical and native traditions in the theatre. In the third and fourth chapters, Jonson's work has been examined from the point of view of its realism, indicating, however, that he is not a narrow transcriber of mere fact. It is shown how there is in Jonson's plays, an interplay between realism and fantasy that gives his comedy the unity and the universality of great art.

The fifth chapter is intended to bring out the didactic and the aesthetic elements in Jonson's comedies while maintaining that Jonson is not a conventional moralist, but essentially a comic dramatist using the didactic theory for literary and dramatic purposes. The sixth chapter seeks to present the satirical content of Jonson's comedies, making it clear that his relentlessness is born of his intellectual indignation as well as of his artistic integrity.

While the seventh chapter is concerned with Jonson's art of comic characterisation, it is indicated that not all his characters are of 'humours' type, and that he is also capable of creating immortal, individualised characters when the occasion demands. It is shown how Jonson's characters have both an intellectual consistency and a universal significance. In the eighth chapter an attempt is made to show how the structural unity of Jonson's comedies is at once linear and thematic or symbolic, two levels of meaning being carried on a single action, each complementing the other. The final chapter is devoted to a close and critical study of *Bartholomew Fair*, revealing that it is a perfect fulfilment of the 'Comedy of Humours,' representing as it does the culmination of Jonson's dramatic art.

In conclusion, it is maintained that Jonson has done what he set out to do, but by remaining a dramatic artist. Being a native classicist, he deliberately imposed a great many limitations on his art as a dramatist. Hence, his so-called deficiencies—exotic locations, a taste for young love, absence of charm, colourful portrayal of characters, the lack of appeal to sentiment and emotion, responsiveness to nature and the vicissitudes of the human lot—are not in truth deficiencies at all, but the outcome of an artistic principle of deliberate exclusion. Jonson's mode of drama is properly and intentionally different from Shakespeare's, and we must necessarily grasp this point to begin enjoying Jonson. Above all, a just appreciation of Jonson's achievement as a dramatist, particularly his greatness as a writer of comedy, demands a careful and close study, and a certain intellectual activity, rather an 'intelligent saturation' in his work as a whole.

This book brings to a close, over thirty years' biographical and critical study of Jonson during which I have incurred innumerable debts of gratitude to friends and scholars throughout the academic world and the libraries that minister to us. Another immeasurable debt is to the work of other Jonsonians, and especially to the eleven volume edition of Jonson's works by C.H. Herford and Percy and Evelyn Simpson (Oxford, 1925-52). All the quotations from Jonson's works are from this monumental edition.

My most profound indebtedness I have tried to acknowledge in my dedication. It is Professor M.V. Rama Sarma, an erudite scholar of the Elizabethan literature, who initiated me into Jonson studies and guided me in my academic career from the beginning with great care, love and affection. I am deeply beholden to Professor Harold F. Brooks and Professor John Russell Brown for their keen interest in my work and for their kind suggestions and invaluable criticisms.

Sri Krishnadevaraya University **K. Venkata Reddy**
Anantapur
January 1994

Abbreviations

EC	*Essays in Criticism*
ELH	*English Literary History*
ES	*Essays and Studies*
HLQ	*Huntington Library Quarterly*
JEGP	*Journal of English and Germanic Philology*
KR	*Kenyan Review*
MLN	*Modern Language Notes*
MLR	*Modern Language Review*
MP	*Modern Philology*
NQ	*Notes and Queries*
PMLA	*Publications of the Modern Language Association*
PQ	*Philological Quarterly*
RES	*Review of English Studies*
SEL	*Studies in English Literature*
SP	*Studies in Philology*
SQ	*Shakespeare's Quarterly*
SR	*Southern Review*
TLS	*Times Literary Supplement*
VQR	*Virginia Quarterly Review*

Ben Jonson and His Times

During the last part of Elizabeth's reign, by the middle of the 1590, there emerged, as successors to the 'University Wits,' a new group of writers aptly called the Elizabethan 'Angry Young Men'[1] who brought about a radical change in the world of theatre. They were ingenious and uncompromising literary men who saw life in a new way. Like the 'University Wits' they were intellectuals; but unlike Marlowe and his friends they were not bohemians. While their predecessors had been essentially romantic and idealistic, the 'Angry Young Men' were down-to-earth. They were fundamentally serious-minded scholars with a satiric bent of mind. Their interest was pre-eminently in the unvarnished, the odd and even the unpleasant sides of life. Hence their determined effort to use the anti-romantic method with the ostensible purpose of presenting social criticism generally satiric in spirit.

The 'Angry Young Men,' however, became dominating men of letters of the day, and their coming to prominence was greatly encouraged by the very spirit of the times. As R.W. Chambers has rightly pointed out, "these later Elizabethan days had been glorious, but yet no 'halcyon days of happy ease.'"[2] Owing to various factors—political, social, economic and literary—the obtaining ethos at this juncture was one of anxiety, despondency and disillusionment, as opposed to the buoyancy, radiance, vitality and gusto of the immediately-preceding period.

Politically a sense of insecurity and instability came mainly from "the memory of the crises of the past three accessions and of the series of plots to assassinate the Queen throughout her reign combined with the knowledge that there was no obvious heir to the throne at her death."[3] Consequently dissent of various kinds seemed to disrupt national unity.

Regarding the social aspect, there began to appear a perceptible change in the structure of society of the day. As a result of the all-absorbing excitement of the Spanish wars and the flux of political and social adjustment, "the lines between the different ranks of the people grew hard and rigid, and the world of fashion evolved a code of manners complex and artifical to a degree previously unknown. The opposition between the court and city circles and between town and country habits was sharply, even bitterly accentuated."[4]

Then, the economic expansion of the period was accompanied by the severe depressions at home[5] largely owing to the closing of continental markets under Elizabeth's control. As L.C. Knights points out, "in the years 1594-1597 there was a great dearth of corn, tillage was described as being very greatly decayed, and there were frequent bread riots; there was much unemployment in the clothing-trade, and 'the whole trade of the city was described as being much impaired and its traffic greatly diminished.' Plague, moreover, had been intermittent throughout the 'nineties."[6]

The economic problems, in this manner, became unavoidably obtrusive "placing in relief the individual struggle to retain some control over one's worldly conditions."[7] It was no longer easy to believe that all things were possible to any man. Thus, step by step, the exaltation and confidence of the heroic age seemed to lose its bloom in the last decade of Elizabeth's reign. The sentiment of expectation changed to a sense of weariness, depression and disillusionment. Then, it looked as though the native hue of Elizabethan resolution was already sicklied over with the pale cast of Jacobean melancholy.

Also, the economic instability of the 1590s resulted in the revival of satire. The concentration of wealth in the hands of a few with its corresponding spread of luxury, the steady drift of gentlemen from the simplicity of country life to the disorder of the town, the domination of the metropolis by a sophisticated and pleasure-loving court – all seemed to cry aloud for the lash of the satirist. And "frustrated in his hopes of patronage, disgusted by the flourishing of social pretenders in City and Court alike, and more conscious than ever before both of the dignity and the insecurity of his calling, the man of letters turned to satire as a corrective of public morals through which he could also give vent to his personal discontent."[8]

Besides, the decade of the 1590s was the flowering time of the English Renaissance. The humanist triumph which had been prepared by Wilson's *Art of Rhetoric* (1553) and *Ascham's Schoolmaster* (1570) and which had been well advanced in the years following *The Shepherd's Calendar* (1579) was by now fully accomplished, with the posthumous appearance of Sidney's *Arcadia* and his sonnets (1590-91) and Spenser's publication of *The Faerie Queene* (1590-96).[9] In consequence, there came over English a tidal wave of neo-classical inspiration. Writers seemed to vie with one another in listing new English poets for comparison with the famous authors of Italy and ancient Rome. The climate of the period was thus congenial to the flourishing of the 'Angry Young Men.'

On top of that, by the end of the century "professional drama was beginning to show a cleavage along class lines."[10] The citizens seemed to take less interest in attending the theatres. Consequently the audiences were made up mainly of courtiers and cavaliers. The theatres were rapidly becoming the exclusive property of the elite. The dramatic companies, therefore, began to concentrate on the private theatres which "evidently attracted more playgoers, since performances in them became more frequent then."[11]

The Elizabethan 'Angry Young Men' soon found that the private theatres suited them best as they offered them more opportunities than the public theatres. They appealed mainly to intellectuals and to their practical experience. Conceivably they aimed at realistic drama dealing with social vices, follies and foibles thereby deliberately limiting their knowledge to a non-spiritual world of man. The type of drama they attempted was, therefore, to reflect rather the mundane lives of the audience than moments of their heightened experience or their desires and demands. In other words, "The stage, which had interpreted life in terms of universal significance, became the mirror of local prejudice and the scourge of social folly."[12]

Thus, with the turn of the century a strong reaction against the pure imagination and robust spirit of the Elizabethan drama began to make itself felt in England. The various conducive factors described above gave an impetus to this movement towards satirical and realistic portrayal of life in drama. This movement found a perfect expositor in Ben Jonson who "was at once a rebel against the stage-technique of the public theatre of his day and an exponent of it."[13] He readily absorbed the tone of the age and the opportune times helped him find himself.

Ben Jonson entered the theatre at a time when the 'University Wits,' on the one hand, and Shakespeare, on the other, were establishing the romantic comedy and the flamboyant tragedy. Beginning with Edwards and Whetstone, followed by Greene, Peele, Nashe, Lodge, Yarington, Lyly, Kyd and Marlowe, a succession of good writers besides many authors of anonymous plays developed the romantic drama evolved from their own genius, as opposed to the classical drama. Particularly Shakespeare played a key role in creating a drama at once popular and poetic.

This dramatic development, while breaking away from classical models, had established no theory or criticism of its own. It had only resulted from the individual innovations of poets and playwrights who strove to meet the persistent demand of the popular stage. They, no doubt, gave specific character to the 'History Play,' 'Domestic Tragedy,' 'Tragedy of Blood,' 'Pastoral Play' and several kinds of comedy. But there were no prescribed rules for all these species. Fervently inspired to give their audiences the thrills and glory of life, these dramatists had dealt with remote places, idealised persons, marvellous adventures, conquests and such other vicissitudes of life. But they had not attempted an ordered analysis and rationalised 'imitation' of life of their day. So, their plays "were neither right tragedies nor right comedies."[14]

Furthermore, the Elizabethan plays, whether comic or tragic, conforming, in the main, to the fashions of the time, offered much that appeared to be glaringly lawless particularly to those familiar with classical drama. For, these plays conveniently flouted the classical tradition. There were hardly any restrictions guiding the plays. The plots were full of improbabilities and happy coincidences. The dramatists seldom observed the Unities of time and place. Their plays, "where you shall have Asia of the one side and Africa of the other, and so many other under-kingdoms,"[15] simply discarded these dramatic laws.

Moreover, with the extravagance of energy which unfailingly characterised the Elizabethans in all things, the splendour and magnificence of the Elizabethan age had their own dangers too. The torrent of Marlowe's eloquence obviously mingled fantastic brutality with sweetness. Shakespeare's tragedies were surcharged with unrelieved pressure of thought, passion and poetry. These things, no boubt, were good in themselves but minor dramatists in trying to imitate them were bound to commit most intolerable excesses. Shakespeare was endowed with such rare dramatic genius that he gave full concession to the popular taste and to the requirements of the Elizabethan theatre, "yet transmuted in the giving, so that what might have been a mere connivance in baseness becomes a miracle of expressive art."[16] Since all the Elizabethan playwrights were not Shakespeares, they could not follow the same method without disaster. There was, however, "a real danger that authority in every sense would be flung to the winds and that every literary fault would be thought justified by genius."[17] Inevitably, therefore, criticism called for classical form and realistic presentation of life in drama.

This call for classical form found its answer in Ben Jonson who could offer the greatly-needed precept and practice through his plays. Jonson began his theatrical career as a strolling player. And the time was ripe for his development. Though he began to write for the theatres as early as 1593, in his nineteenth year, he first challenged public censure only in 1598 with his *Every Man in His Humour* which bore the special stamp of his genius. The play is an important turning point in the course of the Elizabethan drama marking as it does the beginning of a revolutionary movement in dramatic methods. What is more, the play announces Jonson's programme for the rest of his dramatic career apparently signifying a change of plan on his part and his devotion to a new kind of play.[18] This unequivocally pre-supposes that Jonson must have passed through an altogether different period until he reached his characteristic standpoint.

This period from 1593 to 1598 could be said to be the period of Jonson's apprenticeship. When Jonson first threw his lot with the playwrights he frankly followed the current demand for romantic drama, showing no small skill in adopting the full-blooded romantic manner. He had to share almost equally with Shakespeare in the powerful influences of Marlowe's art. Like Shakespeare, Jonson had to mend imperfect scenes, to furnish additions for plays that were becoming stale, to improve faulty verses and also to take part in the representations on the stage. But, unfortunately, nothing is known to have survived from the authorship of this period.

Nevertheless, Jonson gained from Meres the encomium, "our best for Tragedie,"[19] along with several other Elizabethan dramatists. We justly wonder what these plays could be that won for Jonson such a praise. Even Henslowe tells us nothing of these earlier years of Jonson's dramatic apprenticeship. He only refers to Jonson in his *Diary* as a maker of plots as well as a player. All the same, the plays[20] that Jonson wrote for Henslowe from 1597 in collaboration with his contemporaries give us, in their romantic elements and style, some hints that his early work did not differentiate itself much from the current romantic work of his fellow-dramatists. That Jonson must have adopted the dominant romantic style and that he was also a master of that style is proved by his 'Additions'[21] to *The Spanish Tragedy* later. Further evidence that his early work was romantic may be found in the romantic elements of the earliest of his extant comedy, *The Case is Altered*, which stands quite apart from all the rest of his work. Thus Jonson, like Shakespeare himself, during his dramatic apprenticeship had to deal with romantic plays.

But whereas Shakespeare continued in that tradition bringing the romantic style to the very height of perfection, Jonson swerved from that tradition. Shakespeare, with a largeness of vision and flexibility of technique, worked upon the popular dramatic tradition of his time and produced an English poetic drama which developed out of the pressure of its own vitality and its own kind of form and unity without owing much to an external doctrine of correctness. Jonson approached his art from a quite different point of view. Notwithstanding the initial romantic play of his genius and his mastery of that romantic style, Jonson stood apart, as an example of that 'rara avis,' with a diverse object and principle backed by his solid classical training and stirred by his zeal for reform.

In thus dwelling apart from his fellow-dramatists, Jonson challenged the judgment of his times. Shakespeare accepted the conditions of the stage of his time. He was quite aware of its shortcomings and defects but seemed to have resigned himself to them with good humour. Jonson, on the other hand, registered his protest against the dramatic practice of his age, against its extravagance and its carelessness. And in angry defiance of the accepted traditions of the Elizabethan stage, Jonson set up his own tastes, ideas and theories assimilated from the ancients against the popular taste. In the midst of that luxuriant romanticism which culminated in Shakespeare, Jonson emerged essentially as a native classicist with the definite purpose of effecting a reform of theatrical taste and convention both by his precept and example.[22]

Thus, no sooner had Jonson completed his apprenticeship than he came forward as a pioneer, a law-giver and an innovator in dramatic art, assuming the role of a dictator, a laureate and a censor. As D.H. Craig rightly points out, Jonson "set out to establish for the first time in England a literary canon, and to install himself at its centre."[23] The system was to be based on the principles of scholarly industry, careful constitution, observance of the rules and the imitation of the ancients. Having acquired some credit with the managers, he resolved to embody his own conceptions in his future plays and to model them upon the plan of his ancient masters. He consciously appointed himself a teacher and a missionary of literature with a definite creed different from that of others of the time. Jonson, like Donne, was thus in revolt against the artistic principles of his contemporaries, and he sought in the classics a cure for the romantic excesses of Elizabethan drama. Hence he came forward as the champion of classicism.

It may be argued that while the main tendency of the Elizabethan drama was towards romanticism, neither classicism nor realism had, by any means, been lacking in the earlier drama, particularly in comedy. It is true that though classicism had been driven from the stage to the closet in tragedy, in comedy at least Plautus and Terence were still largely followed as models. The Plautian model was anglicised in *Ralph Roister Doister.* This had notable copies in Lyly's *Mother Bombie* and Shakespeare's *Comedy of Errors*. Besides, not only its stock characters—its clever servants, parasites, misers, braggart soldiers—but also its general scheme of a series of tricks, brought about through disguises, had come to be widely used in the early drama.

But the point is that except in rare cases, the use of classicism and realism in the early drama was more apparent than real. It was, on the whole, external and superficial. "The average Elizabethan writer," says Marchette Chute, "agreed in theory that the classics were very valuable and important, but in practice he used his classical education chiefly as a way of showing off."[24] Writers like Nashe and Greene only scattered bits of classical lore through their writings. They could readily have recited whole pages of Cicero and Horace from their retentive memory but neither of them had any idea as to what those disciplined Romans were talking about. A superficial classicism of this kind was one that any intelligent Londoner could acquire by means of a handbook on mythology and an anthology of classical quotations like Aesop's *Fables.*

Unlike the majority of his contemporary writers, Jonson was consciously trained to be a poet and a dramatist. His education at Westminster under Camden, one of Europe's most respected scholars, concentrated very heavily on the study of classical writers, both Greek and Roman. Jonson's classical reading supplied him with ideas and structure, characters, situations, theme and tone. Camden also taught Jonson to see the craft of words as a serious study, demanding whole-hearted, lifelong commitment. Of equal importance to the development of his craft was the inherent emphasis on self-reflection that constantly directed Jonson to examine and perfect his own working methods and artistic life. He advocated an Horatian control over the emotions, an ideal of rationality and self-restraint, because he was keenly aware of his own tumultuous nature, and of the need to impose some discipline upon it. And "even in the heat of his most ill-tempered and ill-judged disputes, Jonson never lost faith in the cool restraint of the classical aims and ideals."[25]

It was left to Jonson, then, to reinforce the classical ideal genuinely on the Elizabethan stage. What made Jonson exceptional was that, unlike most of his contemporaries, he was primarily concerned with the spirit rather than the rigidity and outward trappings of the classics. Also, it was in Jonson, above all the other men of his time, that the classical ideal centred in its application to English conditions.

Jonson's knowledge of the past and his reflective turn of mind, however, enabled him to analyse and take a detached view of the fashion of play-making and play-going and, what is more, to appraise it in the light of dramatic history. We may say that Jonson succeeded in conveying an adequate impression of the drama of his time better than any other author of the period. For Sidney was obviously too early and, moreover, did not have the actual experience of playwriting. Compilers like Meres and Bolton were too categorical. Pamphleteers like Gosson were too prejudiced. Later men like Suckling in his *Sessions of the Poets* were too trivial and superficial in their points of view. Shakespeare was too deeply absorbed in his swift act of creating to take an objective view of his art. But, Jonson, coming to playwriting with a critic's instinct and with a good knowledge of dramatic history and the rules of dramatic structure, was in a competent position to judge and appraise the contemporary drama. The defence of his art of analysing, estimating and appraising the contemporary drama is so clearly and frequently expressed by him in the course of his plays that one can never go wrong in understanding it.

But, more often than not, Jonson is misinterpreted in his attitude to the work of his contemporaries and recent predecessors. The "War of the Theatres" was particularly responsible for such a misconception. The bad temper on both sides in the 'quarrel-plays' has been exaggerated and over-emphasized with the result that personal animosity is supposed to colour all his criticism of the contemporary stage.[26] But if Jonson's specific expressions of opinion are put together and judged disinterestedly, they show a well-supported and constructive criticism based upon sound aesthetic principles.

Jonson's main indictment of the conditions of the Elizabethan drama is precisely formulated in the 'Prologve' to *Every Man in His Humour*.[27] With his unshaken belief in the validity of the classical Unities of time and place Jonson considers it ridiculous

To make a child, now swadled, to proceede
Man, and then shoote vp, in one beard, and weede,
Past threescore yeeres: (ll. 7-9)

Jonson also ridicules the flagrant absurdities of historical plays with their

three rustie swords,
And helpe of some few foot-and-halfe-foote words,
Fight ouer *Yorke,* and *Lancasters* long iarres:
And in the tyring-house bring wounds, to scarres (ll. 9-12)

Further, Jonson condemns the use of the '*Chorus*' to "waft you ore the seas" as a device rendered necessary by failure to observe the unity of place. He disapproves of other such stage artifices as the "creaking throne" let down when Gods interfered, the "nimble squibbe . . . to make afear'd/The gentlewomen," the "roul'd bullet . . . /To say, it thunders," or again the "tempestuous drumme/to tell you when the storme doth come"; (ll. 16-20) – all melodramatic devices called into being by the nature of extravagant plots. Following the track of Whetstone and Sidney, Jonson, in this manner, attacks the inartistic methods of the pure romantic school. Jonson was equally vexed with the bombast and ranting in the revenge tragedies. He ridicules the bombast of Kyd's *Spanish Tragedy* in the light of Bobadill's "ill-judged praise of its well-penned lines":

> I would faine see all the Poets, of these times, pen such another play as that was! they'll prate and swagger, and keepe a stir of arte and deuices; . . . they are the most shallow, pittifull, barren fellowes.
> (*Every Man in His Humour*, I, v, 50-54)

Jonson, thus, disapproved of the course that the English drama had taken since *Tamburlaine* and *The Spanish Tragedy*. He sought to regulate the creative energy of his age which was often apt to tend in the direction of extravagance of language and exuberance of style. For he hopefully felt, that, however great might be the talent and genius now employed on the Elizabethan stage, it was still necessary to introduce a more regular drama than had hitherto appeared. Hence he "applied himself continually to the task of defining and redefining the forms which dramatic art in his own time might naturally and properly assume."[28]

Before proceeding further, we may ask the question whether Jonson's stand was justified. When we think of Shakespeare in whose "hands, the traditions have been overlaid by a new and more comprehensive dramatic purpose,"[29] we, no doubt, find Jonson rather rigid and categorical. But the point to bear in mind is that Shakespeare was a singular exception. He outdistanced his contemporaries. Whatever he touched he rendered, by dint of his rare genius, into pieces of great art. So, to a real genius like Shakespeare he sanctioned liberty and had "lov'd the man" and honoured "his memory (on this side Idolatry)" (*Discoveries*, ll. 654-55) and certified that "he was not of an age, but for all time."[30] Nor was Jonson blind to the glories of English literature. He only saw danger in its unbridled course. A Shakespeare or a Bacon had his own lights to guide him. But what about the rest? Therefore, the restraints and standards that he set were obviously meant for those who belonged to the average level, but claimed licence too easily. From this it is clear that Jonson scarcely failed to realise the greatness of his age or to appreciate the really deserving poets. He knew the strength as well as the weaknesses of his contemporaries. It was only against an unbridled romanticism that Jonson raised his voice.

Jonson's watchword was reform. He earnestly intended to rescue the Elizabethan world of letters from its sloppy and emotional ways. He wanted "to wrest both tragedy and comedy out of romantic extravagance and sloppiness."[31] But his main concern was to free comedy from its romantic entanglements. He, therefore, bent the whole strength of his mind, critical as well as creative, to supply the element of art to the exuberant literature of his age, to ensure its proper development and progress.

Jonson dwelt upon the Greek principle, 'nothing too much,' when he was surrounded by writers who commonly sought to do much more than enough. He pleaded for election and a mean, for proportion, fitness and propriety. He advocated a strict and succinct style wherein you can take away nothing without loss. He proclaimed it to be his sacred office to

> raise the depis'd head of *poetrie* againe, and stripping her out of those rotten and base rags, wherewith the Times haue adulterated her form, restore her to her primitiue habit, feature, and maiesty, and render her worthy to be imbraced, and kist, of all the great and master-spirits of our world. (*Volpone*, Dedication, ll. 129-34)

Thus, Jonson's primary purpose was to alter and reform the current practices of the stage, first, by a strong reaction against all absurdities of current forms of drama, and then, through a recourse to classical standards as a cure for its lawlessness, thereby establishing a comic and tragic form based on rational plan. With this purpose, he attempted to inculcate sounder dramatic methods for comedy and tragedy both by his theory and practice. Jonson's own professional standards were rigorous. He was a staunch defender of the classical unities of time and place and "deplored the fanciful and the romantic."[32] He boldly claimed to write such plays "as other playes should be" (*Every Man in His Humour*, 'Prologve,' l. 14), by observing "the lawes of time, place, (and) persons," and swerving "from no needfull rule." (*Volpone*, 'Prologve,' ll. 31-32)

But this does not mean that Jonson was a slave to the laws of drama derived by the neo-classical theorists from Aristotle and from the practice of the ancient dramatists. Nevertheless, Jonson's primary fault is said to be "a too servile imitation of the classic models."[33] Some recent critics, even after what Eliot and Herford and Simpson have done to place Jonson in the proper perspective, subscribe to the same view of Jonson. Mary Suddard, for instance, refers to Jonson as "this over-docile disciple of antiquity."[34] Edmund Wilson categorically states that Jonson "was a pedant whose cult of the classics had little connection with his special kind of genius."[35] David Daiches thinks that Jonson is "pedantic (and) imitative . . . in his learned art."[36]

The traditional over-emphasis on Jonson's classical inheritance obscures both his native independence of thought and the success of his eclecticism. First of all, the view that Jonson is little more than an imitating and translating scholar is far from being true. On the other hand he is genuinely creative within the self-imposed limits. It is true that Jonson derived motives and ideas and phrases from classical literature, but at the same time, he did not borrow them directly without their passing through a remoulding process in his hands. The point, however, is that Jonson had an altogether different attitude to borrowing from the classics as well as from native sources. To translate a fine classical phrase aptly Jonson regarded as almost an original work while he scorned to steal phrases from *Arcadia*. What is more, this translation is managed with admirable freedom. Jonson did not need to dovetail or weld his borrowings into one another. For, having fused them in his mind, he poured them forth into the mould of his thought. "Jonson's effort," in the words of F.R. Leavis, "was to feel Catullus, and the others he cultivated, as contemporary with himself; or rather, to achieve an English mode that should express a sense of contemporaneity with them."[37] It is this intellectual process behind his borrowing which determines its significance. Jonson certainly "did not copy the Roman writers, he identified himself with them; he did not steal their thoughts, he thought them and felt them, and when he used their words, it was because no fitter ones would naturally occur to him."[38] This kind of borrowing from classical treasures, we should remember, was accounted to be no robbery in that age.

According to Jonson the poet may seek material anywhere so long as he unifies it, thus making it his own by his art. This is the essence of originality for Jonson. He himself illustrates this when he says that a poet should

> bee able to convert the substance, or Riches of an other *Poet*, to his owne use (and). . . . Not, to imitate servilely . . . but, to draw forth out of the best, and choicest flowers, with the Bee, and turne all into Honey, worke it into one relish, and savour:
>
> (*Discoveries*, ll. 2467-78)

As long as Jonson is able to do so, whatever he borrows, the thought, in a genuine sense, is really Jonson's own, being made so by right of complete assimilation.

Thus Jonson had carried scholarship to its highest stage and turned it into a new creation. This creative borrowing and this splendid energy to compass and surmount his sources was one of Jonson's chief gifts. His *Discoveries* is a triumphant metamorphosis of borrowings.[39] How thoroughly the material of *Discoveries* became his own is shown by the very way in which he handled it, sometimes fusing several sentences into one, changing the order, transferring remarks, blending the material of different authors into a more or less coherent whole. This extraordinary ability of Jonson to make the treasure of the past his own was appreciated in his own time. To cite but one instance, T. Carew applauded Jonson's ability

to bring the booty home:
Nor think it theft if the rich spoils, so torn
From conquer'd authors, be as trophies worn.
(*To Ben Jonson*, ll. 40-42)

We may conclude that imitation to Jonson only meant a coming into harmony with the literary instinct, the refined taste, the mode of thought and the art of the master imitated, thus making all that he followed purely his own. Hence there is nothing wrong if Jonson "invades authors like a monarch" as long as "what would be theft in other poets, is only victory in him."[40]

Also, the view that Jonson was a pedant is not correct. In reality, Jonson was no pedant and was far from being a slave to antiquity. For, in his zeal to denounce the extravagance of romantic drama he did not tend to be a neo-classicist of the rigid and pedantic type. His common sense was far too strong to allow him to imitate the ancients blindly.

Jonson always deprecated an unintelligent subservience to antiquity. Jonson himself points out that the unhappy ending of *Volpone* is not in accordance with "the strict rigour of comick law." (*Volpone*, Dedication, l. 110) He asserts that his breach of the law had been intentional and had been dictated by his own doctrine that "the office of a comic-Poet (was) to imitate iustice, and instruct to life." (*Volpone*, Dedication, ll. 121-22) Again, he says that in *Every Man Out of His Humour* he has not followed "the lawes of *Comedie*":

> the equall diuision of it into *Acts*, and *Scenes*, according to the *Terentian* manner, his true number of Actors; the furnishing of the *Scene* with GREX or CHORVS, and that the whole Argument fall within compasse of a dayes business,

on the ground that

> these are too nice obseruations. (Grex, ll. 237-42)

Jonson was thus bold in his readiness to modify classical 'lawes of *Comedie*.'

Further, though Jonson adhered to the three Unities, he would never allow himself to be bound by them. As David Cook has rightly pointed out, "characteristically Jonson did not accept the Unities as laws, but welcomed them as optional aids to artistic discipline."[41] That is why he carefully moderated them so as to suit his dramatic requirements. For instance, the day of twenty-four hours might, on a suitable occasion, extend to two days as happens in *Every Man Out of His Humour*. In *Sejanus*, as history requires Jonson changes the scene completely from Rome to Caprae. In *Catiline* there is a flight from Rome to Tuscany. Thus, though the action of most of his plays generally passes within twenty-four hours and avoids all violent changes of scene, Jonson makes no attempt to stick to the Unities blindly, perceiving that such adherence causes greater absurdities than it avoids. We can, therefore, safely conclude that Jonson observed rules as far as he thought it necessary and ignored them when he thought fit. Jonson not only knew classical drama better than any of his contemporaries but he tried to adapt intelligently and not slavishly its principles and ruled to the peculiarities of the English theatre.

Besides, Jonson's attitude to the classical writers and their precepts was liberal because while revering their memory he refused to be fettered or enslaved by them. For instance, he read Scaliger and admired him but he was well guarded against the extremes of Scaliger's dogmatism. Again, although he had a deep reverence for Aristotle as the first law-giver in antiquity to evolve and systematize the theory of literary criticism, he could not concur with the tendency of blind worship and deification, which was current in the Middle Ages. He was dead against the whole principle of dictatorship in art. He felt that

> Nothing is more ridiculous, then to make an Author a *Dictator*, as the schooles have done *Aristotle*. (*Discoveries*, ll. 2095-97)

The same sturdy independence colours his remarks in respect of rules and precepts. In pursuance of the prescriptions by the ancients, Jonson was quite aware of the scope for the poet's liberty. For, he says:

> I am not of that opinion to conclude a *Poets* liberty within the narrowe limits of lawes, which either the *Grammarians*, or *Philosophers* prescribe. (*Discoveries*, ll. 2555-57)

Above all, the ancients were there only as guides but not as commanders to Jonson, for he says:

> It is true they open'd the gates, and made the way, that went before us; but as Guides, not Commanders: (*Discoveries*, ll. 137-39)

Again, however greatly Jonson admired the ancients, his final authority was not the ancients but Truth. With his conviction that "truth layes open to all," Jonson reiterates his stand:

Stand for *Truth*, and 'tis enough (*Discoveries*, ll. 158-59)

Therefore, if at all Jonson was a slave to any creed it was to Truth. His devotion was not so much to any particular tradition or model as to Truth. With him it was a question not of authorities but of Truth.

From these observations it is clear that classical rules were never a strait-jacket for Jonson. As a recent critic puts it "to Jonson, the classics were pre-eminent; but they were not all-in-all." His employment of classical raw material was never as uncritical as is often assumed.[42] For, he never believed that the salvation of English literature lay in slavishly following the classical ways. He held the principles of the ancients in solution in his spacious memory but "with an intelligent recognition and liberal interpretation of those principles in their adaptation to the needs of contemporary English conditions."[43] This is chiefly because, like Milton, Jonson claimed the right of free thought in the realm of letters as others claimed it in the domain of religion. Small wonder if he made departures from classical practice thereby giving his independent and deliberate assent to the classical standards. Moreover, as Anne Barton rightly observes, "Jonson's classicism was balanced by a compensating attraction towards the irregular, the gothic, the contemporary and the strange."[44] Hence we may safely hold the view that Jonson was usually a classicist but there is a 'substratum' of sanity, moderation and native good sense about his opinions. Moreover, "the emotional content of Jonson's art is much more substantial and immediate than one might suppose in a (normal) 'classicist.'"[45]

Jonson's classicism was, therefore, altogether different from the empirical classicism of men like Sidney and Barnes who experimented with Greek and Roman measures in English lyrical poetry. Also, such classicism as Jonson's was certainly above the reach of the early imitators of and borrowers from Seneca and Plautus. Jonson's classicism, with its unique grasp, understanding and intelligent use of the ideas, the technical practices, the subject-matter and style of the ancient authors, may be called assimilated classicism. For, Jonson assimilated classicism to such a degree that ancient authors like Quintillian, Pliny, Plutarch, Juvenal and Terence became part of his imaginative reaction to the present life. They were woven, as it were, into the very web of his thought. It was as if the classics lived with him.

There is another misinterpretation of Jonson's classicism. The fact that the ancient authors have been the source of Jonson's inspiration and his dramatic power has been often overstressed so as to imply that "Jonson owes everything to classicism."[46] This view is not correct totally denying as it does the originality of Jonson. That Jonson was for originality, for exploring new paths is made clear when he says:

> Let *Aristotle*, and others have their dues; but if we can make further Discoveries of truth and fitnesse then they, why are we envied?
> (*Discoveries*, ll. 2101-3)

Jonson could really "make further Discoveries of truth and fitnesse" by making use of his own personal experience, by his rich knowledge of contemporary English life and also by his close touch with the literary movements of his day.

In formulating critical standards, besides the observation of the ancients, Jonson felt the necessity of utilizing personal experience:

> For to all the observation of the *Ancients*, wee have our owne experience: which, if wee will use, and apply, wee have better meanes to pronounce. (*Discoveries*, ll. 134-37)

Therefore, if Jonson eschewed enchanted islands and impossible seacoasts for the background of his plays, and refused to make his plays hinge on freak circumstances such as "of a duke to be in love with a countesse, and that countesse to bee in love with the dukes sonne, and the sonne to loue the ladies waiting maid: some such cross-wooing," (*Every Man Out of His Humour*, III, vi, 195-99) confusions of identity and misunderstandings, it is not because of his 'trust' from the ancients, but because that part of 'our owne experience' which activated him was observation of human follies in a familiar London setting, rather than the ethereal reaches of the imagination and the emotions.

Hence, the view that Jonson was obsessed with the thought of the ancients is unsound. However interested Jonson was in the literature of the past, he was, by no means, preoccupied with it. In fact, he was more concerned with the contemporary literature which he tried to reform in the light of the principles which those models embodied in them. So, Jonson's interest was not so much in probing the methods of the Greeks and Romans as the methods of the Elizabethans. He only felt the weight of literary tradition while remaining within the current of contemporary life. In short, what Jonson wanted was not to surrender himself to Greece and Rome, but to rival them and to wed ancient form to contemporary substance.

Furthermore, pre-eminently an Englishman of his own day, Jonson had immense belief in the value of English life for the work of the literary man. This is clear when he says:

> Our *Scene* is *London*, 'cause we would make knowne,
> No countries mirth is better then our owne.
> No clime breeds better matter, for your whore,
> Bawd, squire, impostor, many persons more,
> Whose manners, now call'd humors, feed the stage:
> (*The Alchemist*, 'Prologve,' ll. 5-9)

Further, Jonson proclaims that his avowed purpose in the composition of *The Sad Shepherd* was to garner

> such wool
> As from mere English flocks his Muse can pull

This shows how Jonson was a rugged Englishman with a sardonic relish for the varied and colourful London life of his day. Whatever its relation to any Latin or Greek originals, in Jonson's work "the English poet, who remains not the less English and of his own time, enters into an ideal community, conceived of as something with which contemporary life and manners may and should have close relations."[47] But for his English fibre at heart, Jonson might have been easily transmuted into the slavish follower of outworn classical forms and usages. Jonson's characteristic classicism may, therefore, be said to be "a kind of native classicism . . . – obscene, yet moralizing, caustic, thorny, immediate, Londinian and topical. . . . It was Roman satiric technique applied to London vice . . . or recreation of the classic model."[48]

Though Jonson swerved apart, he never stood aloof from the literary movements of his day. However much he stressed his mission as a teacher of classic art, Jonson was in the closest touch with all contemporary literature. He was an Elizabethan by birth as well as by apprenticeship. He seemed to "embody in his own career something of the vigour, restlessness and many-sided activity of Elizabethan life." As a practical playwright eager to appeal to the men of his time, and as a critic who claimed conformity with the local conditions as the prerogative of the poet or dramatist, Jonson had to be responsive to the literary movements of his day. As L.C. Knights observes, "the more we study in minute detail the more clearly Jonson appears both intensely individual and . . . at one with his contemporaries."[49] In developing his characteristic type of play, Jonson almost unconsciously seized upon ideas and methods which had run through English literature of the time. For instance, when Jonson interweaves the two Latin stories – the *Captives* and the *Aulularia* – in *The Case is Altered*, it is in accordance with the current usage of the Elizabethan stage. Jonson seems to be an ultra-Elizabethan when, in the same play, he crowds the canvas with figures, multiplies their motives and marshals almost all the men as rival lovers of Rachal de Price. Further, when he tries to present the theme of love, it looks as if he was an English Plautus trying to write in the Elizabethan style. Hence Jonson's classicism is one that springs from the strength of a native tradition with all its rooted and racy Englishness. As Terry Egleton elucidates, "on the one hand Jonson is admirably learned, judicious, authoritative and neo-classical, the very type of 'high' conservative humanist, on the other hand he is engagingly earthy and boisterous, full of a robust 'English' vitality which disdains metaphysical presentation or frigid formalism."[50]

That is why the arguments as to whether Jonson is to be more correctly regarded as a 'classical' writer on the continental model or as a 'romantic' English writer are beside the point. We may say that he was both as he endeavoured to combine the best in both the traditions. Jonson seems to have wished to have the seriousness of purpose, the polish, the concentration, the restraint and the precision of the classics without losing the richness, the vitality and the raciness of the freer native drama. It is because of this rare phenomenon that Jonson appears to be at once classical and romantic. We may, therefore, conclude that Jonson's classical work, on the whole, is thoroughly English in spirit and tone and conforms, in the main, to the prevailing currents of English literature.

Possessed of the assimilated knowledge of ancient literature together with a wide knowledge of contemporary English life and literature, it must have seemed quite possible to Jonson that he could bring back single-handed the original function of the poet and dramatist as Sidney had described it, and that he could reform the contemporary theatre by raising it to the level of Greek and Roman theatres.

But in view of some presumptions that Jonson did not have any higher education, that seven years of his formal education had been merely spent in learning to lay bricks, and, what is more, that his sole experience in the theatre had been only as a hired actor and as a hack writer for Henslowe, it has often been assumed that Jonson had given himself "an impossible assignment" of reforming the English drama. But Jonson, being what he was, had never thought so. No doubt, Jonson set himself to a great task and his claim was quite bold. All the same, he had no doubts of his abilities to carry out the self-appointed task. A man who could write a play for presentation before the Queen and end it with the injunction:

By (—) 'tis good, and if you lik't, you may.

(*Cynthia's Revels*, 'The Epilogve,' l. 20)

could hardly have suffered from any lack of self-confidence. We may, by all means, say that Jonson was eminently fitted to carry out the task he assigned to himself, however difficult the task might be.

Jonson came to the theatre possessed of many advantages. He was already a great master of learning although he had not received any university education. Jonson's learning was not only wide, varied and deep but solid and thorough. He was worthy of being the pupil of Camden and the friend of Selden. He had, like Milton, an unusual thirst for learning and scholarship. All the treasures of ancient literature were open to him. He was familiar not only with the perfect productions of the Greek dramatists but with the fragments among the works of the sophists and grammarians. His studies, while by no means confined to the Greek and Roman classics, included the Greek philosophers as well as the Roman historians and poets.

Then, we are simply astounded at the wealth of Jonson's knowledge. Having studied the most minute details and understood the true spirit of ancient life, his knowledge was vast and as deep as it was accurate. He was not merely satisfied with the best writers. He dug into the orators, critics, scholiasts and compilers. He seemed to have a speciality in all branches of knowledge and to have acquired a very considerable degree of information of every topic connected with the arts then known and cultivated. Yet, his massive learning and vast knowledge in no way marred his vigour.

While his diversified learning bore him into nobler spheres of comprehension, Jonson's keen power of observation gave him rich experience of men and manners. In the course of his life he had passed through vicissitudes of fortune. He had been a student, a tradesman and a soldier before he became a public actor and dramatic author and an agent in the amusements of the court. He had travelled widely. He knew something of the Flemish plains and Paris streets. He lived for twenty years with the beauties and wits of the court. He was closely familiar with London. Thus, Jonson had a good knowledge of life down to its lowest haunts.

But, all these – his solid learning, rich knowledge, accurate observation, first-hand experience of men and life – are merely the instruments a dramatist works with. A successful dramatist is also expected to be in possession of certain requisites of the stage.

Jonson was thoroughly conversant with the stage conditions of both the public and private theatres of the time. As W.A. Armstrong points out "no Jacobean playwright had a richer knowledge than his of the various amateur and professional stages of the period."[51] He had an acute sense of the theatre. He had been an actor himself. Richard Allen Cave, Professor of Drama and Theatre Arts, Universtiy of London, in his recent book, *Ben Jonson*, focuses on Jonson's plays in performance and highlights the dynamic relationship between the stage and the audience whom Jonson learned to manipulate with dazzling skill.[52] Jonson was undoubtedly a past master of the stagecraft—the art with which the playwright selects and integrates the various physical media such as the architecture, machinery, properties, the conventions of the stage, the voices, gestures, attitudes, movements, stage-business and dress of the actors which would enable him to communicate what he has written to an audience in a theatre. Jonson seems to have watched performances by his fellow-pupils while he was at Westminster school, and Dekker's *Satiromastix* reveals that he was a professional actor in the provinces and at the Swan Theatre in the early 1590s. Moreover, his collaboration with Inigo Jones, the eminent designer of stage machines, must have greatly helped him in mastering the stage-craft. Small wonder, therefore, if "Jonson was acknowledged to be the great and cunning craftsman of the Elizabethan Age, both in his own time and after."[53]

Besides, Jonson's knowledge of human nature was extensive and profound. He was next only to Shakespeare in this regard. Jonson was also a man of "correct judgment," "strong crabbed sense," "retentive memory," "great honesty," and, above all, "fidelity of description" which made it possible for him to reproduce his thorough knowledge of human nature faithfully and fully.

Jonson also had the necessary literary gifts. He had industry, constancy, versatility, a powerful and original vein of humour, nimbleness of wit, a keen sense of satire, a quick and almost intuitive faculty of discerning the ridiculous and an insight into contemporary life and manners. But these alone could not have made him a great dramatist. For, it is necessary that the application of these should be directed by a high purpose and informed of original genius.

Regarding high purpose, Jonson had a deep conviction of the sacredness and gravity of his vocation. He was a great moralist, and "of all styles he loved most to be named Honest."[54] Jonson, like Sidney, "conceived of the poet as a poet-moralist, a poet-preacher, and adhered to the Renaissance 'credo' that comedy was an instrument of ethical reform."[55] Although, as a practical playwright, Jonson found it necessary to please in order to be successful, transitory applause was never the goal of his ambition. He was strongly determined to satisfy only competent judges, for, as he himself says:

> To judge of Poets is only the facultie of Poets;
> and not of all Poets, but the best. (*Discoveries*, ll. 2578-79)

Jonson had a highly original dramatic genius. He had an astonishing power for inventing plots. While his fellow-dramatists, particularly Shakespeare, were busy in borrowing plots from other sources, Jonson exerted himself in making his own plots. He could construct with lucidity and effectiveness. He was an adept in the art of comic characterisation. In fact, Jonson was the only dramatist of the day who was not either directly produced or very greatly modified by Shakespeare. He remained the most original of the dramatists of Shakespeare's age. Of course, it is true that Jonson was not original in the same way as Shakespeare was original. But after a fashion of his own, Ben Jonson is most truly original.

Jonson was particularly fitted for the task of reforming the Elizabethan drama by virtue of his being "a born-critic." Jonson's own learning, the influence of the Renaissance humanism, and his own distinguished temperament led him to put careful and studious craftmanship before imaginative boldness both in his theory and in his practice. This helped to make Jonson "one of the most significant 'neo-classic' critics in English.[56]

It was Jonson who for the first time, systematized the classical critical ideas and the classical practice into a set of rules for guidance. For Puttenham's treatise, *The Arte of English Poesie*, made only a beginning in this regard narrowly scholastic as it was. Sidney's *Apology for Poetry* gives us "the poetry rather than the art or the theory of criticism."[57] Spenser's treatise is lost to us. We have only his correspondence with Harvey, dealing in a narrow spirit with the minor question of rhyme and metre. It was Jonson who worked out a set of principles which have all the inner consistency of a system.

Apart from what he says in his Prologues, Epilogues or Inductions to his plays, Jonson's critical utterances include his translation of Horace's *Ars Poetica*,[58] his *Conversations with Drummond*,[59] and his *Discoveries*.[60] About two thirds of Jonson's *Discoveries* are concerned with literary criticism. The most sustained literary discussion is that on poetry, tragedy and on comedy.

Jonson is the first English critic who deliberately faced the practical problems of contemporary literature. He stood in the full stream of the vigorous literature of his age, fully alive to its problems and inherent dangers. Being conscious of his critical mission, he bent the entire energy of his erudite mind to its fulfilment. His greatness lies not so much in the originality and novelty of his critical precepts as in the soundness and discrimination of his judgment in selecting the right principles, and the persistent vigour in enforcing them for the guidance of the creative literature, particularly drama, of his age. The discipline he sought to impose upon the wild and reckless growth of contemporary literature was timely, because it underlined the dignity and seriousness of the craft of letters and the perseverance and preparation required for its proper practice. He wisely struck a balance between nature and art, freedom and restraint and imitation and originality. Jonson showed the way towards an intelligent synthesis between respect for authority and freedom to go forward in the direction determined by the changing conditions of the times, thereby achieving a harmonious fusion of the best in the academic and popular traditions.

Thus, with his many-sided acquirements, embracing all that was best in the literature and criticism of antiquity as well as in the contemporary writers on the continent, combined with his artistic conscience, his sturdy independence of spirit, his refined literary sensibility, his impersonal urbanity and poise and his instinctive love of order and neatness in the composition, Jonson was well fitted for the task he set before himself, namely, reformation and regeneration of the Elizabethan drama. Above all, he created the taste of the period by combining existing elements into a new whole. And what Dudden says of Fielding as a novelist, we may as well quite appropriately say of Jonson that no dramatist "ever proceeded to his task with a finer intellectual outfit."[61]

NOTES

1. Allardyce Nicoll, *British Drama* (Harrap, 1961), p. 97. These were, as J.B. Bamborough explains, "the sons of professional men or of the minor gentry, and many of them had been trained as lawyers in the Inns of Court, the legal colleges in London which formed almost a third University in England." *Ben Jonson* (London, 1970), p. 97.
2. R.W. Chambers, *Man's Unconquerable Mind* (London, 1938), p. 253.
3. Una Ellis-Fermor, *The Jacobean Drama* (London, 1936), p. 2.
4. C.F. Tucker Brooke, *Tudor Drama* (Boston, 1911), p. 393.
5. This aspect of Elizabethan life has been brought into prominence only recently. E.P. Cheyney describes the 'turbulence' of the years 1596-1597: "There was . . . the whole miserable mass of distress, crime and vagabondage that crowded the gallows, prisons, streets and highways of the time." (*History of England from the Defeat of the Armada to the Death of Elizabeth*, vol. II, p. 36).
6. L.C. Knights, *Drama and Society in the Age of Jonson* (London:

Chatto and Windus, 1937), p. 134.

7. H.M. Robertson, *Aspects of the Rise of Economic Individualism*, p. 184.
8. L.G. Salingar, "The Elizabethan Literary Renaissance," *The Age of Shakespeare*, ed. Boris Ford (London, 1964), vol. 2, p. 74.
9. *Ibid.*, p. 69.
10. Louis B. Wright, *Middle-Class Culture in Elizabethan England* (Folger Shakespeare Library, 1958), p. 614
11. William A. Armstrong, "The Audiences of the Elizabethan Private Theatres," *RES*, X (1959), p. 242.
12. C.F. Tucker Brooke, p. 393.
13. F.S. Boas, *An Introduction to Stuart Drama* (London, 1946), p. 49.
14. Sir Philip Sidney, "An Apology for Poetry," *English Critical Texts*, ed. Enright and Chickera (London, 1962), p. 48.
15. *Ibid.*, p. 41.
16. Walter Raleigh, *Shakespeare*, p. 27.
17. N.L. Clay, *The English Critic*, p. 13.
18. It is rather difficult to agree with the most recent opinion, put forth by W. David Kay ("The Shaping of Ben Jonson's Career: A Reexamination of Facts and Problems," *MP*, 67 (Feb. 1970, p. 225), that it is with *Every Man Out of His Humour* that Jonson established himself as a leading dramatist. On the other hand, it is more plausible to think with Herford and Simpson that it is *Every Man in His Humour* "which placed Jonson at a stride in the foremost rank of English playwrights." (*Ben Jonson*, vol. I, p. 18) Because we have the authentic proof from Aubrey that after some unsuccessful plays produced at the Curtain Theatre, Jonson "undertooke againe to write a playe and did hitt it admirably well, viz. Every Man. . . which was his first good one." (Quoted in Herford and Simpson, vol. I, p. 179) Besides, in 'The 'Indvction' to *The Magnetic Lady* (1632) Jonson writes of himself as "beginning his studies of this kind, with *Every Man in his Humour*. (ll. 99-100) From this it is clear that Jonson thought of *Every Man in His Humour* as the foundation of his achievement.
19. Francis Mores, "Palladis Tamia," *Elizabethan Critical Essays*, ed. Gregory Smith, vol. II, p. 319.
20. The plays include *Hot Anger Soon Cool'd* written in collaboration with Porter and Chettle, *Page of Plymouth* with Dekker, *Robert II, King of Scots* with Dekker and Chettle and another tragedy *Hichard Crookback*. See *Henslowe's Diary*, ed. R.A. Foakes and R.T. Ricket, pp. 96, 123-24.
21. The 'Additions' to *The Spanish Tragedy* have been ascribed to Jon-

son on the strength of two entries in *Henslowe's Diary* to the effect that on "the 25 September 1601" and "the 22 of June 1602," Jonson was paid a substantial sum by Henslowe "for new Adicyons for Jeronymo." (*Henslowe's Diary*, I, 149, 168) But there have been various objections to Jonson's authorship of the "Additions." (See E.K. Chambers, *The Elizabethan Stage*, vol. III, pp. 429-30; H. Levin, "An echo from *The Spanish Tragedy, MLN*, LXIV (1949), pp. 297-302) The main objection to Jonson's authorship, however, is internal evidence of style. Herford and Simpson remark that Henslowe's entries "cannot guarantee, if there is strong internal evidence to the contrary, that the work undertaken by Jonson was not carried out by some one else." (vol. II, p. 245) Various critics have suggested various probable authors such as Webster (Lamb, *Specimens of English Dramatic Poets*, p. 111), Shakespeare (Coleridge, *Table Talk*, p. 210) and even Dekker. (H.W. Crundell and H.G. Howarth, *NQ*, March 4, 1933; April 7, 1934; January 4, 1941) But as far as we know there is no Elizabethan dramatist who wrote quite in this style. Moreover, we wonder what happened to those "new adicyons" for which Jonson was paid in 1601 and 1602, if they are not his? Hence, we are not unjustified in believing that Jonson was the author of the 'Additions' to *The Spanish Tragedy*.

22. Jonson's disciplined, reasoned and restrictive art was, perhaps, precisely what was needed in his day to check the exuberance of the romanticists.
23. D.H. Craig, *Ben Jonson: The Critical Heritage* (London and New York: Routledge, 1990), p. 1.
24. Marchette Chute, *Ben Jonson of Westminster* (New York: Dutton, 1953), p. 27.
25. Rosalind Miles, *Ben Jonson: His Craft and Art* (London and New York, 1990), p. 7.
26. See Gregory Smith, *Ben Jonson* (London: Macmillan, 1919), pp. 11-20.
27. The 'Prologue,' which might be said to have replaced Lorenzo Junior's Defence of Poetry of the Quarto version, was added to the play for the first time in the Folio version. There is every reason to accept Herford and Simpson's argument (vol. I, p. 333) that the Prologue belongs to 1612 when Jonson was almost certainly writing the revised version of *Every Man in His Humour* as part of his preparation for the 1616 Folio. The Prologue, however, was very important to Jonson because in effect it prefaced his entire Folio collection.
28. J.A. Bryant, Jr., "The Significance of Ben Jonson's First Require-

ment for Tragedy: 'Truth of Argument,'" *SP*, XLIX (Jan. 1952), p. 195.

29. John Russell Brown, *Shakespeare and His Comedies* (London: 1957), p. 36.
30. All the same, it has often been questioned by Jonson's contemporaries like Leonard Digges whether Jonson gave Shakespeare "his due." (See, John Freehafer, "Leonard Digges, Ben Jonson and Shakespeare Idolatry," *SQ*, XXI (Winter, 1970), p. 66. However, G.E. Bentley has corrected these misconceptions about Shakespeare's seventeenth-century reputation in *Shakespeare and Jonson: Their Reputations in the Seventeenth Century Compared.* (1945)
31. *TLS*, July 30, 1915, p. 502.
32. Margaret Alexander, *Shakespeare and His Contemporaries* (London: Heinemann, 1979), p. 300.
33. R.G. Noyes, *Ben Jonson on the English Stage*, p. 5.
34. S.J. Mary Suddard, *Studies and Essays*, p. 191.
35. Remund Wilson, "Morose Ben Jonson," *Ben Jonson: A Collection of Critical Essays*, ed. Jonas A. Barish (N.J: Prentice Hall, 1963), pp. 63-64.
36. David Daiches, *A Critical History of English Literature* (London, 1956), vol. II, p. 309.
37. F.R. Leavis, "English Poetry in the Seventeenth Century," *Scrutiny*, IV (Dec. 1935), p. 243.
38. Elisabeth Woodbridge, *Studies in Jonson's Comedy* (Boston and New York: Lamson, Wolffe, 1898), p. 19.
39. Jonson borrowed principally from sources like Daniel Heinsius's treatises, "De tragoedioe constitione," "Ad Horatii de Plauto et Terentio judicium dissertatio" published in 1611, and Jacobus Pontanus's treatise on poetry "Poeticarum institutionum libri tres" published in 1594.
    See J.E. Spingarn, "The Sources of Jonson's *Discoveries*," *MP*, II (April 1905), pp. 451-60.
40. Dryden, "An Essay on Dramatic Poesy," *English Critical Texts*, ed. Enright and Chickera, p. 90.
41. David Cook, ed., *Volpone*, 'Introduction' (London, 1967), p. 18.
42. A. Rosalind Miles, p. 7.
43. F.E. Schelling, "Ben Jonson and the Classical School," *PMLA*, XIII (1898), p. 234.
44. Anne Barton, *Ben Jonson, Dramatist* (New York: Cambridge University Press, 1984), p. x.
45. W. Speed Hill, "Biography, Autobiography, and *Volpone*," *SEL*,

XII (Spring 1972), p. 319.

46. See W.S. Johnson, Review of Baskervill's *English Elements in the Early Comedy of Jonson*, *JEGP*, XII (1913).
47. F.R. Leavis, p. 243.
48. W.K. Wimsatt Jr. and Cleanth Brooks, *Literary Criticism*, p. 175.
49. L.C. Knights, p. 195.
50. Terry Egleton, ed., *Ben Jonson* (New York: Basil Blackwell, 1987), p. vi.
51. William A. Armstrong, "Ben Jonson and Jacobean Stagecraft," *Jacobean Theatre* (Stratford-Upon-Avon Studies I), ed. John Russell Brown and Bernard Harris, p. 43.
52. Richard Allen Cave, *Ben Jonson* (London: Macmillan, 1991)
53. E.E. Stoll, "The Old Drama and the New," *MLR*, XX (April 1925), p. 150.
54. *Jonson's Conversations with Drummond*, p. 37.
55. E.W. Talbert, "The Classical Mythology and the Structure of *Cynthia's Revels*," *PQ*, XXII (July 1943), p. 194.
56. David Daiches, *Critical Approaches to Literature*, p. 177.
57. Wylie, *Evolution of English Criticism*, p. 12.
58. Jonson's translation of *Ars Poetica*, 'an Ars of his own,' is supposed to have been lost when his library burned in 1623. See Leah Jonas, *The Divine Science*, p. 16.
59. These consist of a few pungent 'obiter dicta' upon English contemporaries made when Jonson walked to Scotland in 1619, and conversed with the poet, Drummond.
60. "As the title suggests, the work is a stock book of established classical ideas collected and translated, somewhat at random, by a practising man of letters for his several purposes." (Wimsatt, Jr. and Cleanth Brooks, p. 176) Though borrowed, *Discoveries* represents essentially Jonson's own critical inclinations. Hence it may be treated as Jonson's own.
61. F.H. Dudden, *Henry Fielding* (Oxford, 1952), vol. II, p. 1092.

Jonson's Theories of Comedy and Tragedy

All dramatic literature, we may say, broadly divides itself into two kins – the comic and the tragic – in spite of their frequent inter-mixture. "There are," as L.J. Potts points out, "only two literary modes of thought; tragedy and comedy."[1] All the same, the two cannot possibly be treated in isolation as watertight compartments, for the simple reason that tragedy and comedy are not altogether dissimilar, nor are they fundamentally opposed to each other. Aristotle's conception of tragedy and comedy[2] too accommodates no such fundamental opposition between the two species. For that matter, we may go even to the extent of saying that "there is, in point of fact, more in common between high tragedy and fine comedy than there is between certain types of tragedy and certain types of comedy."[3]

As fully developed conventions of art, tragedy and comedy are parallel both in their history and in their character. Both tragedy and comedy took their shape not only at approximately the same time, but out of the same forms. The choral song chanted round the altar of God in Greece developed along the twin lines of tragic and of comic expressions. In England, the services of the church gave rise both to the tragic themes and to the comic interludes.

Again, both the species have been produced by the same nations contemporaneously. In Greece, comedy was allowed to enter consciously and of a set purpose in the flourishing period of tragedy. In France, Racine and Moliére were simultaneously producing neo-classical tragedies and sparkling comedies. In Italy, the great comic dramatist Goldoni and the fine tragic dramatist Vittorio Alfieri flourished in the same age.

Also, there have been many individual writers who excelled in the two great branches of drama, and, what is more, combined the two in a single composition. For instance, "Shakespeare has united the powers of exciting laughter and sorrow not only in one mind, but in one composition."[4] From these observations it is clear that comedy and tragedy are, after all, not fundamentally opposed to each other.

The doctrine that the two species are fundamentally opposed to each other seems largely to be the development of later criticism. The broad distinction between the two species has development not so much from the 'free' criticism as exemplified in Aristotle and the romantics, as from the 'derivative' and artificial criticism as exemplified in Horace, whose *Ars Poetica* had virtually preserved the substance of Aristotle's lost discussion of comedy, and in the neo-classical writers of France. For instance, the Renaissance critics in Italy made distinctions between tragedy and comedy, advocating a strict separation of themes of the two species.[5]

In England the question of dramatic species arose in the sixteenth century and we find the distinction between tragedy and comedy made by the early Renaissance critics. The scholastic view of the difference between tragedy and comedy is expressed by Webbe thus:

> There grewe at last to be a greater diuersitye between Tragedy wryters and Comedy wryters, the one expressing onely sorrowfull and lamentable Hystories, bringing in the persons of Gods and Goddesses, Kynges and Queenes and great states, whose partes were cheefely to expresse most miserable calamities and dreadfull chaunces, which increased worse and worse tyll they came to the most wofull plight that might be deuised. The Comedies, on the other side, were directed to a contrary ende, which, beginning doubtfully, drewe to some trouble or turmoyle, and by some lucky chaunce alwayes ended to the ioy and appeasement of all parties.[6]

Puttenham also distinguishes between comical poets and tragical poets more or less on the same grounds.

Kyd, who may be said to be the author of *Soliman and Perseda* (1583),[7] voices his opinion regarding the distinction between tragedy and comedy when Death says to his two companions:

> Packe, *Loue, Fortune,* play in Commedies;
> For powerfull *Death* best fitteth Tragedies. (V, v, 29-30)

Kyd gives his verdict regarding the relative dignity of the two species in his stern remark:

> A Comedie?
> Fie, Comedies are fit for common wits:
> But to present a kingly troup withall,
> Give me a stately written Tragedie;
> *Tragedia cothurnate*, fitting kings,
> Containing matter, and not common things.

(*The Spanish Tragedy*, IV, i, 155-60)

Comedy was, thus, apparently classed as a lower form of art than tragedy. And this must have been the popular judgment as well; or else Kyd would not have spoken before a public audience in that fashion.

Thus, critical theory and theatrical practice combined in devoting more attention and importance to tragedy than to comedy. Let us examine the reasons for this phenomenon. In the first place, Aristotle himself may be said to be responsible for this. While devoting the greater part of his Poetics to tragedy thereby sufficiently stimulating others to devote more attention to its problems, Aristotle dismissed comedy almost in a few sentences. This naturally resulted in making the coming generations of critics concentrate on the tragic form. Consequently comedy tended to receive only perfunctory treatment. Secondly "until very lately there has been a failure to recognize the existence of several distinct strains or kinds within the general field of the comic."[8] This, in turn, has resulted in the production of many comedies marred by uncertainty of fundamental objectives. Lastly, the looking down upon comedy was due to the common equation of comedy with laughter. So the comic in the field of drama was obviously associated merely with the idea of merriment.

However, even to the time of Scaliger, it was traditional in criticism to begin with tragedy and end with tragedy only with sporadical references to comedy. The approach to comedy had been a negative one since it was allowed to exist simply because it was akin to no other form of literature. Similarly comedy was granted its individual rights as a literary genre only because such rights could not be claimed by tragedy. Comedy was also considered unfit to hold an honourable place beside tragedy and epic.

On top of that, notwithstanding the romantic extravagance of English tragedy, there were rules governing its composition, but "to such a disordered thing as English comedy no tests had been applied, for none had been seriously sought."[9] Besides, the relationship of comedy and tragedy, both in criticism and in the writing of plays, had been considered only from the point of view of their antithesis. Thus, for long, comedy had been viewed as the opposite to tragedy. And by the close of the sixteenth century, the differentiation between the two species had grown more and more artificial.

At this critical juncture appears Ben Jonson on the scene, upholding the view that the English theatre has misunderstood the functions of comedy. No doubt, Sidney had already discussed the differences between comedy and tragedy along classical lines. But Sidney's criticism of the

English stage could make very little impact on acted drama, because it was merely academic. Hence Jonson's earnest attempt to translate a persistent doctrine of study to the practice of the theatre. In all Jonson's work the pressure of his literary conscience is clear, but it is in comedy that it is more pronouncing and its working most deliberately disclosed. Disapproving of the conventional views, Jonson unequivocally declares that

> the parts of a Comedie are the same with a *Tragedie*, and the end is partly the same. (*Discoveries*, ll. 2625-26)

Thus, in Jonson's conception of the relations of tragedy and comedy, the fostered opposition between the two species disappears. This is not, however, surprising, because "wherever a critic of the neo-classical school breaks away into a more independent or natural position there vanishes from him the necessity for any strict division between the two moods or species."[10]

Therefore, in Jonson's critical view, if tragedy works out its morality by the effects of pity and fear, comedy achieves its aim, which is also ethical, by mockery of baseness and folly in their lesser degrees. In both the genres the process is cathartic and corrective but the material differs. Tragedy deals with greater and rarer things while comedy deals with lesser and more familiar matters. And, if tragedy works with the emotions and with incidents produced by their clashing with each other and with Fate, comedy works with contrasts in character with incidents or intrigue. It is on this analogy that Jonson based his defence of comedy.

As an Elizabethan dramatist, Jonson had before him two traditions of comedy – the intrigue or satiric comedy, and the narrative or romantic comedy – with different antecedents. As John Russell Brown points out "intrigue comedy was the purer form deriving principally from classical and neo-classical models; narrative comedy was both the more pervasive and, being of very mixed origin, the more fluid form. In the broadest sense the former may be said to have aimed at making a certain number of characters look ridiculous, the latter to have aimed at telling a story."[11] So, Jonson, like any dramatist in Elizabethan England, could choose between these two basic comic forms. And "faced by a choice in such matters, a writer is wise if he follows his temperament. . . . Shakespeare reached for his Chaucer. . . . Ben Jonson knotted his cat-o'-nine-tails."[12] Thus, if Shakespeare exemplifies the Romantic comedy Jonson exemplifies the Satiric comedy existing in Elizabethan times. There were hybrids: but Jonson is undoubtedly a pioneer in the critical comedy of his time.

In his attempt to define the chosen kind of comedy, Jonson naturally went to classical antiquity in search of models. He made a meticulous study of the Greek and Roman masters of comedy. He clearly derived some of his ideas of comedy from the works of Renaissance adherents to the Aristotelian tradition in dramatic theory. He seems to have known best the critical theories of Scaliger, Pontanus, Heinsius and Vossius. He was intimately acquainted with the early Italian commentators on Aristotle, like Robertelli and Vittori, and the creators of complete critical systems like Minturno.[13] Also, Jonson appears to have been familiar with Plato's ideas of comedy, particularly as they found expression in the *Philebus* and the *Laws*.

All these concepts had worked their way into the main current of English Renaissnce criticism. The Renaissance view of comedy, offering no antithesis to tragedy, shows that "the ends of either form are often alike, namely ethical, both in theory and practice."[14] The English Renaissance critics are of almost unanimous opinion that punishment of vice is the proper object of comedy. George Whetstone expresses his view thus:

> For by the rewarde of the good the good are encouraged in wel doinge: and with the scowrge of the lewde the lewde are feared euill attempts.[15]

Sir Philip Sidney defines comedy as

> an imitation of the common errors of our life, which he representeth in the most ridiculous and scornefull sort that may be; so that it is impossible that any beholder can be content to be such a one.[16]

George Puttenham discussing the name and nature of comedy says how comedy deals with

> merchants, souldiers, artificers, good honest householders, and also . . . (with) vnthrifty youthes, yong damsels, old nurses, bawds, brokers, ruffians, and parasites, with such like, in whose behauiors lyeth in effect the whole course and trade of mans life, and therefore tended altogither to the good amendment of man by discipline and example.[17]

Jonson adopted these concepts for his own theory of comedy, but not in toto. For, steeped in earlier native drama, Jonson could never have abandoned the English traditions. Moreover, "popular taste still demanded the kind of satisfactions provided by native drama, and only the closet dramatist could afford to ignore this demand completely."[18] Hence, Jonson's endeavour to achieve a harmonious fusion of the classical and native traditions in the theatre, and the combination of the two is a marked characteristic of Jonson's work. Besides, with his intellectual independence, Jonson was willing to accept Renaissance critical theory only when it agreed with what he himself believed to be true. Further, he had the courage to modify the classical theories so as to suit his own dramatic purposes and genius. All this only testifies to the extent to which Jonson realised the truth that "tradition without the individual talent cannot make an important artist."[19] He was certainly "one, that knowes the strength of his owne *muse*" (*Poetaster*, 'Prologve,' l. 24), and so he

> . . . presents quick *comoedie,* refined,
> As best Criticks haue designed, (*Volpone*: 'Prologve,' ll. 29-30)

The comedy that Jonson presents is the realistic, satirical comedy which is generally known as the 'Comedy of Humours,' however, is not so much a novelty as an elaboration of a long accepted dramatic practice. Naturally it derives itself largley from the didactic content of the Mirth Interludes which ridiculed conceit and braggadocio as in the *Thersytes* and *Ralph Roister Doister*. It also draws on the didactic content of the youth Interludes such as *Hyckescorner* and the *Interlude of Youth* which portrayed the conflict of the spirit with the excesses and lusts of the flesh, with their Vice and Deadly Sins. It may also have derived from the didactic element of still later survivals of the Moral Interludes such as *Trial of Treasure* directed against cupidity, and as Lupton's *All for Money*. In all these, the Vice is but a 'Humour.' Besides, Robert Wilson's reorganized Moral Interludes such as *Three Ladies* and *The Lords and Ladies* contained in germ the critical and satiric which were so powerful as to effect the development of the 'humours' school.

But, in spite of the fact that the 'Comedy of Humours' owes a great deal to the old Morality plays, the period of its gestation was between 1590 and 1598 when Chapman, Porter, Marston and Jonson were associated as playwrights in Henslowe's Company. Chapman was the first to achieve success in the critical school of 'humours.' He preceded Jonson, as has already been observed, in putting a comedy of 'Humours' upon the stage as Henslowe himself evidently stated. But despite Henslowe's statement, we cannot possibly agree with Kreider that Chapman's *An Humourous Day's Mirth* is "a 'bone fide' 'Comedy of Humours'."[20]

What, in this regard, we have to bear in mind is that Chapman was only an experimenter who did not develop any finished product illustrative of the genre—'Comedy of Humours.' Only the 'humour motif' is clearly evident in the entire range of his comedies. His earliest extant play *The Blind Beggar of Alexandria* (1596), is described on its title page as "most pleasantly discoursing the variable humours of Irus in disguised shapes full of conceite and pleasure." The words 'humour' and 'humours' are conspicuous in the dialogues. Particularly the character Cleanthes, like the women in Lyly's *Women in the Moon,* has as many 'humours' as disguises.

No doubt, in his *An Humourous Day's Mirth* the technique of the genre, 'Comedy of Humours,' is displayed to a great extent. All persons characterised are dominated by 'humours.' Chapman, moreover, devotes entire scenes to character-exposition even neglecting to advance his story. Particularly the two characters, Blanuel and Dowsecer are genuine creatures of 'humours.' Also, in his *All Fools,* Cornelia, the jealous husband of Gazette, is largely a 'humours' type. Again, in his *Sir Giles Goosecap* the three characters—Sir Giles, Captain Foulweather and Sir Cuthbert Rudesby—are good studies in 'humours.' Thus, in all of Chapman's comic plays are present characters and situations dependent on 'humours.' All the same, it cannot be maintained that Chapman perfected the genre—'Comedy of Humours.' At best it can be said that he inaugurated the 'Comedy of Humours.'

However, Chapman was not the only 'humour' dramatist in 1597, nor necessarily the first to offer Henslowe a comedy of 'Humours.' Henry Porter has already sold his *What Will Be Shall Be* on December 26th, 1596 to the Admiral's Company, the play that bears some resemblance to the 'Comedy of Humours.' Then followed his famous play *Love Prevented* on May 30th, 1598, a 'humours' comedy of historical distinction. Later, but certainly before *Every Man in His Humour,* he wrote in collaboration with Chettle and Jonson another play evidently of 'humours'—*Hot Anger Soon Cool'd.*

But the point is that the leaders of the critical school of humours were themselves not free from uniting with the portrayal of humours the interest of romantic intrigue also. Although Chapman's *The Blind Beggar* advertises itself as "pleasantly discoursing the variable humours," its plot is an absurd romantic intrigue. The best of his later comedies, including *An Humorous Day's Mirth*, involve extravagant romance. Chapman made very little attempt to bring his plot into organic relation with his Humours. The central interest in the plot of Chapman is provided by the tricks of mischief. But the tricks themselves are of a fantastic ingenuity, far removed from everyday homeliness. Such fantastic romance and passion are peremptorily excluded from Jonsonian 'Humour' plot. In Jonson alone does the 'Comedy of Humours' become conscious and it is closely consistent with the fundamental requirements of the genre.

Finally, Chapman's *An Humorous Day's Mirth* though mentioned by Henslowe as a 'Comedy of Humours' was "a piece of no distinction and of no perceptible influence in its own day."[21] On the other hand, Jonson's much better thought out and better constructed comedy, *Every Man in His Humour,* ushered in a new era, creating a new epoch in dramaturgy thereby firmly establishing the 'Comedy of Humours' as a dramatic form. Therefore, though Chapman anticipated Jonson in using the 'humour motif' in drama, he was not the innovator of the 'Comedy of Humours.' Ben Jonson, then, was, in the highest degree, responsible for the 'Comedy of Humours' regarding both the structural form it took and the critical principles,

> deedes, and language, such as men do vse:
> And persons, such Comoedie would chuse,
> When she would shew an Image of the times,
> And sport with humane follies, not with crimes.
>
> (*Every Man in His Humour*, 'Prologve,' ll. 21-24)

upon which it was mainly based. These critical principles which mainly constitute Jonson's 'Comedy of Humours' unmistakably align it with the satiric tradition of comedy, where comedy is didactic offering as it does moral correction, and is concerned with people placed low in the social scale, people of the city and the streets.

The 'Comedy of Humours,' however, is "one of the most confusing for critical analysis, mainly owing to the fact that all comedy, be it of 'humours' or of romance or of manners, deals with types of character rather than with personalities, and therefore employs what are, to all intents and purposes, the 'humours' which are often assumed to be the sole property of Ben Jonson."[22] Hence, it becomes imperative to specify the elements which particularly distinguish the 'Comedy of Humours' from the other types of comedy so that the specific title given to this kind of drama is seen fully justified.

Surprisingly enough, Jonson, who is always at pains to explain and elucidate the principles of his dramatic technique, is silent regarding the origin and history of the term 'humour.' The general idea, until recently, has been that the 'humour' is purely Jonsonian in origin as well as in development. Critics have been inclined to think that Jonson's most characteristic use of the word humour was at any rate new in drama and that the 'Comedy of Humours' sprang full-grown from the brain of Jonson in *Every Man in His Humour*. This idea is incorrect since 'humour' was already a catchword in literature when Jonson began to write, although it was carelessly used.

Spingarn thinking that the origin of this term, as that of all other critical ideas throughout the sixteenth century Europe, must be looked for in the aesthetic literature of Italy, traces the origin of Jonson's conception of humour to the definition of 'humour' given by Salviati in his manuscript lecture "Del Trattato della Poetica" in about 1586.[23] But, it is not likely that Jonson owed any direct meanings of 'humour' in England much earlier than Salviati's manuscript lecture, and the prevalence of the idea of humour in the didactic literature of England belonging to the last twenty years of the sixteenth century[24] prevent us from considering the Italian influence on Jonson's conception of 'humour' as likely. As Baskervill points out "both the conception of 'humours' and the corresponding treatment of character may well have been independent of foreign influences, though doubtless Italian and classical ideas had the effect of crystallizing native tendencies."[25]

The conception of 'humour,' however, did not begin with Jonson. The term is not of literary origin at all.[26] Like many metaphors in England, the idea of humour comes from Medieval physiology. According to the Medieval physiologists like Galen "there are four elements or simple bodies in creation – earth, fire, air and water which are thought to possess certain qualities. Corresponding with these four elementary qualities are the four bodily humours, namely, melancholia, cholera, phlegm, and blood, generated in the brain, heart, liver and stomach. And arising from the compounding of these humours in the body come four complexions or temperaments of men, viz., the melancholic, the choleric, the phlegmatic and the sanguine."[27] In average and normal persons these conflicting elements were blended in varying proportions to make for individual variations. But this normal balance was sometimes disturbed when a man came to possess one element in excess over the others.[28] Then it was regarded as plethora or in the Italian phrase, an overboiling of the dominant humour.

English literature in the late sixteenth century was full of metaphors and allusions derived from the physical idea of humour. There was a flourishing crop of humour books. The term 'humour' was immensely popular. But in popular parlance 'humour' did not long retain its technical meaning of psychological master-bias rooted in the very nature of the individual. It had passed from the physiologists and doctors into common speeches and pursuits and was used very loosely. It came to express any tendency or disposition. Any mood, condition or habit, for that matter, might he called a 'humour.'

And, by 1598 'humour' lapsed into a catchword to connote sheer extravagance or eccentricity. What is more, it had become a tiresome social convention—a cloak worn threadbare by a fop or the mere apish strain which led a coxcomb to don or anything that he tried to flaunt. The most common meaning of the word was that explained by Cash in *Every Man in His Humour*. To Cob's question, "what is that humour?," Cash replies:

> Mary, I'le tell thee, . . . It is a gentleman-like monster, bred, in the speciall gallantrie of our time, by affectation; and fed by folly.
>
> (III, iv, 18-22)

It was characteristic of Jonson that he endeavoured to formulate the inexact and ill-used term and to present it as the symbol of a literary type. He had no English theories to guide him. He took the popular term and gave sharpness of definition. The clearest statement of what Jonson intended to be the true idea of 'humour' is embedded in the induction to *Every Man Out of His Humour* by way of enlightening an undiscriminating public. His purpose was

> To giue these ignorant well-spoken dayes,
> Some taste of their abuse of this word Humour.

To those who were compelled

> Daily to see how the poore innocent word
> Is rackt, and tortur'd

he offered a definition:

> Why, Humour, (as'tis *ens*) we thus define it . . .
> As when some one peculiar quality
> Doth so possesse a man, that it doth draw
> All his affects, his spirits, and his powers,
> In their confluctions, all to runne one way,
> This may be truly said to be a Humour.
>
> (*Every Man Out of His Humour:* 'Grex,' ll. 79-109)

So, humour, according to Jonson, is not an aberration from average human nature but an intensification of one trait in human nature. Giving his own standpoint thus defined, Jonson glanced at the popular misconception of 'humour':

But that a rooke, in wearing a pyed feather,
The cable hat-band, or the three-pild ruffe,
A yard of shooetye, or the Switzers knot
On his *French* garters, should affect a Humour!
O, 'tis more than most ridiculous. (*Ibid.*, ll. 110-14)

This shows that Jonson was only angry with the people who mistook a 'humour' for a mere trick of speech or dress.

But Jonson's actual depiction of 'humours' is supposed not to be in conformity with his own definition of humour as given in the Induction to *Every Man Out of His Humour.* Gregory Smith says that Jonson "does not always follow his own counsel."[29] Baskervill thinks that many of the 'humours' in Jonson are but affectations.[30] Paul Mueschke and Jeannette Fleisher point out that in his definition of 'humour,' "Jonson himself . . . limits the use of the term 'humour' to a psychological master-bias, but in practice he used it to apply also to more superficial attributes."[31]

To this crux Jonsonian critics have come because they have somehow missed seeing the relationship of the definition to its context in the Induction. A close and careful study of the Induction reveals that Jonson intended to portray affected and eccentric 'humours' as well, 'humours' which are not in accord with his own definition along with the 'humours' of his own definition.[32] When Asper gives examples of affectations as not genuine but pseudo-humours, Cordatus adds:

He speakes pure truth now, if an Idiot
Haue but an apish, or phantasticke straine,
It is his Humour. (*Ibid.*, 'Grex,' ll. 115-17)

Asper's immediate rejoinder is the key to an understanding of Jonson's meaning:

Well I will scourge those apes;
And to these courteous eyes oppose a mirrour,
As large as is the stage, whereon we act:
Where they shall see the times deformitie
Anatoniz'd in euery nerue and sinnew,
With constant courage, and contempt of feare (*Ibid.*, ll. 118-22)

Asper, the mouthpiece of Jonson unequivocally says here that in the play those apes will be well scourged, that is, their affectations and their eccentricities will be portrayed as 'humours' in the popular sense of the word. In other words, Jonson through his presenter tells us that he is fully aware of the meaning of 'humour' in the genuinely psychological sense and that he defined it for us. But, at the same time, he says that those apish and 'phantastic' strains ridiculously called 'humours' in those times would serve not only to show the age its vices and vanities going under the guise of 'humours' but incidentally to give those "ignorant well-spoken days" some taste of their abuse of the word 'humour' and to illustrate how the "poor innocent word is rackt and tortured."

So to speak, when Jonson called his plays 'Comedies of Humours,' he did not mean that he was going to represent the 'humours' only in their limited genuinely psychological sense of which he was fully aware. What he meant was that he would represent 'humour' in its affected apish sense as well, as was in vogue in his times thereby seizing an opportunity not only to mirror the contemporary social follies and foibles but also to anatomize and scourge them with a whip of steel. Then, "like Aristotle's doctrine of catharsis which it strikingly resembles, Jonson's theory of 'humours' is less analytic than apologetic, less a system of literary criticism than an exercise in ethical justification."[33]

To illustrate the critical principles upon which the 'Comedy of Humours' is based, Jonson's first care was to insist on the need for realism so as to bring comedy into closer touch with life. He was of the firm view that unlike tragedy which dealt with far-off, stately and portentous matters, comedy ought to deal with the familiar, immediate and ordinary surroundings that a play-goer could see about him. Hence he genuinely felt that

> to present all custard, or all tart,
> And haue no other meats, to beare a part,
> Or to want bread, and salt, were but course art.
>
> (*The Silent Woman*, 'Prologve,' ll. 16-18)

Considering the contemporary dramatic art to be "course," he confesses that

> Hee is loth to make Nature afraid in his *Playes*, like those that beget *Tales*, *Tempests*, and such like *Drolleries,* to mixe his head with other mens heeles, (*Bartholomew Fair*, 'The Indvction,' ll. 128-31)

Making, thus, clear to his audience how he differs from his fellow playwrights, he asks them not

> to looke backe to the sword and bucklerage of *Smithfield,* but content himselfe with the present. (*Ibid*., ll. 116-17)

Jonson, in this manner, wants his audience to concern themselves not with the things of the past but with those that occur in the present.

Further, Jonson states, almost with a dig at the most unrealistic romantic comedies of his day, that in his comedy

> . . . neither *Chorus* wafts you ore the seas;
> Nor creaking throne comes downe, the boyes to please;
> Nor nimble squibbe is seene, to make afear'd
> The gentlewomen; nor roul'd bullet heard
> To say, it thunders; nor tempestuous drumme
> Rumbles, to tell you when the storme doth come;
> (*Every Man in His Humour,* 'Prologve,' ll. 15-20)

Instead, Jonson purports to give only

> deedes, and language, such as men doe vse
> (*Ibid.*, 'Prologve,' l. 21)

So, the Jonsonian comedy is to deal only with the ordinary and familiar things most common to human experience.

Jonson's comedy, as the line quoted above indicates, is also to employ only such language as is normally used by people in daily life. For, in Jonson's view,

> though . . . language differ from the vulgar somewhat; it shall not fly from all humanity, with the *Tamerlanes* and *Tamer-Chams* of the late Age, which had nothing in them but the *scenicall* strutting, and furious vociferation, (*Discoveries*, ll. 775-79)

Thus, Jonson pleads for realism in his comedy through the treatment of common things in common language. One can easily discern how Jonson's vigorous plea for realistic presentation of things is almost in conformity with Sidney's statement that we "delight . . . in things that have a conveniency to ourselves, or to the general nature."[34]

Regarding the scope or province of his comedy, Jonson thinks that it is to be

> neere, and familiarly allied to the time,

because he

would have a *Comoedie* to be *Imitatio Vitae*
Speculum consuetudinis, Imago Veritatis;
(*Every Man Out of His Homour*, III, vi, 200-7)

So Jonson intends to hold the mirror to the world:

And to these courteous eyes oppose a mirrour,
As large as the stage, whereon we act:
Where they shall see the times deformitie
(*Ibid.*, 'Grex,' ll. 118-20)

In other words, the scope of Jonson's comedy, to put in a nutshell, is to

shew an Image of the times
(*Every Man in His Humour*, 'Prologve,' 23)

Regarding the object of his comedy, Jonson was fully in agreement with Horace that

> The poet's aim is either to profit or to please, or to blend in one the delightful and the useful.[35]

So, the Horatian couplet

Aut prodesse volunt, aut delectare poetae
Aut Simul et iucunda et idonea dicere vitae. (*Ars Poetica,* ll. 333-34)

forms the basis for many of Jonson's formal statements about the profits and pleasure which he included in his comedy.

Uncompromisingly asserting "the impossibility of any mans being the good Poet, without first being a good man," Jonson reveals the function of his comedy when he says that "the office of a *comick-poet*" is "to imitate iustice, and instruct to life . . . or stirre vp gentle affections."[36] He also says:

> I haue labour'd, for their instruction, and amendment, to reduce, not onely the ancient formes, but manners of the scene, the easinesse, the propriety, the innocence, and last the doctrine, which is the principall end of *Poesie,* to informe men, in the best reason of liuing. (*Volpone*, Dedication, ll. 122-23)

When Jonson says that instruction is the "principall end of poesie" he implies that there are possible subsidiary ends. Pleasure is such an end. Again believing with Horace that

> the man who mingles the useful with the sweet carries the day,[37]

Jonson anounces that

> In all his *poemes,* still, hath been this measure,
> To mixe profit, with your pleasure; (*Volpone,* 'Prologve,' ll. 7-8)

With most of his contemporaries the amusement of the playgoers was the chief end. But with Jonson, however pleasant comedy was in its aim and in its method, laughter was not its chief end:

> Nor, is the moving of laughter alwaies the end of *Comedy,* that is rather a fowling for the peoples delight, or their fooling. For, as Aristotle, saies rightly, the moving of laughter is a fault in Comedie, a kind of turpitude, that depraves some part of mans nature without a disease. (*Discoveries*, ll. 2629-32)

Delight is the first consideration and laughter may be a means to it. He finally declares that

> The ends of all, who for the *Scene* doe write,
> Are, or should be, to profit, and delight.
> (*Epicoene*, II 'Prologve,' ll. 1-2)

Even towards the close of his career he tells us how he has had this "double scope" maintained in his plays:

> Thus haue you seene the Makers double scope,
> To profit, and delight. (*The Staple of News*, 'The Epilogve,' ll. 1-2)

Then, Jonson has a definite aim in writing comedy. He starts saying how

> of old, the art of making plaies
> Was to content the people; and their praise
> Was to the *Poet* money, wine, and bayes.
> (*Epicoene*, 'Prologve,' ll. 1-3)

Further, he complains how

> in this age, a sect of writers are,
> That, onely, for particular likings care,
> And will taste nothing that is populare. (*Ibid.*, ll. 4-6)

But Jonson categorically says that his intention is not to play a 'rival' to such 'a sect of writers' that

> make themselues a name with the multitude, or (to draw their rude, and beastly claps) care not whose liuing faces they intrench, with their petulant stiles; *(Volpone,* Dedication, ll. 72-74)

Moreover, he appeals to his judicious spectators that he is not there

> to begge your patience,
> Or seruilely to fawne on your applause,
> Like some drie braine, despairing in his merit:
> (*Every Man Out of His Humour,* 'Grex,' ll. 57-59)

Because his Muse never

> hunts . . . . after popular applause,
> Or fomie praise, that drops from common lawes:
> (*Cynthia's Revels*, 'Prologve,' ll. 13-14)

Hence, Jonson's aim is not to hanker 'after the applause' of the audience but to

> Sport with humane follies, not with crimes
> (*Every Man in His Humour,* 'Prologve,' l. 24)

in keeping with Sidney's "common errors." Jonson could discover classical warrant too for embarking upon this enterprise. He found such sanction in Renaissance theories of "vetus comoedia" and its relation to 'Satyra' and Latin Satire.

As regards the dramatis personae of his comedy Jonson has a particular view. He considered the character of the contemporary drama as 'stage monsters.' He was sorry that the drama had

> nothing but kings and princes in it. (*The Case is Altered*, I, ii, 69)

Jonson further furiously complains:

> take anie of our play-bookes without a CVPID or a MERCVRIE in it, and burne it for an heretique in *Poetrie.*
> (*The Staple of News*, 'Indvction,' ll. 47-49)

He was also vexed with the conventionality of certain characters like fool and devil.

Besides, in the creation of characters the contemporary art aimed at the portrayal of personalities blended with a multiplicity of motives as they usually are in life. It is here that Jonson diverged most radically from the English drama in his age. Jonson's contention was not to present the characters that the dramatist would choose to, but to present only

> persons, such as *Comoedie* would chuse
> (*Every Man in His Humour*, 'Prologve,' l. 22)

So, unlike his fellow-dramatists of the romantic school, Jonson would start with characters set, already formed, fully developed and absorbed in specific 'humours.' These characters he seeks to unfold before our eyes in the course of the play.

Finally, regarding plot-construction in his comedy, Jonson has his own definite views. To him plot must be original. Unlike Shakespeare, he does not believe in borrowing plots from other sources and bettering them. Being sensitive of his right to his own invention of his plots, Jonson was proud of his originality. He proclaims:

> In this alone, his MVSE her sweetnesse hath,
> Shee shunnes the print of any beaten path;
> And proues new wayes to come to learned eares:
> (*Cynthia's Revels,* 'Prologve,' ll. 9-11)

Further, Jonson lays down two principles for plot. The first principle deals with the bound or extent of a play that it should not exceed "the compasse of one Day," but

> there be place left for digression, and Art. For the *Episodes*, and digressions in a Fable, are the same that houshold stuffe, and other furniture are in a house. (*Discoveries*, ll. 2747-49)

The second principle is concerned with the complexity and unity of the plot. Repudiating the single plot as practised by the Greek tragedians,

Jonson insists on the necessity of having more than one strand of action, and these different strands being related, a higher unity is then attained. Jonson reiterates that the plot

> should be one, and intire. One is considerable two waies: either, as it is only separate, and by it self: or as being compos'd of many parts, it beginnes to be one, as those parts grow, or are wrought together. (*Discoveries,* ll. 2751-54)

However, recent critics like Harold F. Brooks are rightly of the view that Jonson's paramount concern, so far as we can deduce from his dramatic practice, was with the 'dramatic design' of each play as a whole. And 'dramatic design' can be regarded as, in a certain sense, plot inasmuch as it belongs to the dramatist's plotting of his play. When Aristotle regards ethos ('character') as subordinate to mythos ('plot'), mythos is a good deal nearer to 'design' than to what we designated 'plot' in the narrow sense of 'intrigue.' We may say that Jonson is Aristotelian and subordinates characterisation, with rare exceptions, to design.

This is, in brief, Jonson's theory of comedy—the 'Comedy of Humours.' We cannot possibly agree with Palmer that "there is, indeed, little that is original or peculiar in Jonson's humours, or the theory of comedy which he constructed upon them."[38] Nor can we subscribe to the view that the 'Prologve' to *Every Man in His Humour*, which is regarded as Jonson's dramatic manifesto, is 'a positive collage of Sidneyisms' and that "Sidney nearly encapsulates both Jonson's aim and his method in the laser comical satires."[39] No doubt, Jonson enthusiastically borrowed Sidney's critical precepts, but he thoroughly assimilated them and, what is more, applied them to his own ends. It is also true that Jonson found in Spenser 'grist to his mill' and in Nashe 'a fellow-spirit and an emotional source,' but Jonson worked most consistently from the outset to re-create the status of the dramatist and to demonstrate authentic poetic genius.

Most of the elements of Jonsonian comedy, as has already been shown, may be found sporadically in previous drama as early as Tudor Interludes and as recent as the first comedies of Shakespeare, but never before had they deliberately been sought and brought together as the essential matter of comedy and systematised. Hence Jonson could justly claim that in the 'Comedy of Humours' he had evolved something new, something different from ancient comedy. In his plea for realism and moral elevation through satire, in his adoption of 'humours' as the basis of his character-creation, in his observance of the Unities and in the originality of his plots, Jonson, beyond doubt, made a departure from the native tradition of comic writing.

Jonsonian comedy, then, is essentially an intellectual, not an emotional, affair. Naturally, its appeal is to the head and not to the heart. It is to be 'an interpretation of life, a criticism of society and an embodiment of values.' Its supreme interest is in character which is sometimes stressed at the expense of plot. Its chief concern is with the dramatic design of each play as a whole. It is this combination of features that gives a distinct character to Jonsonian comedy and not merely the use of 'humours' which has been given "a somewhat fictitious importance in criticism."[40] Perhaps, Jonson was right in choosing a realistic satirical comedy, since in the work which he made characteristically his own he had no equal, whereas in the realms that he abandoned he would have had even a superior.

When we turn from Jonson's theory of comedy to his theory of tragedy, it looks almost as if we had passed from a great talker to a mute. Because Jonson is quite reticent on the theory of tragedy though he is said to have been a good tragedian. Even long before he wrote *Sejanus* and *Catiline*, Jonson was named by Meres in 1598 as one of the nine poets who "were our best for Tragedie."[41] Moreover, even after he had found his strength in comedy in 1598 Jonson did not renounce tragedy altogether. He collaborated in 1599 with other playwrights in the missing *Page of Plymouth* and *Robert II, King of Scots.*[42] Even as late as 1602 he was engaged in his preparation of *Richard Crookback* and his 'Additions' to *The Spanish Tragedy.*[43] Notwithstanding this considerable work he did and the high reputation he earned in writing tragedies Jonson, surprisingly enough, is silent about his achievement in tragedy.

This most unusual silence on the part of Jonson has puzzled critics and has taken literary critics like Atkins by surprise. Atkins comments: "in view of this serious attempt to legislate for a new English comedy it is somewhat surprising to find that Jonson has but little at this date to say regarding tragedy."[44] The surprise on the part of critics becomes all the more intensified especially because of greater popularity of tragedy at this date. Following Aristotle, Italian critics wrote at length on tragedy and, what is more, it was tragedy that had been the greatest of Elizabethan triumphs.

Nevertheless, a close examination of Jonson's dramatic career would certainly dispel all our sense of surprise over his unexpected reticence on the theory of his tragedy. We may say that tragedy was merely an accident in Jonson's dramatic career. Because, but for the unfriendly and discouraging attitude on the part of the public to his Comic Muse, perhaps, Jonson would not have turned to tragedy and we would not have had his two Roman plays. His first regular comedy *Every Man in His Humour* (1598) was a tremendous success and was a "proof that his theory could be translated into practice, even on the popular stage."[45] But with *Every Man Out of His Humour* (1599) Jonson got into difficulties by over-committing himself. In *Cynthia's Revels* (1600) and *Poetaster* (1601) he became too peremptory and too keen to anatomize, to receive good reception from the audience. The public showed a thoroughgoing disregard of his play and Jonson was greatly disappointed and even disgusted, so much that he wanted to forsake the very dramatic form—comedy for the time being—and try his luck in tragedy. This he makes clear in the 'Apologetical Dialogue' that immediately follows *Poetaster:*

> And, since the *Comick* MVSE
> Hath prou'd so ominous to me, I will trie
> If *Tragoedie* haue a more kind aspect. (ll. 222-24)

This is how and why Jonson took to the writing of tragedy by mere force of circumstances and out of sheer necessity.

We have no tragedies of Jonson surviving except *Sejanus* (1603) and *Catiline* (1611). Also, curiously enough, not a line remains of the tragic work to which Meres alludes in *Paladis Tamia.* Naturally enough, critics like Palmer have gone to the extent of doubting whether Jonson had ever written "a full tragedy single-handed except for the two which he acknowledged."[46] This kind of questioning can hardly be brushed aside as there is no evidence or support other than that of Meres to prove that Jonson ever wrote complete and original tragedies of his own in those early years.

Even if Jonson had really written some tragedies earlier, it was not by his will and pleasure, but by force of circumstances. After, all, Jonson had to work for Henslowe to earn his livelihood. So he had to do any work that was assigned to him whether he had aptitude for that sort of literary work or not. Whatever Jonson wrote before 1598 (before he became independent) he wrote for a fee and wrote in the current fashion. Perhaps he did not wish that his apprenticeship work, particularly the tragedies, should survive.

However, if Jonson took to the writing of a tragedy, soon after *Poetaster*, it is because in his state of deep despair and unabated impatience he suddenly, rather accidentally felt that

> There's something come into my thought,
> That must, and shall be sung, high, and aloofe,
> Safe from the wolues black iaw, and the dull asses hoofe.
> (*Poetaster,* 'To The Reader,' ll. 237-39)

The "something" that had come into his thought was Roman tragedy as he would have been attracted by Shakespeare's *Julius Caesar* (1600) which was still one of the resounding successes of the day. We may believe with Robert Ornstein that "*Sejanus* was Jonson's attempt to rival the tremendous success of Shakespeare's drama of Roman conspiracy, *Julius Caesar*."[47]

In view of this, it is less surprising to find that Jonson has but little to say regarding tragedy. However, what Jonson does say is highly significant. Jonson's conception of tragedy may be gathered from his claim to have embodied in *Sejanus* what he regarded as the essential qualities of that dramatic form.

In the preface to *Sejanus* Jonson briefly enumerates the technical points which a writer of tragedy must observe. He begins with a confession that *Sejanus* is "no true *Poeme*" in that it has not observed, judged by ancient standards, "the strict Lawes of *Time*," and "the want of a proper *Chorus*." At the same time he pleads quite reasonably that "in these our Times, and to such Auditors, as commonly Things are presented," it is not needful or almost possible "to obserue the ould state, and splendour of *Drammatick Poemes,* with preseruation of any popular delight." (ll. 6-15) Now he says that he has "discharg'd the other offices of a *Tragick* writer," in observing the laws of

> truth of Argument, dignity of persons, grauity and height of Elocution, fulnesse and frequencie of Sentence.[48]
>
> ('To the Readers,' ll. 18-20)

The primary reason why Jonson put "truth of Argument" in the first place is the belief that fiction is naturally displeasing in a serious work. "Truth of Argument" implied to Renaissance critics a historical argument capable of being presented with verisimilitude. Jonson's view too encompasses this traditonal definition with its corollary but takes a step further. According to Jonson "the argument of a tragedy must not only be drawn from history; it must also be historically verifiable – not merely in the main outline, but even in small, significant details."[49] Jonson himself elaborates his point in the same preface. He says that though he abhors the method of the use of quotations in a play, he has done it in *Sejanus* only "to shew my integrity in the *Story*" with the purpose of "(saving) my selfe in those common Torturers, that bring all wit to the Rack." (ll. 28-30) And in the words of the Oxford Editors Jonson meant 'truth of Argument' and 'integrity in the Story' "in a sense and to a degree which no one before him in the English drama had attempted."[50] For, the

Elizabethan joy in sheer abundance and multiplicity which Jonson so openly displayed in his comedies is, in his conception of tragedy, fortified by the scholar's meticulous particularity in rendering historic facts.

The second tragic law, 'dignity of Persons,' refers to the kind of characters that the Jonsonian tragedy treats. The 'persons' for his comedy are those 'such as *Comoedie* would chuse.' Similarly Jonson might have meant that the persons for his tragedy are those such as tragedy would choose. If his comedy chooses already-formed types from low life, his tragedy is to choose characters that come from high life with gravity and sobriety.

The third essential quality of Jonson's tragedy—'grauity and height of Elocution'—is clearly a reference to a lofty style. Jonson used 'gravity' in the sense of the Latin 'gravitas,' a peculiarly Roman quality denoting both weight and dignity. If the characters of his comedy speak in the ordinary, simple language of day-to-day life, the characters of his tragedy are to use an elevated language with heightened diction.

The last tragic law—'fulnesse and frequencie of Sentence'— adverts to the didactic function of the Jonsonian tragedy. The tragedy is to be fraught with sententious precepts. 'Fulnesse and frequencie of sentence' is also a Roman tradition. The sentence, or moral maxim expressed with point and brevity, is a legacy of Seneca, and it was popular in Elizabethan writing. And, 'fulnesse and frequencie of Sentence' is quite analogous to the dictum, 'to imitate justice and instruct to life,' of the Jonsonian comedy.

From this brief theory of tragedy it is clear to us that Jonson has in mind the Senecan conception of tragedy, a conception previously illustrated by Sidney in his *Apology for Poetry,* rather than the Aristotelian conception. Also, it is obvious that Jonson's conception of tragedy was largely dictated by the same considerations as had given rise to his idea of comedy. And "we cannot say that the qualities which made Jonson triumphant in comedy were unsuited to tragedy."[51] A close study of Jonson's theory of comedy and of tragedy, however, would certainly confirm his idea that "the parts of a *Comedie* are the same with a *Tragedie,* and the end is partly the same." (*Discoveries,* ll. 2625-26) Nevertheless, there is a significant difference between Jonson's comedies and tragedies. While the follies of his comedies are concerned with human motives, speech and actions, the crimes of his tragedies almost duplicate historical fact. In other words, when Jonson represents idealized folly on the stage he produces comedy, but when he presents on the stage actions which have actually occurred one time or other in history, he produces tragedy.

Disapproving of the conventional conception of the relations of comedy and tragedy, Jonson thus comes forward with his own definite theories of comedy and tragedy whrein the fostered oppositon between the two species disappears. Like Dryden, Pope, Wordsworth, Arnold and T.S. Eliot, later in the sphere of poetry, Jonson was potent in moulding the taste of his own age as well as the course which English drama was to take in times to come.

Both in view of the contemporary plight of comedy and by virtue of his own genius for comedy, Jonson focused all his attention on the theory and practice of comedy. In the following chapters, an attempt is made to discuss how far Jonson's theories of comedy have been applied and worked out in his plays.

NOTES

1. L.J. Potts, *Comedy* (London, 1949), p. 10.
2. "Comedy is an imitation of those who are worse than ourselves, yet not in every sort of evil but only in that baseness of which the ridiculous is a species."
   "Tragedy is an imitation of an action that is serious and complete and has sufficient size in language that is made sweet, and with each of the kinds of sweet language separately in the various parts of the tragedy, presented by those who act and not by narrative, exciting pity and fear, bringing about the catharsis of such emotions."
   ("The Poetics," *Literary Criticism*: *Plato to Dryden*, ed. Allan H. Gilbert, pp. 74-75).
3. Allardyce Nicoll, *An Introduction to Dramatic Theory* (London, 1931), p. 23.
4. Johnson, "Preface to Shakespeare," *English Critical Texts*, ed. Enright and Chickera (London, 1962), p. 136.
5. Daniello (1536) distinguishes tragedy from comedy in that the comic poets 'deal with the most familiar and domestic, not to say base and vile operations; the tragic poets, with the deaths of high kings and the ruins of great empires.' Giraldi distinguishes tragedy from comedy on somewhat the same grounds as Daniello. "Tragedy and comedy" he says, "differ in that the former imitates the illustrious and royal, the latter the popular and civil." (J.E. Spingarn, *A History of Literary Criticism in the Renaissance* (New York, 1899), pp. 61-62.
6. "Discourse of English Poetrie," *Elizabethan Critical Essays,* ed. Gregory Smith (Oxford, 1904), vol. I, p. 249.

7. Though published anonymously, there is sufficient scope for attributing *Soliman and Perseda* to Kyd. The very fact that the story of Soliman and Perseda forms the subject of Hieronimo's play in Act IV of *The Spanish Tragedy* indicates that "it must . . . have deeply interested Kyd and been looked upon by him as suitable material for the stage." (F.S. Boas, ed., *The Works of Thomas Kyd*, p. vi). Also, see James E. Routh Jr., "Thomas Kyd's Rime Schemes and the Authorship of *Soliman and Perseda* and of *The First Part of Jeronimo*," *MLN*, XX (1905), pp. 49-51.
8. Allardyce Nicoll, *The Theatre and Dramatic Theory*, p. 116.
9. Gregory Smith, *Ben Jonson* (London: Macmillan, 1990), p. 76.
10. Allardyce Nicoll, *An Introduction to Dramatic Theory*, p. 24.
11. John Russell Brown, *Shakespeare and His Comedies* (London, 1957), p. 28.
12. Nevill Coghill, "The Basis of Shakespearian Comedy," *ES*, III, (1950), p. 9.
13. See J.E. Spingarn, ed., *Critical Essays of the Seventeenth Century*, vol. I, pp. xvi-xviii. Spingarn, of course, observes that Jonson's "knowledge of critical developments on the continent was limited by his small French and less Italian." (p. xvi) But Jonson's comparative ignorance of Italian, as shown by O.J. Campbell ("The Relation of *Epicoene* to Aretino's *IlMarescalco*," *PMLA*, XLVI (1931), p. 762), is inferred only from Drummond's ill-natured and suspicious report. Hence it need not be taken very seriously.
14. Nevill Coghill, p. 7.
15. "Dedication" to *Promos and Cassandra* (1578), *Elizabethan Critical Essays*, vol. I, p. 59.
16. "An Apologie for Poetrie" (1583), *Ibid.*, pp. 176-77.
17. "The Arte of English Poesie" (1589), *Ibid.*, vol. II, p. 33.
18. J.B. Bamborough, *Ben Jonson* (London, 1959), p. 19.
19. Harold F. Brooks, "Marlowe and Early Shakespeare," *Christopher Marlowe* (Mermaid Critical Commentaries), ed. Brian Morris (London, 1968), p. 84.
20. Paul V. Kreider, *Elizabethan Comic Character Conventions as Revealed in the Comedies of Chapman*, p. 146.
21. C.F. Tucker Brooke, *Tudor Drama* (Boston, 1911), p. 405.
22. Allardyce Nicoll, *An Introduction to Dramatic Theory*, p. 182.
23. See J.E. Spingarn, *A History of Literary Criticism in the Renaissance* (New York, 1899), pp. 88-89.
24. The word 'humour' occurs with several meanings in stories, in Greene's numerous treatments of jealousy, in plays as in Lyly's *Women in the Moon* and in character sketches as in Lodge's *Wits*

Miserie and Nashe's *Pierce Penilesse.*

25. C.R. Baskervill, *English Elements in Jonson's Early Comedy* (Austin: University of Texas Press, 1911), p. 45.
26. See Percy Simpson, ed., *Every Man in His Humour*, 'Introduction,' p. xxxvi.
27. W.C. Curry, "Doctor of Physic and Mediaeval Medicine," *Chaucer and the Mediaeval Science* (New York, 1926), p. 10.
28. See W.W. Skeat, *Oxford Chaucer*, vol. V, pp. 32, 40-42.
29. Gregory Smith, *Ben Jonson* p. 85.
30. See Baskervill, *English Elements in Jonson's Early Comedy*, pp. 33-36.
31. Paul Mueschke and Jeannette Fleisher, "Jonsonian Elements in the Comic Underplot of *Twelfth Night*," *PMLA*, 48 (1933), p. 723.
32. See Henry L. Snuggs, "The Comic Humours: A New Inerpretation," *PMLA*, 62 (1947), p. 119.
33. Harry Levin, "An Introduction to Ben Jonson," in ed. Jonas A. Barish, p. 41.
34. Sidney, 'Apology for Poetry,' *English Critical Texts*, pp. 42-43.
35. Allan H. Gilbert, ed., p. 139.
36. "Jonson here aligns himself with the central tradition of Christian-Humanist defenders of poetry as the union of eloquence and wisdom in the setting forth of moral truth, as posited by Sidney in his *Defense of Poesy* and by Milton in *An Apology for Smectymnuus*." (W. Speed Hill, "Biography, Autobiography and *Volpone*," *SEL*, XII (Spring, 1972), p. 310).
37. Allan H. Gilbert, ed., p. 139.
38. John Palmer, *Ben Jonson* (New York: The Viking Press, 1934), p. 30.
39. Rosalind Miles, p. 9.
40. W.S. Johnson, "Review" of Baskervill's *English Elements in Jonson's Early Comedy*, *JEGP*, XII (1913), p. 340.
41. "So these are our best for Tragedie, The Lorde Buckhurst, Doctor Leg of Cambridge, Doctor Edes of Oxford, Master Edward Ferris . . . Marlowe, Peele, Watson, Kyd, Shakespeare, Drayton, Chapman, Decker, and Beniamin Johnson." (Meres, "Palladis Tamia," *Elizabethan Critical Essays*, vol. II, p. 319)
42. See *Henslowe's Diary*, ed. R.A. Foakes and R.T. Ricket, pp. 96, 123-24.
43. *Ibid.*, pp. 182-203.
44. J.W.H. Atkins, *English Literary Criticism: The Renascence* (London, 1947), p. 259.
45. Gregory Smith, *Ben Jonson*, p. 100.

46. John Palmer, p. 124.
47. Robert Ornstein, *The Moral Vision of Jacobean Tragedy* (Madison, 1960), p. 90.
48. The importance of these critieria in the criticism of the Italian Renaissance is discussed by J.E. Spingarn in *A History of Literary Criticism in the Renaissance*, pp. 74-81.
49. J.A. Bryant, Jr., "The Significance of Ben Jonson's First Requirement for Tragedy: Truth of Argument," *SP*, XLIX (Jan. 1952), p. 203.
50. Herford and Simpson, vol. II, p. 8.
51. Robert Ornstein, p. 85.

Deeds and Language Such as Men Do Use

The basic principle which Jonson accepted from the ancients and which was further reinforced from his study of Sidney was that comedy should be patterned after real life. Hence his determination to recall comedy from its romantic entanglements "at a time when there was a fear of comedy's vanishing altogether into those fantastic and impossible realms of make-believe."[1] Jonson's endeavour was to bring comedy to the levels of ordinary existence through presenting in his plays

> deedes, and language, such as men doe vse.
>
> (*Every Man in His Humour,* 'Prologve,' l. 21)

What he meant by this was that his characters were to live and move and have their being in a world of recognizable experience and that his plays, rendering artistically the real and familiar, would breathe an aura of realism. Thus, proclaiming himself to be a stubborn realist, Jonson was seeking to present men and things as he saw them.

It is, of course, true that "realism was no new element in English comedy."[2] Already change was in the air. A reaction against the excesses of the romantic playwrights had already set in both in theory and practice. Sidney in his *Apology for Poetry* (1583) had condemned the gross absurdities of the Elizabethan stage and clearly discussed the need for realism in comedy. Realism had been present in the early English plays like *Gammer Gurton's Needle* (1552-63) which was truly English in its realism, set in an English village with its miry roads and its cozy but badly kept houses. In the words of Rossiter, "the play deals solely with low-life types in a village rumpus."[3] Lyly's *Mother Bombie* (1590), with its contemporary character, has realistic touches about it. We witness marks of realism in historical plays like *The Famous Victories of Henry V* and particularly in Shakespeare's *Henry IV Part I* and its successors. Historical and 'low-life' scenes roughly alternate in *The Famous Victories.* The incidents of the play include the robbery by the prince and his confederates, and their riotous mirth leads to a quarrel and the interpositon of the sheriff and mayor of London. There are certainly 'low-life' scenes interspersed here and there in the three parts of *Henry VI*. Then, in *Henry IV Part I*, we have the realistic comedy of London life which the Elizabethan dramatists knew so well. Especially the Eastcheap scenes are steeped in realism. Furthermore, a movement in that direction had already become visible in the plays of Chapman and Porter, particularly in the former's *An Humorous Day's Mirth* (1597).

But the point is that if Jonson was not the first to express the change, he was certainly the first to emphasize the far-reaching importance of realism as an element in comedy. As Nicoll puts it "realism, added to intensified 'humour,' treated in a satirical spirit, was first given to the theatrical world by Jonson."[4]

Realism, however, was vital to Jonson's comedy. Jonson's acceptance of humours entailed a certain amount of exaggeration. It meant that his creatures were to be the embodiments of one particular quality, to be the walking illustrations of an idea or a theory. Secondly, it involved the danger of their becoming uniform and standardised and, thus, dramatically unreal like the symbolical figures of the old Morality plays. It was to guard against these dangers that Jonson strove for realism. And in this endeavour he succeeded admirably, thanks to his keen observation, his first-hand knowledge of contemporary life, his grip on concrete facts and his emphasis on individual and local traits and colour.

The term 'realism,' as its etymology suggests, denotes attachment to fact, or the tendency to regard things as they really are. In other words, pure realism implies absolute fidelity to nature or impartial transcription of the phenomenal world. But such realism is neither possible nor desirable in literature. For, "the idiosyncrasies of human perception, the multiple zones and levels that constitute the real, as well as the alchemy of the creative process, forbid, strictly speaking, any objective account of the world in art."[5] Realism at best can only be approximate inasmuch as "art cannot give us 'la chose meme' except by resorting to artifice; the theatre has its trick mirrors, its optical illusions; the playwright, like the painter, manipulates techniques and calculates impressions."[6]

Jonson endeavours to make his comedies realistic in texture, tone and temper by making the setting, incidents, characters and dialogue realistic. He openly set his scene in London and made his characters English in a systematic way. He had a great belief in the value of English life for the work of the literary man. He frankly and boldly announces:

> Our *Scene* is *London*, 'cause we would make knowne,
> No countries mirth is better then our owne.
> No clime breeds better matter, for your whore,
> Bawd, squire, impostor, many persons more,

Whose manners, now call'd humours, feed the stage:
(*The Alchemist*, 'Prologve,' ll. 5-9)

The basis of Jonson's satirical comedy which is the reflection of follies and vices of the contemporary society invites him to draw upon the very world in which he lives for his material. Naturally enough, his plays are rich in details taken from real life and glimpses of actual manners. They are full of contemporary allusions to the theatre, the scholarship, the new Royal Exchange and commerce, the money-lenders, usurers, alchemists and other swindlers which the London swarmed with, to the fashionable pastimes of fencing, hunting, smoking and living by wits—so popular in Elizabethan-Jacobean London—and to the actual events of the period like plagues.

The early comedies of Jonson—*The Case is Altered* and *A Tale of a Tub*[7]—contain only incidental suggestions of the realistic method. They illustrate the formative stage in the playwright's realistic method. *The Case is Altered* is, in the main, an attractive piece of Jonson's romantic apprentice-work based on the old motive of infant confusion. Though Plautian in plot and introducing personal satire on Munday, it is romantic in tone with its scene set in Milan and its element of averted tragedy. However, the most individual part of the play and the only part which has significance in the light of Jonson's later career is that dealing with the subsidiary 'humours' of Juniper, the cobbler, Peter Onion and their companions.

A Tale of a Tub is far more a Jonsonian work than *The Case is Altered* in that it concerns itself exclusively with contemporary London types most of which are presented with real wit and appreciation. Limiting its action strictly to the compass of a single day and to the immediate suburbs of London, the play develops quite amusingly a thin story of mutual deceit and misunderstanding.

Every Man in His Humour (1598) is Jonson's first mature play. Conceived as a kind of 'domestic panorama,' the play is a realistic presentation of a series of sharply contrasted characters—an old father over-concerned about a son, a jealous husband and his wife, a plain squire, a sharp-minded servant, a water-bearer and his wife, a country gull and a town gull, and a merry magistrate.

Every Man in His Humour was first set in Italy, but with the revision of the play,[8] the scene was changed to London with the sole purpose of making it more realistic to the English audience. The process of transformation was unquestionably a process of improvement. The names of the characters are changed, vague references are particularised, excesses and imbalances of plot are toned down, and the whole action gains in realism.

The discarding of the Italian convention by the change of scene, naturally gives point to a picture of London life and manners. Transplanted from the imaginary or fantastic Italy, in which at first they lived and had their being, to the actual and immediate atmosphere of contemporary London, the characters gain even more in life-like and interesting veracity or verisimilitude. The people are made livelier and more recognizable, the dialogue more relaxed and realistic, and the whole thing is planted firmly in a London climate. Naturally the play is redolent of London life in its varied aspects. The whole racy action is instinct with the life of Jonson's own time. The jealousy of Kitely, the pretence of Cob, the absurdities of the gulls, Matthew and Stephen, the up-to-date oaths, the skill in the tobacco art and the latest duelling strokes of Bobadill—all these derive from the native sources as well as from Jonson's own imaginative power.

Thus, *Every Man in His Humour*, in its deliberate and successful adaptation of the Latin methods of realism as opposed to the unregulated and sensational devices adopted by the dramatists of the day, becomes a classic. However sharply it traversed certain romantic proclivities of the stage, it "powerfully appealed to the ingrained realism of the Elizabethan audience and gave them with a vigour and brilliance paralleled yet only in the contemporary glory of Falstaff's Eastcheap what they wanted most."[9] Thus the play was a tremendous success.

Jonson did not simply set out to capitalise on the success of *Every Man in His Humour* by repeating its effects in the immediately following 'Humour' play, *Every Man Out of His Humour* (1599). He now seems to have been more interested in considering seriously what the proper form and role of Comedy were. As a result, despite the similarity of title, *Every Man Out of His Humour* is a different sort of play from its predecessor.

The action of the play is slight. The stage is crowded with a great variety of strongly defined characters—an envious poor man, a vainglorious knight, a profane jester, an affected courtier, a doting citizen, a proud wife, a light-witted lady, a misanthropical knave—all intensive studies in realism as they are all representatives of social follies in contemporary London. They are kept in their 'humours' till the close of the fourth act and finally every one is shaken out of his 'humour' by suitable exposure. It is, indeed, "a play of verbal and psychological rather than bodily combat."[10]

Though Jonson himself felt that in this comedy "his art appears most full of lustre, and approcheth nearest the life" (IV, viii, 166-67), his realistic method is marred by excess. Here Jonson gets into difficulties by over-committing himself to the mood of Asper. In his zeal for emphasis, he so crowds the stage that he himself justly wonders:

is't possible there should be any such Humorist? (II, iii, 41)

Also, the unravelling of the 'humours' at the end sounds a little perfunctory. Yet, in spite of its excesses and all the Italian names,[11] *Every Man Out of His Humour* is also a London play, full of the atmosphere of contemporary London.

In *Cynthia's Revels* (1600) we have a play only partly realistic, despite its truthfully-presented theme of self-love, because here Jonson combines his realistic comedy with the allegoric and symbolic techniques of the artificial myth-world of the masque, perhaps, by way of evolving a new kind of play.[12] No doubt, "Lyly had faced the same problems that Jonson was facing in the attempt to write comedy that was at once topical enough for the fashionable, serious enough for the intellectuals, and robust enough for the vulgar, and had managed (especially in his *Mother Bombie*) to combine homeliness, raciness and vigour with the most polished and rigorous artistic control."[13] But Lyly was out of favour and his euphuistic style had become a stock subject for parody by the time Jonson wrote *Cynthia's Revels.* So, while making no attempt to reproduce the artifices of euphuism, Jonson follows the symmetry and balance of the characters and plots of Lyly's plays.

In *Cynthia's Revels* Jonson applies classical myth to the dramatic presentment of Elizabeth's court. Naturally enough there arises a 'strange encounter' between the realist and the symbolist in Jonson. The courtly fops and pretenders – Hedon, Anaides, Amorphus, Asotus and their ladies – so obviously indigenous to Jonsonian London get mingled in the palace chambers with antique gods and allegorical personifications – Mercury and Cupid, Arete and Hesperus. The very scene of the action, though always in or near the palace, changes its complexion and latitude with the changing persons.

However, with all its heavy mythological and allegorical superstructure and its explicitly-stated moral idealism, *Cynthia's Revels* is not totally devoid of realistic flavour. For, Jonson, all through the play, insists on the existence of universal ideals as well as temporal absurdities. Jonson's direct observation of contemporary human life, no doubt, suffers a large intrusion of fanciful and abstract elements. But, at least clearly in details and in single characters the great realist painter of Elizabethan court cannot be missed. Most of the action is concerned with the courtiers and their ladies who represent the kind of follies and vices – self-love, frivolity, voluptuousness, impudence, extravagance – that were most prominent at Elizabeth's court.

Poetaster (1601) is a play about poets and their problems. In spite of its title, "the subject of the play is not bad poets, but the good poet and the education of the poet."[14] He does not merely devote his energies to attacking his enemies, but restates his positive views of the nature of true poetry. Taken as a defence of poetry, *Poetaster* clearly states Jonson's views of the different 'kinds' in poetry, their relative importance, and the value each had for humanity.

However, what in this play Jonson is finally concerned with is the relationship between poetry and the body politic, poetry and the state. Whenever he is concerned with such literary problems he chooses to present them not on the usual realistic level of action but on a symbolic level, of course, implied in the realistic level.

Jonson presents in *Poetaster* the dissolute society of his own age under cover of scholarly reconstruction and imaginative revival of the literary life of Augustan Rome. Through that society of historical fiction, Jonson presents "a symbolical picture of the relations of true poets and poetasters to frivolous and dissolute London society of the last years of Elizabeth's reign."[15] What is noteworthy is that in painting an accurate picture of the manners, temper and taste of Augustan society Jonson is ingeniously emphasizing the features that resemble the pageant of London life in 1601. The historical setting remains Rome, but the situation is sharply relevant to the actual world of Jonson's England. Thus, in *Poetaster,* Jonson achieves considerable verisimilitude by forcing one period of Roman history to yield its experience to portray the dangerous tendencies in the society of his own day.

If Jonson has preferred London to Italy for the scene of action of *Every Man in His Humour* with a view to gaining more in realism, he prefers Venice to London for the scene of action of *Volpone* (1605) with the same view.[16] Here Jonson takes for his theme the most universal passion of mankind susceptible of indefinite exploration—the inflation of the will at the expense of the spirit.

However, it is not as though "in choosing such a subject as this Jonson . . . necessarily abandoned one of his surest holds upon the play-going public, his powerful presentment of the London life at their doors."[17] It is also not correct to say that "neither the events of the play nor the dialogue through which they are conveyed could possibly be described as 'realistic,' even by the standard of most other contemporary urban comedies."[18] Because the worlds created by such consummate artists as Jonson could not be merely fanciful inasmuch as "they have a logic of their own; and the logic illuminates the actual world, because it gives us a new point of view from which to inspect it."[19]

The subject of *Volpone* need not necessarily be the narrow theme of avarice as presented in the masterpieces of Plautus and Moliére, but can be considered as a more spacious one—the attraction and power of effective wealth—which compels even a jealous husband to procure his virtuous wife, an old gentleman to disinherit his own dutiful son, an advocate to perjure himself twice in open court, and an Italianate English lady to risk her reputation. Almost every scene in the play is so designed as to exhibit the consequences of wealth, the insolence which it breeds and the infamies which one would commit for the love of it. Hence, in the modern theatre one would find an opulence of production and 'decors' as necessary to emphasize the preoccupation with affluence and acquisitiveness which the play exposes.

The subject of *Volpone* can also be related to Jacobean London. *Volpone* presents a powerful picture of the moral depravity of the age. The issues with which Jonson deals here—gold-fever, passion for sensuous beauty, craving for sensual pleasures with a spirit of revolt against conventional morality—"were among the most deeply ingrained preoccupations of his age."[20] They were all the offshoots of the English Renaissance which, here, are 'deglamourized.'

Moreover, with the introduction of the three English characters—Sir Politic Would-be, Lady Politic Would-be and Peregrine—Jonson fully recovers the normal temper of his realistic comedy. Sir Politic is a contemporary satirical portrait of the English traveller, and Lady Would-be a minor Mrs. Malaprop. Turning from the Venetians of his invention to those quaintly refreshing English personages of his familiar experience, Jonson is reflecting the life in Fleet street and Westminster.

Thus *Volpone* is in essentials as English as it is Venetian while superficially taking advantage of the current fascination of Italy as a land of supposedly exotic and sensational crime. So Jonson loses little in immediacy and realistic flavour because of the foreign setting. On the other hand, as David Cook rightly argues, "the very slight distancing which does result from the foreign mise-en-scéne partly explains why the satiric sweep is bolder and larger in *Volpone* even than in that tremendous comedy *The Alchemist*, which is so vividly localised in London."[21]

Epicoene (1609) is Jonson's "first play fully and frankly set in London and dedicated to a realistic representation of contemporary society, distorted only to the limits of probability."[22] Yet, there are some critics who consider it as a farce.[23] This is chiefly because the plot of the play turns upon a mere trick—the entrapping of Morose, the hater of noise, into marriage with the loquacious and proves ultimately to be a boy. The fun drawn out of this is said to be so wildly improbable as to be out of place in a comedy. But these critics seem to have missed the rich symbolic suggestion of the whole play which lends it realistic significance.

The point is that the title, *Epicoene*, as Partridge very rightly suggests, "refers to much more than a central twist of the plot in which

Morose's wife turns out to be a boy."[24] It symbolically applies to the aberrant and topsy-turvy society represented in the play. Below the farcical surface action of the play can be found the serious themes of courtly affection, unnatural sexuality and pretence to authority. Fundamentally concerned with deviations from a norm, the play explores, in the main, the question of 'decorum' of the sexes and the 'decorum' of society. Its various scenes explore comically and searchingly certain standards of what is masculine and what is feminine, as well as what is natural and what is artificial in dress, behaviour and beauty, standards which the spectators bring to the theatre with them. This kind of thematic approach, as Slights rightly observes, "helps to account for the complexity of thought which is easily over-looked when the play is compared to the rather simple continental farces of the early sixteenth century."[25]

Almost every one in the play is epicene in some way or other. The Collegiate Ladies are portrayed as too bold to be feminine. They look women but act like men. Truewit describes how they are

> an order betweene courtiers, and country-madames . . . with most masculine, or rather *hermaphroditicall* authoritie: (I, i, 75-80)

The epicene natures of the women throw the masculine natures of the men out of gear. For instance, Tom Otter's nature is dislocated by his wife's masculinity. La Foole, the man, apparently speaks in an effeminate manner.

Then to observe how the play explores the question of what is natural and what is artificial, we have to note the allusions to the prodigies and to the strange, the unnatural and the monstrous. Just as Morose thinks that any one (except himself) who makes noise is a prodigy, Truewit thinks that complete silence is a prodigy. He says

> There was neuer such a prodigie heard of. (I, ii, 3)

Epicoene's loquacity which seems 'monstrous' impertinency to Morose, appears quite normal and natural to the Ladies Collegiate, because they themselves are most loquacious. Furthermore, the famous song—"Still to be neat, still to be drest"—Clerimont writes being offended by Lady Haughty's artificial beauty, highlights the dichotomy between nature and artifice. Clerimont upholds simplicity and nature because the artifices of powder and perfume may only conceal what is not sweet and sound. The natural to him is to be simple, careless and free. Approached in this fashion, *Epicoene* comes to us as a comedy about nature, normality and 'decorum.'

Besides, the milieu of the play is realistic. The scene of action is London. The plot itself depends strictly on the facts of the local setting. The characters—idle gallants, ladies of pleasure, a barber, a page, a henpecked captain—are all recognizable London types. What is more, the subjects of their conversation are the fashionable topics of the day. Thus "in its grace, its verve, its hard-won realism, and its appeal to the coterie instincts of a social elite *Epicoene* became almost a model for future English Comedy."[26]

Rooted in the Jacobean London of Jonson's own day, and based on an actual event of the times, *The Alchemist* (1610) gives us a tremendous impression of reality, transmuting some of the everyday affairs of Jonson's own contemporary surroundings into poetry, poetizing the affairs of cheats, conjurers, panders, knaves and gulls. It has the vigour and veracity of *Volpone* with none of its bitterness. Jonson attempts here another large canvas of tricksters and gulls. He shows how the desire to become suddenly rich brings a grocer, Drugger, a lawyer's clerk, Dapper, a city knight, Sir Epicure Mammon, a country squire, Kastrill, the puritans, Ananias and Tribulation Wholesome severally into the clutches of a pseudo-alchemist, Subtle. We watch with astonishment the unfolding of the realistic action which continues with increasing complexity through a series of crises to the return of Lovewit, the houseowner.

The Alchemist stands apart from all Jonson's previous comedies in sheer realism of subject. For, when Jonson turned to alchemy as a subject for his realistic comedy he found "the material ready to his hand of the right admixture of pretentious learning and bizarre humbug perfectly suited to his comic genius."[27] He uses alchemy as one of the principal means toward the amazing complication of the simple tight plot. The multiplicity of cants and high-flown jargon of the alchemists go a long way-in making the play realistic. Subtle and Face are masters at juggling the various meanings of such words as 'grace,' 'virtue' and 'price' in order to befuddle their dupes. Face, for instance, confides to Dapper:

> You doe not know
> What grace her *Grace* may doe you in cleane linnen. (I, ii, 174-75)

The plot of the play hinges upon an actual event—the plague that visited London in the summer of 1610, the year in which it was written and produced. Besides, the play is full of contemporary allusions to commerce, the money-lenders and swindlers, the cheats and tricksters, the gamblers and the gambling houses. What is more, it "reproduces the rhythms of ordinary life in a great, Renaissance city."[28] It also points to the practice of rich country people coming to town to learn fashions, the mathematical aspect of fencing, the new Royal Exchange, the new water works, the famous scholars of physics and mathematics and the coins like Harry's sovereign. Interwoven thus with everyday events of Jonson's time, *The Alchemist* is a brilliant picture of London life in 1610.

After *Bartholomew Fair* (1614)[29] Jonson reverts, in *The Devil is an Ass* (1616), to a fervently popular class of subject, the devil lore – a crude supernaturalism inherited from Mysteries and Moralities. Jonson himself ridiculed those who would

> desire rather to see fooles, and deuils, and those antique reliques of barbarisme retriu'd with all other ridiculous, and exploded follies:
> (*Volpone*, Dedication, ll. 79-81)

Yet, he himself now seems to 'retrieve' the 'antique relic' by producing a devil play, but only to "make comic capital out of the dust and cobwebs of its antiquity."[30] This he achieves through a constant interplay of literary caricature and realistic portraiture.

The Devil is an Ass concerns itself with the adventures of a minor devil, Pug, during a day's sojourn on earth, his purpose being to introduce new corruption into the affairs of men thereby to gain new and greater triumphs for hell as well as glory to himself.[31] But the main theme is provided by the projectors, monopolists and patentees whose activities had alarmingly increased by the middle of the reign of James I.[32]

That Jonson presents the contemporary world in all his plays we are conscious. But, perhaps, never before has he handled a major political issue of the day so effectively as he does in the present play. If in *Volpone* he has concerned himself with attitudes and impulses permanent in human nature, now he brings the events themselves upon the stage with the result that "a study of the leading characters in *The Devil is an Ass* . . . would be by far the best introduction to the economic history of the period."[33] Meercraft, for instance, was an absolutely contemporary figure, making use of a notorious economic abuse of the day.

If *The Devil is an Ass* were merely a political pamphlet, it would have been ephemeral and would have died a natural death. The effectiveness and success of the play is due to the fact that it is much more than a political pamphlet. However close the play is to the contemporary scene, Jonson's incisive handling of the satiric material raises it well above the level of a mere documentary. The projects presented in the play are carried through in such a way as to keep close to reality. The audience is kept "shifting uneasily from fantastic caricature to sober truth, and back, until reality itself is seen in the same critical light as the caricature."[34] Thus the combination of the traditional, the contemporary, and the timeless is brilliant in *The Devil is an Ass.*

The Staple of News (1625) is not simply a hasty putting-together of ill-assorted parts. There is much lively comic invention as well as a serious intellectual theme in it. The play treats a quite recent feature of London social life—"hunger and thirst after publish'd pamphlets of *News* . . . no syllable of truth in them." ('To The Readers,' ll. 12-15)[35] The staple office, we may say, is a variant of the alchemist's laboratory devised for the fabrication of news instead of gold. The staple is built upon money-greed and it collapses upon the failure of funds. Jonson's imaginary office of the staple had such a bland air of reality about it that he had to add a note to his readers:

> Wherein, although our *Title,* Sir, be Newes
> Wee yet adventure, here, to tell you none;
> But shew you common follies, and so knowne,
> That though they are not truths, th' innocent Muse
> Hath made so like, as Phant'sie could then state,
> Or *Poetry*, without scandall, imitate.
>
> ('The Prologve for the Covrt,' ll. 9-14)

thus assuring them that the whole thing was a joke and that his parody of European news had no sinister interpretations.

The notion of the staple, however, permits Jonson to satirize the new news industry as well as the behaviour of those who buy and sell the news. Jonson's "technique is to make the Staple Office a holiday joke in which the new business of newsmongering is blown up into a large-scale monopolistic enterprise like the venerable Wool Staple."[36] News is issued under the 'Office-Seale' as 'Staple Commodittie'. And as Fitton exclaims

> . . . if a man will assure his Newes, he may:
> Two-pence a Sheet he shall be warranted,
> And haue a *policie* for't. (I, v, 64-66)

Jonson, however, mixes this matter-of-fact business of the piece with the allegory of Lady Pecunia and the Pennyboys in which again money and its various uses and abuses are the primary theme. Hence the play involves a curious mixture of allegoric abstraction and moral symbolism—the elements that seem so discrepant. Nonetheless, Jonson brings to this problem he has created all the resources of his tried stagecraft and of his invention and shows an astonishing talent for giving abstractions—Gossips, Tattle, Mirth, Expectation, and Censure—the semblance of life. Like Beaumont's Citizen and his Wife, these lively characters "remain a credible and vivid depiction of unsophisticated theatre-goers, speaking for ever in the colloquial forms and rhythms of early seventeenth-century Londoners."[37]

The New Inn (1629) has been cordially damned by critics simply as an old man's whim for romance. The play has simply been taken as Jonson's "unique attempt to give dramatic expression to idealized love."[38] G.B. Tennant concludes that Jonson here bungles in trying to write a 'Comedy of Humours' with a theme of love and valour which was unfit for such satiric treatment.[39]

The adverse criticism of the play, perhaps, for want of salutary perceptiveness, has thoroughly failed to grasp the play's exact argument and its tone. What precisely the critics have missed to notice here is the consistent ironic tone of the play. The play is essentially an ironic reflection on the current theatrical medium itself. As Douglas Duncan has recently pointed out Jonson by now was "sadly aware that 'the drama's laws the drama's patrons give,' and his burlesqued romantic revelations suggest wry recognition that the theatre in a declining age was bound to have more in common with a puppet-show than a philosophical feast."[40] Hence, irony seems to have been the only solution to the 'serious dramatist's dilemma,' the only means by which the cook – to use Jonson's favourite metaphor – could please his own taste – as well as the guest's.

The entire action of the play, *The New Inn*, takes place in the inn. If the inn on the realistic level is a place of resort, frequented by all kinds of people from all walks of life, on the symbolic level it represents the theatre. This is specifically indicated to us when the Host describes himself as watching life like a comedy being enacted in his inn:

> If I be honest, and that all the cheat
> Be, of my selfe, in keeping this Light Heart,
> Where, I imagine all the world's a Play;
> The state and means affaires, all passages
> Of life, to spring new *scenes,* come in, goe out,
> And shift, and vanish; and if I haue got
> A seat, to sit at ease here, i' mine Inne,
> To see the Comedy; and laugh, and chuck
> At the variety, and throng of humors,
> And dispositions, that come iustling in,
> And out still, as they one droue hence another; (I, iii, 126-31)

This reminds us of *Cynthia's Revels* and *Bartholomew Fair* where again the stage becomes respectively the court and the fair, both of which in turn are shown to be mirrors or microcosms of society as a whole.

The New Inn, then, is not a romance of love and valour, but an ironic representation of the contemporary state of the theatre which gave undue concession to the cheap demands of its audience. This is made clear in the ironical assurance of Jonson to the audience of the play:

> You sha' not looke
> Long, for your bill of fare, but euery dish
> Be seru'd in, i' the time, and to your wish: ('The Prologue,' ll. 4-6)

The action of *The Magnetic Lady* (1632), Jonson's last 'Comedy of Humours,'[41] is relatively simple, as it does not depend much on irony or symbolism. The realistic action is inherently amusing dealing as it does with "the fantastic tricks which the neighbourhood of a young woman with a fortune will induce in a worldly community, the jealousies of rival suitors, the plots and counter-plots of domestic factions, the opinionativeness of guardians, the partisanship of aunts and the craft of nurses."[42]

The play seeks to present marriage purely as a financial affair, dramatizing the story of a wealthy heiress, Placentia, who is sold off to the highest bidder. Compasse, observing Sir Moth Interest, Bias and Practise talk about marrying Placentia to Practise, says:

> 't will be a bargaine, and sale; (II, v, 51)

Practise only confirms this when he concludes the "Contract" with the statement:

> A direct bargaine, and sale in open market. (II, vi, 23)

The play is fully realistic in so far as it reflects the institution of marriage in the seventeenth century England in which contracts were used and money and property were exchanged. Thus the material of Jonson's comedy is soaked in realism.

The realism of the matter naturally demands an equal realism in its expression. Hence Jonson's determination to have the 'deeds' of men couched in such language "as men doe vse." In his programmatic effort to evolve a vital comic speech out of the raw materials of everyday conversation, Jonson forms one of the pillars of the comic tradition. Strenuously seeking to copy 'nature' Jonson displays an increasing preoccupation with life-like speech. He endeavours to make his characters talk no better or worse than they do, or, at least, to give the illusion of doing so. Similarly Shakespeare achieved 'a lively image of life' in his plays. "This achievement," as John Russell Brown explains, "is in large part due to his ability to imagine total human reactions and write down words that give actors and readers the power to create from the words that full reality: verbal utterance in his plays is part of a complicated illusion of life."[43]

However, when Jonson said that he would write his comedies in "language such as men doe vse," we should bear in mind that he was not simply stating a need for verisimilitude in language. He was in part echoing the commonly held opinion that a man's talk was the clearest revelation of his personality. Jonson himself says elsewhere:

> *Language* most shewes a man: speake that I may see thee. It springs out of the most retired, and inmost parts of us, and is the Image of the Parent of it, the mind. No glasse renders a mans forme, or likenesse, so true as his speech. (*Discoveries*, ll. 2031-35)

The same idea underlies his proclamation that he aims to provide

> Words, aboue action: matter, aboue words.
> (*Cynthia's Revels*, 'Prologve,' l. 20)

in his comedies. In saying this he is clearly indicating that he proposes to create his characters not so much by what they do as by what they say.

This, we know, is purely a Renaissance doctrine where the concept of Decorum is involved:

> In Commedies, the greatest Skyll is this, rightly to touche
> All thynges to the quicke: and eke to frame eche person so,
> That by his common talke, you may his nature rightly know:
> A Royster ought not to preache, that were too strange to heare,
> But as from vertue he doth swerve, so ought his woordes appeare:
> The olde man is sober, the yonge man rashe, the Lover triumphing
> in joyes,
> The Matron grave, the Harlot wilde and full of wanton toyes.
> Which all in one course that in no wise doo agree:
> So correspondent to their kinde their speeches ought to bee.[44]

So, it was vital to the dramatist that he should be able to master the varieties of common speech in this way and thus reveal character in language. Jonson is at great pains to give his characters a vocabulary and style appropriate to their nature and profession.

Committed as he is to critical comedy, Jonson tends to present a world composed of fops and eccentrics. The language of the critical comedy naturally demands attention not merely to its own agility and gusto, but to its own absurdity. The speakers of his comedy being endowed with 'humours' or 'vapours,' all speech in the Jonsonian theatre tends to tingle with absurdity latent if not explicit. Telltale quirks of diction, tag ends of phrase, bits and pieces of expletive associated with recognizable social attitudes, spring to the surface. Jonsonian comedy, then, takes the total moral reprehensiveness of language as a major premise and activates it so as to create 'a circuit between language and folly.'

Rhetoric, therefore, becomes "the most suitable expression for Jonson's realism."[45] Some kinds of rhetoric are, no doubt, incompatible with realism but the rhetorical speech which is characteristic of Jonson is the language of life as Jonson sees it. In the words of John Russell Brown, "similes, metaphors and other figures of speech, when read in conjunction with the rhythm and tempo of speech, can indicate physical performance. . . . But, perhaps more powerfully, images also display a general, overall excitement, a state of being in which fantasy becomes real."[46] Hence simile, metaphor, image, jargon and hyperbole become integral parts of Jonson's language and enhance the comic irony he aims at. The language also constantly plays upon the dramatic situation and enriches its meaning. It is this kind of richness that is Jonson's distinction.

In his early comedies, the themes of which have a closer affinity with everyday life, Jonson uses a greater amount of prose and even when he uses blank verse he avoids all unnecessary ornament. The quality of his verse is eminently suited to the everyday tone of the plays and the prosaic character of the speakers. Let us take, for example, Old Knowell's speech in *Every Man in His Humour*:

> I cannot loose the thought, yet, of this letter,
> Sent to my sonne: nor leaue t' admire the change
> Of manners, and the breeding of our youth,
> Within the kingdome, since my selfe was one.
> When I was yong, he liu'd not in the stewes,
> Durst haue conceiu'd a scorne, and vtter'd it,
> On a grey head; age was authoritie
> Against a buffon: and a man had, then,
> A certaine reuerence pai'd vnto his yeeres,
> That had none due vnto his life. So much
> The sanctitie of some preuail'd, for others. (II, v, l. 11)

While the norm of five accents to the line is generally kept, there is no stiff monotony; the verse flows into brief yet varied periods with an almost colloquial ease. It is unadorned, incisive and terse, but there is no stiffness or monotony.

Even the poetic speeches of Sir Epicure Mammon, the dreamer of magnificence, are realistic reflecting as they do his true nature. Let us examine his most poetic speech in the play:

> I will haue all my beds, blowne vp; not stuft:
> Downe is too hard.And then, mine oual roome,
> Fill'd with such pictures, as TIBERIVS tooke
> From ELEPHANTIS, and dull ARETINE
> But coldly imitated. . . .
> My meat, shall all come in, in *Indian* shells,
> Dishes of agate, set in gold, and studded,
> With emeralds, saphyres, hiacynths, and rubies.
> The tongues of carpes, dormise, and camels heeles,
> Boil'd i' the spirit of SOL, and dissolu'd pearle,
> (APICIVS diet, 'gainst the *epilepsie*)
> And I will eate these broaths, with spoones of amber,
> Headed with diamant, and carbuncle. (II, ii, 41-49, 72-79)

Thoroughly poetic though the passage is, we cannot say it is unrealistic. Here dramatic poetry is performing an essential function by delightfully, concisely, and sharply displaying the personality of the speaker. In the sort of situation Mammon is placed, only such poetic speeches, through variations in rhythm, phrasing, and mannerisms, can convey his inner reality rather than 'the miserable words of everyday speech.' "To use spoken poetry for the medium of drama, is, therefore, to obey, simply and without violence, the fundamental nature of drama right through, from the first conception to ultimate expression."[47]

When the occasion and character of the person demand it, Jonson can also rise to great heights of poetic magnificence as in passages like Volpone's morning invocation to gold:

> Good morning to the day; and, next, my gold:
> Open the shrine, that I may see my *saint*,
> Haile the worlds soule, and mine. More glad then is
> The teeming earth, to see the long'd-for sunne
> Peepe through the hornes of the celestiall *ram*,
> An I, to view thy splendor, darkening his:
> Thy, lying here, amongst my other hoords,
> Shew'st like a flame, by night; or like the day
> Strooke out of *chaos*, when all darknesse fled
> Vnto the center. (I, i, 1-10)

and Mosca's description of Celia's beauty:

> O, sir, the wonder,
> The blazing starre of *Italie*! a wench
> O' the first yeere! a beautie, ripe, as haruest!
> Whose skin is whiter then a swan, all ouer!
> Then siluer, snow, or lillies! a soft lip,
> Would tempt you to eternitie of kissing!
> And flesh, that melteth in the touch, to bloud!
> Bright as your gold! and louely, as your gold! (I, v, 107-14)

If such passages are rare in Jonson's dramatic work it is because the situations and characters deserving them are rare.

However, much of the dialogue in Jonson's plays is in prose, a vigorous and basically colloquial prose which bears the impress of the idiosyncrasy of the speaker. A high percentage of it is cast in speeches of less than one line. Uncommitted to any prior metrical pattern, Jonson's prose rhythm "permits the rhythms of live speech to be traced intimately, and it accommodates with less strain the masses of petty detail, the tautologies and slovenly usages, with which daily speech is loaded."[48] Also the prose is singularly free from false wit. There are, here and there, a few cliches and pert phrases but they are certainly rarer than the fashion of the day allows. Again, the words usually follow in the just and measured cadence of a thought that is trained but not overpowered by scholarship.

Moreover, there are no literary flourishes in Jonson's prose, as was the vogue in the first half of the seventeenth century. His prose style carefully avoids all ornamentation, all unnecessary graces. Witty wording for its own sake is eschewed. The sparkle of promiscuous epigram is unsought for. Although it lacks the brilliance, the polish and the sparkling wit, so abundantly found in the style of the Restoration comic writers, Jonson's prose is sinewy, incisive and lucid. It may want in relaxed sureness of Shakespeare's best prose. It may seem tense and high strung to the last. But within his range Jonson achieved a remarkable success. Jonson's prose is a monumental achievement in that it "gives definitive shape to one aspect of the language of a generation, and makes that language not merely an adjunct of comedy, but comedy itself."[49]

Jonson's prose is essentially racy of the soil. It is eminently fitted to the situations and the speakers. It reflects the commonplace actuality of the language of characters who are drawn mainly from low life. The complete matter-of-factness of Jonson's prose is achieved in no small measure by his use of words and phrases and allusions, slang expressions and oaths and colloquialisms peculiar to contemporary London. Bobadill's speech, propounding his scheme of killing forty thousand enemies of the queen, illustrates this best:

> Why thus, sir. I would select nineteene, more, to my selfe, throughout the land; gentlemen they should bee of good spirit, strong, and able constitution, I would choose them by an instinct, a character that I haue: and I would teach these nineteene, the speciall rules, as your *Punto,* your *Reuerso*, your *Stoccata*, your *Imbroccata*, your *Passada*, your *Montanto*: till they could all play very neare, or altogether as well as my selfe. This done, say the enemie were fortie thousand strong, we twentie would come into the field, the tenth of March, or thereabouts; and wee would challenge twentie of the enemie; they could not, in their honour, refuse vs, well, wee would kill them; challenge twentie more, kill them; twentie more, kill them; twentie more, kill them too; and thus, would wee kill, euery man, his twentie a day, that's twentie score; twentie score, that's two hundreth; two hundreth a day, fiue dayes a thousand; fortie thousand; fortie times fiue, fiue times fortie, two hundreth dayes kills them all vp, by computation. (IV, vii, 73-90)

Thus Jonson's colloquial prose runs without effort. It carries its meaning without strain. "In a sense Jonson, like more than one Renaissance poet, let the colloquial language itself 'poeticize' for him."[50]

Thus, Jonson uses both verse and prose for his dramatic medium. And one cannot possibly discern any single principle governing his use of prose and verse. Jonson appears to have made his decision regarding the use of prose or verse separately for each play in accordance with its individual nature. Where he found the mixed form suitable he freely employed it as in the two 'Humour' plays and in *Poetaster*; where a single medium seemed preferable, he used prose for *Epicoene* and verse for *The Alchemist.* Thus he wrote two plays—*Epicoene* and *Bartholomew Fair*—entirely in prose, and two plays—*Sejanus* and *Volpone*—entirely in verse but for a few prose passages.

One would wonder why Jonson introduced prose passages into these two plays otherwise in verse. In *Sejanus* the first four acts are without prose. But the opening of V, x, in which Jonson presents a meeting of the senate, and Tiberius' letter, which during the meeting proclaims the fall of Sejanus, are in prose. An explanation for this could be that the circumstances under which the letter in prose is read contribute to the vigour and movement of the scene. The whole of *Volpone* is in verse but for Volpone's sales-talk, in the Mountebank scene (II, i), which is in prose. The reason is that Jonson wants here a street-scene which his instinct compels him to portray realistically. Similarly, for reasons of convention and dramatic necessity we have in *The Alchemist* two scenes (IV, i and ii) in which prose figures. These scenes present Surly in his Spanish disguise, speaking Spanish prose. Thus, what appears to underline Jonson's way of restricting himself to prose or verse in his dramatic medium is a certain self-consciousness about his craft.

Jonson's plays thus display his exquisite mastery of linguistic realism as well as linguistic satire. To conclude with Jonas A. Barish, "if linguistic realism is a valuable artistic technique, no playwright before Jonson copied live speech more tellingly, and few since have more powerfully worked it into a design that transcends mere realism. If linguistic satire is a perennial feature of European comedy, no dramatist has perceived its relevance to life more acutely or plumbed its possibilities more exhaustively, or elevated it into such a major comic insight. None, certainly is more responsible for making it one of the hallmarks of English dramatic literature."[51] However, in his deliberate aim to keep the language as true to life as possible for an artist, Jonson, more than any other Jacobean playwright, has anticipated Ibsen, Shaw and Galsworthy.

Jonson's learning is often said to make his medium difficult. It is true that Jonson's verse, like his prose, carries allusions from classical mythology. And there are references to medieval medicine and natural sciences, folk lore and contemporary events. But, Jonson, like all neo-classicists, wanted his borrowings, allusions and other references to be recognized and enjoyed by the educated listeners. Much of Jonson's learning, however, is embedded in consciously written rhetorical speeches which are normally understood by the audience to have a rhetorical purpose. Perhaps, as Partridge points out, "we think Jonson's language laboured and excessively learned because we have become ignorant of the things he knew about—the fine points of Latin history alchemy, medicine, law, food, London low life, and ancient high life. His alleged laboriousness may be only our real ignorance."[52] The learned playgoers of Jonson's day must have thoroughly enjoyed his plays. And even today the audience would, more or less, equally enjoy Jonson's plays if only they take the trouble to find out before they come to the theatre what Jonson refers to in a particular play.

In a way, even Jonson's learning proves to be of great help in creating verisimilitude. As Alexander H. Sackton rightly points out, "the abundance, even the excess of learned terms or allusions is often Jonson's artistic intention."[53] For instance, it was definitely the scholar in Jonson that enabled him to put into Subtle's mouth something more than the usual jargon of a swindling alchemist or an astrologer, and also made him give Subtle as erudite a case as a confirmed adherent of alchemy could have put forward. Moreover, as a critic suggested, "without the aid of his learning, his self-consciousness would have been without an adequate vocabulary, and Jonson would have been just another neurotic."[54] Although Dryden could think that Jonson wove his language too closely and laboriously, by the time of Coleridge the works of Jonson called forth great praise. "The more I study his writings," says Coleridge, "the more I admire them; and the more the study resembles that of an ancient classic, in the 'minutiae' of his rhythm, metre, choice of words, forms of connection etc., the more numerous have the points of admiration become."[55]

Thus, dealing with "deedes, and language, such as men doe vse" Jonson succeeds well in fulfilling his aim of creating verisimilitude, a semblance of life in his characteristic comedy. No doubt, he portrays excess and abnormality for the purpose of correcting human lapses, but the roots of his art are firmly grounded in the normal and the representative. This kind of realism that he achieved had its own advantages. It raised among the spectators a feeling of affinity with the new comedy with which he had come forward. In his comedy they saw almost their own deeds and language as well as the deeds and language of their fellowmen. His use of local colour and his more general national sentiment as well as his patriotic pride in his use of London as the material of his comedy, gave his plays a generous reception and a more sustained vogue.

Jonson's realism as revealed in his treatment of background, subject-matter and language is undoubtedly most minute and convincing. And his comedies could even be considered as invaluable social documents since they present a brilliant picture of life in England during the great Elizabethan-Jacobean age.

But we shall be doing great injustice to Jonson the dramatic artist if we think of him as a literal-minded transcriber of mere fact. It is not as if his plays were heavy transcripts of real life chopped into an arbitrary shape as some have felt. For, his realistic comedies themselves would have been less great if they had been only realistic in this narrow sense. As his plays bear ample evidence, Jonson's power over the real was invariably accompanied by an almost equal command over the world of fantasy. Though a realist in thought, Jonson was never a slave to the pedantry of realistic technique. Even though the passion for things classical had gone deeper into Jonson's mind than with most of his contemporaries, the imagination of an Englishman remained in him, though disciplined by the Roman virtues of form and order. As a critic puts it, "the compulsive Asper of *Every Man Out of His Humour* closely resembles the satirist-playwright in his moral vigilantism, reflecting Jonson's imagination in its most neurotic aspect."[56]

Jonson's Horatian pose of sanity and moderation seems to have been considerably subdued in the genesis of his dramatic art.[57] To realise this one has only to recall how grotesque are some of the conceits Jonson invents for his comedies – the obsessive fear of noise in *Epicoene,* the alchemical con-game in *The Alchemist,* the Boschian world of *Bartholomew Fair*, the staple of news and the magnetic lady which form the titles of the two plays respectively. "These are the products," in the words of Marotti, "of a bizarre imagination flirting with a vision closer to madness than rational calm."[58]

The conceits of Jonson's invention are exquisitely dramatised in the 'infected imaginations' of many of his characters. We have Morose of *Epicoene* with his daylight nightmares, Kitely of *Every Man in His Humour* who refers to his troublesome "imaginations" (III, iii, 50), Littlewit of *Bartholomew Fair,* who most enthusiastically exclaims: "I do feel conceits coming upon me than I am able to/ turn tongue to" (I, i, 31-33), and Peirce in *The New Inn* who remarks: "we are all mortall/And haue our visions." (III, i, 129-30)

Furthermore, we have an interesting anecdote in which Jonson says that he

> consumed a whole night in lying looking to his great toe, about which he hath seen tartars and turks Romans and Carthaginions flight in his imagination. (*Conversations with Drummond,* ll. 322-24)

This sort of night-time day-dreaming seems to lie behind much of Jonson's work. But, as Freud suggests, the creative artist has got to soften the egotistical character of his daydream in order to transform his private vision into his art.[59] We may say that Jonson accomplishes this in his dramatic practice by putting his 'poetry of the agitated imagination' into the mouths of some of his characters. There is, for example, the veritable explosion of fancy in Volpone's seduction speech to Celia:

> The heads of parrats, tongues of nightingales,
> The braines of peacocks, and of estriches
> Shall be our food: and, could we get the phoenix,
> (Though nature lost her kind) shee were our dish. . . .
> Thy bathes shall be the iuyce of iuly-flowers,
> Spirit of roses, and of violets,
> The milke of vnicornes, and panthers breath
> Gather'd in bagges, and mixt with *cretan* wines.
> Our drinke shall be prepared gold, and amber;
> Which we will take, vntill my roofs whirle round

With the *vertigo* . . . (III, vii, 202-5; 213-19)

Volpone elaborates his fantasy further, dreaming as he does a succession of disguises which he and Celia can wear for their love-making:

we may so, trans-fuse our wandring soules,
Out at our lippes, and score vp summes of pleasures,
    That the curious shall not know
    How to tell them, as they flow;
And the enuious, when they find
    What their number is, be pind. (III, vii, 234-39)

In this most fascinating poetry given to Volpone we find what Jonson himself specially identifies as artistic vices—far-fetched metaphors, rhetorical amplification and hyperbole, "faint, obscure, sordid, humble, improper, or effeminate *Phrase*" (*Discoveries,* ll. 798-99)—become 'delightful viciousness.'

We have the same kind of fascinating poetry given to Sir Epicure Mammon in *The Alchemist.* Though a man of "voluptuous mind" (IV, v, 74), too, Sir Epicure is more spontaneously and hyperbolically fantastic than Volpone. Particularly when he dreams of the kind of life the philosopher's stone can create for him, his profligate imagination is excited. He fantasizes 'the perfect setting for the banquet of sense,' yearning for a luxury beyond luxury—an "oual roome" (II, ii, 42) filled with "pornographic art, mirrors Cut in . . . subtill angles, to disperse/And multiply the figures, as I walke/Naked betweene my *succubae*," (II, ii, 46-48) perfumed mists, and baths "like pits to fall into" from which he and his harem can emerge to dry themselves "in gossamour and roses." (II, ii, 52) For his food he longs to have

The tongues of carpes, dormise, and camels heeles,
Boil'd i' the spirit of SOL, and dissolu'd pearle, . . .
The beards of barbels, seru'd in stead of sallades;
Oild mushromes; and the swelling vnctuous paps
Of a fat pregnant sow, newly cut off,
Drest with an exquisite, and poynant sauce (II, iii, 75-76; 82-86)

For his dress, he craves for "shirts of taffeta-sarsnet, soft and light/As cob-webs," (II, ii, 89-90) "gloves of fishes, perfum'd/with gems of *paradise* and eastern aire." (II, ii, 93-94) Thus, Jonson reaches his loftiest poetic heights in creating 'the Hollywood-extravaganza visions of voluptuous bliss' which Sir Epicure means to enjoy on gaining the sweet fruition of the philosopher's stone.

It is, however, in the course of Sir Epicure's courtship of Dol Common that Jonson attains the highest effect a comic poet can:

MAM: Aboue the art of AESCVLAPIVS,
That drew the enuy of the Thunderer;
I know all this and more.
DOL: Troth, I am taken, Sir Whole, with these studies, that contemplate nature:
MAM: It is a noble humour. But, this forme
Was not intended to do so darke a vse!
Had you beene crooked, foule, of some course mould,
A cloyster had done well; but, such a feature
That might stand vp the glorie of a kingdome,
To liue recluse! is a mere *soloecisme*,
Though in a nunnery. It must not be.
I muse, my lord your brother will permit it!
You should spend halfe my land first, were I hee.
Do's not this diamant better, on my finger,
Then i' the quarrie?
DOL: Yes.
MAM: Why, you are like it.
You were created, lady, for the light! (IV, i, 92-106)

Particularly, the last line, "you were created, lady, for the light!" has the perfection of Chaucer's comment on Chauntecleer's passion for Pertelote:

He loved hire so that wel was hym therwith.
(*The Nun's Priest's Tale*, l. 110)

and would adorn *Antony and Cleopatra* and *The Duchess of Malfi.* Thus, in the intensely poetic speeches given to Volpone and Sir Epicure, Jonson, to put it in the words of Mosca, "make(s) so rare a musique out of discordes." (V, ii, 18)

Thus, Jonson's plays could be approached even as products of poetic imagination no less than of permanent human experience. As a critic has rightly pointed out: "if the follies, meannesses, affectations, and lesser vices of mankind provide the subject-matter for comedy, then the comic poet is he who can transmute these ingredients into poetry."[60] We may say that Jonson achieved this alchemy as fully as a dramatic poet can. Written in blank verse of amazing variety and vigour that rise at times to intoxicating splendour, particularly plays like *Volpone* and *The Alchemist* have power to charm us into a state of comic ecstasy.

Yet, they are related to reality in the same manner and to more or less the same degree as Shakespeare's tragedies. For, Jonson's fantastic exaggerations like Volpone's explosion of fancy to seduce Celia, Sir Epicure's dreams of the kind of life the philosopher's stone can create, or Morose's hatred of noise and Troubleall's search for a warrant, provide the lenses through which the behaviour of more realistically conceived characters can be observed and brought into focus.

Therefore, one need not necessarily regret with Herford and Simpson the "deep-seated contrarieties in Jonson's own artistic nature, where the bent of a great realist for truth and nature never overcame the satirists and humorist's weakness for fantastic caricature."[61] As in Aristophanes, we have in Jonson a deliberate mingling of realism and fantasy as well as a comic structure centred not on a formal plot but on the exploration of an exaggerated conceit. It is chiefly in his grand comic conceits that, what T.S. Eliot calls, Jonson's "unity of inspiration" resides, for in them the interplay of realistic satire and 'fantastic caricature' is most highly concentrated. It is this interplay between realism and fantasy which seems to give Jonson's comedy not only the unity but also the universality of great art.

NOTES

1. Allardyce Nicoll, *An Introduction to Dramatic Theory* (London, 1931), p. 184.
2. J.W.H. Atkins, *English Literary Criticism*: *The Renascence* (London, 1947), p. 257.
3. A.P. Rossiter, *English Drama from Early Times to the Elizabethans* (London, 1950), p. 140.
4. Allardyce Nicoll, *An Introduction to Dramatic Theory*, p. 184.
5. Jonas A. Barish, *Ben Jonson and the Language of Prose Comedy* (Cambridge: Harvard Univ. Press, 1960), p. 144.
6. Levin, "Notes on Convention," *Perspectives of Criticism*, p. 67.
7. Both these comedies are essentially pre-Jonsonian in their nature. *The Case is Altered* was never admitted by Jonson among his collected 'Works' as it was not approved by his later standards. *A Tale of a Tub* has come down to us only in the second Folio (1631-40). Nonetheless, "Jonson may have dallied with this 'prima facie' un-

Jonsonian kind of matter in the obscure experimental years before the well-defined new departure of 1598." (Herford and Simpson, vol. I, p. 283)

8. *Every Man in His Humour* was first printed, in Quarto, in 1601. It was published for the second time in Jonson's edition of his collected works, the Folio of 1616. Between 1601 and 1616 the play had undergone a thorough revision. When exactly during this period the revision was made is uncertain. However, various dates – 1601, 1606 – have been put forward, but the most convincing is that suggested by Herford and Simpson in their collected edition of 1925-52. According to them (vol. I, p. 333) Jonson undertook the revision in the year 1612 when he was busied in the preparation of his plays for the Folio publication. There is every reason to accept their argument that the change of scene from Florence to London was subsequent to Jonson's successful choice of a London setting for *Epicoene* in 1609 and *The Alchemist* in 1610.
9. Herford and Simpson, vol. I, p. 376.
10. Anne Barton, p. 71.
11. All the important characters except Fastidius Briske in the play, so English in its setting, bear Italian names. This has often puzzled the readers. But Jonson's use of Italian names only indicates his belief in their value. In accordance with the habit of comic writers since Aristophanes, Jonson wanted the names to be self-expressive of their characters. Sordido and Sogliardo, for instance, are completely described by their names. It is this great expressive power of their names that seems to have led Jonson willingly to risk puzzling the readers unacquainted with Italian. (See Allan H. Gilbert, "The Italian Names in *Every Man Out of His Humour,*" *SP*, XLIV (Jan. 1947), pp. 195-208)
12. As an experimental work the play is an ingenious attempt to combine modern satire with the mythological machinery that Lyly had used so successfully. In this respect *Cynthia's Revels* undoubtedly anticipates *The Staple of News* and *The Devil is an Ass* as well as many of the devices Jonson was afterwards to use in his Court productions, including the antimasque.
13. J.B. Bamborough, *Ben Jonson* (London, 1970), pp. 37-38.
14. C.G. Thayer, *Ben Jonson: Studies in the Plays* (University of Oklahoma, Norman, 1963), p. 39.
15. O.J. Campbell, *Comicall Satyre and Shakespeare's "Troilus and Cressida,"* p. 110.
16. Jonson lays the scene of *Volpone* in Venice because the custom of making presents to someone in the hope of becoming his heir – the

motif which plays a key role in the play—was not an English but a Roman custom known as 'captatio.' Besides, the exorbitances and enormities of evil he has chosen to depict and repudiate would have gained but little credence if the action had taken place in London instead of in Venice "where flourished, in popular knowledge, an autonomous judicial system sufficiently severe and righteous to frustrate and to punish the villainy its society presumably tolerated." (Richard H. Perkinson, "*Volpone* and the Reputation of Venetian Justice," *MLR*, XXXV (Jan. 1940), p. 11) It should, however, be noted that 'captatio' is no more a prevalent abuse of Venice than of Jonson's England.

17. Herford and Simpson, vol. II, p. 53.
18. Anne Barton, p. 105.
19. T.S. Eliot, *Elizabethan Dramatists* (London, 1962), p. 78.
20. L.C. Knights, "Ben Jonson, Dramatist," *The Age of Shakespeare,* ed. Boris Ford, p. 309.
21. David Cook, ed., *Volpone*, 'Introduction,' p. 28.
22. Rufus Putney, "Jonson's Poetic Comedy," *PQ*, XLI (Jan. 1962), p. 203.
23. See Henry W. Wells, *Elizabethan and Jacobean Playwrights*, p. 203. The most recent exponent of this thesis is L.G. Salingar in "Farce and Fashion in *The Silent Woman*," *ES*, XX (1967), pp. 29-46.
24. Edward B. Partridge, *The Broken Compass* (London: Chatto and Windus, 1958), p. 162.
25. William W.E. Slights, "*Epicoene* and the Prose Paradox," *PQ*, XLIX (April 1970), p. 178.
26. Jonas A. Barish, p. 185.
27. Edgar Hill Duncan, "Jonson's *The Alchemist* and the Literature of Alchemy," *PMLA*, 61 (1946), p. 710.
28 Anne Barton, p. 143.
29. *Bartholomew Fair*, does not, as in the following chapters too, figure here as one later chapter is exclusively devoted to it with a definite purpose.
30. C.M. Gayley, *Representative English Comedies*, vol. III, p. 14.
31. The basic idea of a devil coming to earth to tempt mankind and finding men are a good deal worse than he is, was not, however, a new one. It had been already used in the anonymous play, *Grim the Collier of Croydon*, and in Dekker's *If it is not a Good Play, the Devil is in't*, but it was still capable of development.
32. See G.B. Harrison, *The Elizabethan Journals*, vol. IV, pp. 221-31. L.C. Knights, *Drama and Society in the Age of Jonson*, pp. 211-18; 254-55.

33. George Unwin, "Commerce and Coinage," *Shakespeare's England*, vol. I, p. 339.
34. L.C. Knights, p. 216.
35. Jonson had already written a brief and graceful satire on the growing news business in the court masque entitled *News from the New World Discover'd in the Moone* (1620).
36. D.R. Kifer, "*The Staple of News*: Jonson's Festive Comedy," *SEL*, XII (Spring 1972), p. 331.
37. *Ibid.*, p. 337.
38. F.S. Boas, *An Introduction to Stuart Drama*, p. 127.
39. See G.B. Tennant, ed., *The New Inn* (Yale Studies in English), p. XXXII.
40. Douglas Duncan, "A Guide to *The New Inn*," *EC*, XX (July 1970), pp. 325-26.
41. *The Magnetic Lady* is in a consistent line of development from Jonson's earliest work, looking back not merely to *The New Inn*, but nearly thirty-five years, to the first 'Humour' plays.
42. Herford and Simpson, vol. II, p. 206.
43. John Russell Brown, *Shakespeare's Dramatic Style* (London, 1970), p. 32.
44. Richard Edwards, *Damon and Pythias*, 'Prologve,' ll. 24-32.
45. Alexander H. Sackton, *Rhetoric as a Dramatic Language in Ben Jonson* (New York: Columbia University Press, 1948), p. 167.
46. John Russell Brown, *Shakespeare's Plays in Performance* (London, 1966), p. 19.
47. L. Abercrombie, "The Function of Poetry in Drama," *English Critical Essays*, ed. P.M. Jones, p. 267.
48. Jonas A. Barish, p. 274.
49. *Ibid.*, pp. 297-98.
50. Edward B. Partridge, p. 217.
51. Jonas A. Barish, pp. 298-99.
52. Edward B. Partridge, p. 223.
53. Alexander H. Sackton, p. 166.
54. W. Speed Hill, "Biography, Autobiography, and *Volpone*," *SEL*, XII (Spring 1972), p. 319.
55. *Coleridge's Miscellaneous Criticism*, ed. T.M. Raysor, p. 49.
56. Arthur F. Marotti, "All About Jonson's Poetry," *ELH*, 39 (June 1972), p. 212.
57. We have evidence that Jonson, often wrote under the inspiration of wine. We have in "Memorandums of the Immortal Ben" the following remarks attributed to Jonson: "I laid ye Plot of my Volpone, and wrote most of it, after a present of 10 dozen of palm Sacke. . . .

The first Speech in my Catiline, spoken by Scylla's Ghost, was writ after I parted from my Boys at the Devil-Tavern; I had drunke well yt night, and had brave notions." (Herford and Simpson, vol. I, p. 188)

58. Arthur F. Marotti, p. 211.
59. See "The Relation of the Poet to Day-Dreaming," *Collected Papers*, trans. Joan Riviere, vol. IV, p. 183.
60. Rufus Putney, p. 191.
61. Herford and Simpson, vol. II, p. 76.

An Image of the Times

With his firm opinion that a conscientious artist has no right whatsoever to play about with improbable fairy tales set in imaginary background and in remote countries, Jonson felt that the function of the playwright is to mirror the life he sees around him and thereby "show an image of the times." That is precisely why he chose as a vehicle for his expression that kind of comedy which Cicero had defined as "imitatis vitae, speculum consuetudinis, image veritatis,"[1] that is, imitation of life, a mirror of manners, an image of truth.

Since Aristotle's time, 'imitation' has been frequently echoed both by critics and playwrights. Aristotle asserts that

> Comedy is an imitation of those who are worse than ourselves, yet not in every sort of evil but only in that baseness of which the ridiculous is a species.[2]

The Italian critic, Trissino, states:

> Comedy is an imitation of the wicked and the vicious, yet not in every extremity of the vices, but merely of that which is ugly, whence springs the ridiculous.[3]

The usual interpretation is seen in Sir Thomas Elyot's description of comedy as "a picture or as it were a mirror of man's life,"[4] or in Ascham's idea that drama was a "perfect *imitation,* or fair lively painted picture of the life of every degree of man." Sir Philip Sidney declares that "Comedy is an imitation of the common errors of our life."[6] The phrase is constantly repeated. Lodge and Heywood all claimed on Cicero's authority.[7]

Coming to the playwrights, Shakespeare upholds the same view when he expresses through Hamlet that the end of playing is

> to hold, as 'twere, the mirror up to nature; to show virtue her own feature, scorn her own image, and the very age and body of the time his form and pressure. (III, ii, 25-29)

Webster seems to be of the same opinion when he praises the Queen's Men at the Red Bull for their acting in *The White Devil* (1612 or 1613):

> For the function of the play 'twas generally well, and I dare affirm, with the joint testimony of some of their own quality, (for the true imitation of life, without striving to make nature a monster) the best that ever became them.

So also an imitation of life is praised in *The Second Maiden's Tragedy* (1611):

> Thou shalt see my lady
> Play her part naturally, more to the life
> Then she's aware on.[8]

Thus the Elizabethan dramatists attempted to imitate life in their plays.

All the same, we would be thoroughly mistaken if we think that these dramatists tried to make their plays exactly the same as real life. The point, however, is that they did not endeavour, to put it in Marston's words, to "relate anything as an historian but to inlarge everything as a poet."[9] Naturally "their plays were more exciting and colourful, more full of meaning, than real life."[10] To cite but a few examples, the mirror held up in the courtly plays of Lyly and in his *Eupheus* was unequivocally a flattering one. The same is the case with Shakespeare. In *The Merchant of Venice*, Bassanio, when he finds Portia's picture in the leaden casket, exclaims:

> What demi-god
> Hath come so near a creation? (III, ii, 115-16)

To Ophelia, Hamlet had been

> The glass of fashion, and the mould of form. (III, i, 153)

Paulina in *The Winter's Tale* claims that her 'statue' can show life "Lively mock'd." (V, iii, 10) This the Elizabethan dramatists could easily afford because of the fact that "for an Elizabethan to imitate was to interpret and not to reproduce: a mirror would either flatter or warn, but would not simply reflect: and truth involved the revelation of eternal forms behind the distorting veil of events."[11] Yet, the Elizabethan audience was prepared to take all this as real while the plays were in performance. Thus, "within the charmed circle of the theatre, a new world could be accepted as real, and what they saw personated could be accepted as truly done before them."[12]

With this licence that has belonged to the drama of the times, Jonson does not simply 'imitate' the life around him, but slightly exaggerates the follies of life which he means to correct. Because, his purpose was not simply to present the world of common experience, uncriticized and unstructured. Jonson's mirror, then, is a kind of "magic mirror which slightly distorts the objects it shows, heightening their deformity and making more obvious to the spectators their normal proportions."[13]

The resulting picture of contemporary life in his plays, therefore, cannot be taken at its face value. His picture of life, then, is like the 'perspectives'[14] of pictorial art which were at first designed to deceive the external eye. If one looked at them as one did at a usual picture, they appeared to be too distorted to be recognised. But the artist provided a small hole and by looking through it from a precise particular angle one could see the picture restored to its normal proportions. Similarly Jonson provided the small holes in his careful instructions to the readers through Prologues, Inductions and interpretative choruses which explain to us 'the springs and mechanism' of his art. Jonson repeatedly demanded that the audience should

thinke nothing true:
Lest so you make the maker to iudge you.
For he knowes, *Poet* neuer credit gain'd
By writing truths, but things (like truths) well fain'd.
(*Epicoene,* 'II Prologve,' ll. 7-10)

Thus Jonson repudiates mere literal reproduction of contemporary life in plays. The principle is repeated in the court prologue to *The Staple of News*. Jonson appealing to the audience makes it clear:

Wherein, alothough our *Title,* Sir, be *Newes,*
Wee yet aduenture, here, to tell you none;
But shew you common follies, and so knowne,
That though they are not truths, th' innocent *Muse*
Hath made so like, as Phant'sie could them state,
Or *Poetry*, without scandall, imitate. (ll. 9-14)

Hence, we have to approach the 'perspectives' of Jonson's plays through the 'small holes' of irony, distortion, exaggeration, pretence, disguise and indecorum, which are Jonson's comic ways of presenting the contradictions to the ideal, in order to have the apparently distorted picture of contemporary life restored to its "full reality and flesh-and-blood existence."

Jonson, however, was not the only Renaissance writer to create the contradiction to the ideal. Jonson's sense of a perverted age appears in the pamphlet literature of both the Elizabethan and Jacobean ages. Greene, Nashe and Dekker, whose prose-pamphlets[15] testify to the Elizabethans' intense interest in the sheer mechanics of roguery, present the life of the London underworld from the perspective of a sweeter, simpler past or of a religious ideal.

Particularly Greene's 'conny-catching' pamphlets, purporting to be an expose of ingenious tricks of the card-sharpers, confidence men, cut-purses, and other disreputable characters of the underworld of Elizabethan England, are of great relevance to our study of Jonson's comic world. In strong contrast to his love-pamphlets, which give us none of the characteristics of contemporary society, the 'conny-catching' pamphlets are full of realistic traits and hints and sketches of the times. As A.B. Grosart has rightly pointed out, "having himself frequently fallen into the clutches of London courtesans, Greene was an authority on the subject."[16]

The first of these is *The Notable Discovery of Coosnage* (1591). In 'To The Reader,' Greene says that 'Conny-catching' and 'Cros-biting' are

> such pestilent and preiudiciall practices, as of late haue been the ruine of infinite persons, and the subuertion and overthrow of many Marchaunts, Farmers, and honest minded yeomen,

and that he has "written faithfullie to discover these coosening practices."[17] The purpose of this pamphlet, then, is to warn inexperienced country people coming up to London, of the cunning snares laid for them by the London sharpers. To achieve his purpose Greene minutely describes the favourite arts of these 'conny-catchers,' and acquaints the reader of their thieves' language.

In the preface to his pamphlet, *A Disputation between a He Conny-Catcher and a She Conny-Catcher*, Greene informs his readers that he is going to acquaint them with the manners and customs of the London 'domi-monde.'[18] This pamphlet is a tale of how a courtesan, Nan, succeeded in duping and overreaching one of the sharpest 'conny-catchers,' Laurence, who was ultimately obliged to confess himself vanquished. The tale is concluded with an account of the repentance and reformation of a prostitute. A postscript is added wherein Greene assures his readers that this account had been taken down from the words of the woman herself, and was not fictitious. He says that what he described is

> A merry Tale taken not far from Fetter Lane end, of a new foamed Conny-catcher, that was Conny-catcht himselfe.[19]

Thus, the realistic, satirical 'conny-catching' pamphlets of Greene reveal his extensive knowledge of London's underworld.

Nashe's rambling narrative, *The Unfortunate Traveller* or *The Life of Jack Wilton*, perhaps suggested by the Spanish *Lazarillo de Tormes*,[20] offers a fictional biography of a rogue. The writing has a vivid pictorial quality as though everything is seen in brilliant sunlight. Let us take, for example, the description of the tapster:

> he was an old servitor, a cavelier of an ancient house, as might appeare by the armes of his ancestors, drawen verie amiably in chalke on the in side of his tent dore.[21]

Then, Nashe's description of a heatwave, as Brian Gibbons points out, "brings us closer to the physical stuff of Elizabethan London than all Greene's pamphlets put together."[22] With a pose of confident assertion, Nashe depicts the effects of "a vehement hot summer":

> Felt makers and Furriers, what the one with the hot steame of their wool new taken out of the pan, and the other with the contagious heat of their slaughter budge and connieskinnes, died more thicke than of pestelence: I have seene an old woman at that season, having three chins, wipe them all away one after another, as they melted to water, and left hir selfe nothing of a mouth but an upper chap. . . . Masons paid nothing for haire to mixe their lyme . . . it drooped off mens heads and beards faster than any Barber could shave it.[23]

Nashe's pose of confident assertion combined with such flat statements as "I have seene" drive home to us the point in hand.

Dekker followed Greene and Nashe in producing realistic, satirical accounts of the London underworld, as in *The Wonderful Year, The Seven Deadly Sins of London, The Belman of London* and *The Gull's Horn Book.* These prose pamphlets contain accounts of

> an Army of insufferable abuses, detestable vices, most damnable villainies, abominable pollutions, inexplicable mischiefs, sordid iniquinations, horrible and hell-hound-like perpetrated flagitious enormities.[24]

The Wonderful Year "consists of desultory gossip together with rhetorical accounts of events that were known to everybody, larded with 'tales cut out in sundry fashions, of purpose to shorten the lives of long winter nights.'"[25] *The Seven Deadly Sins of London* presents landlords who rack rents, cheating tradesmen, brewers and bakers who give false measure, fraudulent executors, and usurers

> who for a little money and a great deal of trash (as fire-shovels, brown paper, motley clock-bags, etc.) bring young novices into a fool's paradise till they have sealed the mortgage of their lands, and then like pedlars go they (or some familiar spirit for them, raised by the usurer) up and down to cry *Commodities*, which scarce yield the third part of the sum for which they take them up.[26]

The Gull's Horn Book, offering a lively picture of varieties of fools and rogues in London, "shows the beneficial influence of Jonson and the early Jacobean vogue for dramatic satire."[27] Thus, the prose pamphlets of both the Elizabethan and Jacobean periods show a remarkable knowledge of London low-life.

Jonson's contemporary life forms the life of London at one of its most fascinating moments. The London in which Jonson had to battle for a livelihood was enormously rich in stimulus and provocation for an eye and mind like his.[28] Socially, intellectually and politically it exercised a great influence. Since the fall of Antwerp in 1576 London had become a chief Centre of European commerce.[29] Professional adepts – medical, metallurgical, commercial and financial – found it worth their while to flock from Italy and France to the English metropolis. The ground was being prepared for the Jacobean projectors.[30]

The rapidly expanding Inns of Court[31] were the nucleus of a society. Numerous and accomplished of wits and men about town – lawyers, courtiers, young graduates from the universities – thronged the aisles of Paul's and discovered the middle classes by their free living and free talk. In addition, a crowd of provincials, country squires and their sons gathered in the capital bent on seeing plays, learning to take tobacco and conversing with the wits. Thus, "half of the matter of Jonson's future play-making was being enacted daily before his eyes."[32]

The literary world was in its full swing. University wits and courtiers shared its honours and failures with men of small education and learning. The world of scholarship was spacious and exhilarating. Scholarship was pursued in a spirit of adventure and conquest. It was a time when a scholar like Bacon could profess that he took all knowledge to be his province.[33] It is at this time that Raleigh thought it possible for a single man to write a history of the whole world. Raleigh studied most of his sea voyages where he "carried always a trunk of books along with him and had nothing to divert him."[34]

The everyday life of London was full of theatrical contrasts. It surged through the Strand and Cheapside and overflowed into the narrow lanes and by ways. It was a time when luxury and poverty ran parallel courses. The contrasts, however, became so marked that the society was growing more and more class-conscious.[35] This resulted in social unrest. The relationships of classes and groups to one another were critically examined and carefully studied. And whenever they were faulty and untoward they were immediately challenged. Thus, the modern world, as we know it, was already begun.

Jonson, the dramatist, came into the midst of these times with the purpose of holding a mirror up to it in his comedy. With his full and first-hand knowledge of men and manners combined with a certain power of detachment he had in his nature, Jonson could successfully accomplish the task he set before himself. Even at the moments of most whole-hearted absorption in life, he was able to hold himself a bit outside of his experience, so as to reduce it to order. The result was that the various phases of contemporary existence assumed a pattern when reflected in his orderly mind. It was Jonson's object, then, to give this ordered reflection back to the world through the vehicle of his comedy, in the earnest hope of clarifying its vision and correcting its follies.

This was also the object of most of Jonson's contemporaries like Chapman, Marston, Middleton, Dekker, Heywood and Massinger. In Chapman and Marston, of course, we have only a limited presentation of London life and its manners. Chapman's plays like *An Humorous Day's Mirth, All Fools* and *Sir Giles Goosecap* show his detached and analytic view of life and a satiric outlook.

Marston seems to have reached excellence in the portrayal of the abnormal excesses of contemporary manners. His plays abound in violent railings at the corruption and hypocrisy of courts and courtiers. *The Malcontent,* for instance, is full of the poisonous air of a jaded court. Paserello, the court fool, touches on all things with a 'meditative cynicism.' *The Dutch Courtesan,* in its opening part, offers a vivid picture of tavern life.

It is, however, to the delightful comedy, *Eastward Ho,* on which Chapman and Marston collaborated with Jonson,[36] that we have to turn in order to get a successful picture of contemporary life. The play is set in London, and the city setting is accurately achieved with many placing references to street and district names. The play deals with the conflict of the industrious and idle apprentices of a London goldsmith, Touchstone. The typical interests of the gallant in Jacobean society are summarised when Sir Petronell, after having lost his country estates to usurers, laments:

> Taverns growe dead: Ordinaries are blowne up; playes are at a stand; Howses of Hospitallitie at a fall; not a Feather waving, nor a Spurre gingling any where . . . my creditors have laide to arrest me. (II, ii, 220-22)

We get "a malign view of the motives and 'adventurous' spirit of Elizabethan merchant investors and colonisers,"[37] when Sir Petronell and the idle apprentice, Quicksilver, set out on a voyage to Virginia to make their fortunes there:

> I tell thee, Golde is more plentifull there then Copper is with us; and for as much redde Copper as I can bring, Ile have thrice the waight in Golde. Why man all their dripping Pans, and their Chamber pottes are pure Gold. (III, iii, 25-28)

Thus, *Eastward Ho* is unmistakably realistic, but the trouble with Chapman and Marston is that, both being more interested in tragic themes, they do not follow up their entry into realistic comedy by any consistent development. For this, one has to look to Middleton.

Although we cannot completely agree with T.S. Eliot "that Middleton's comedy was 'photographic,' that it introduces us to the low-life of the time far better than anything in the comedy of Shakespeare or the comedy of Jonson, better than anything except the pamphlets of Dekker and Greene and Nashe,"[38] we may say with K.M. Lynch that "Middleton's keen concentration on the spectacle of the interplay of different social classes marks an important development in realistic comedy."[39] Middleton accurately reflects the low-life of libertines and loose women, tricky lawyers and swindlers, drunkards and usurers, wanton wives and complacent husbands needy knights and harsh creditors of Jacobean London.

Middleton's early comedies like *Your Five Gallants* and *Michaelmas Term* are remarkably interesting as realistic studies of 'social confusion.' "They portray an age in which medieval standards have broken down, in which 'degree' has been disregarded, in which all sense of social responsibility has been completely lost. They show class struggling against class, individual against individual; they show the sons of toothdrawers rising to affluence and the sons of gentlemen losing their estates. They show that money, land, and women—the only prizes in the social struggle—are quickly gained and quickly lost."[40] We are thus introduced to an unsavoury London.

In his comic masterpieces—*A Trick to Catch the Old One, A Mad World, My Masters* and *A Chaste Maid in the Cheapside*—Middleton presents, with a profound sense of irony, "a moral and critical analysis of City society."[41] *A Trick,* like *Volpone* brilliantly illustrates the power of wealth as well as the gullibility of the unscrupulous men who pursue it. Witgood successfully dupes both his creditors and his uncle, the citizen-usurer Lucre, by passing off his Courtesan as a rich widow and circulating the rumour that he is about to marry her. Similarly Follywit in *A Mad World* gulls others "without conscience." He says:

> I go without order, swear without number, gull without mercy, and drink without measure. (I, i, 23-24)

Disguising himself as Lord Owemuch he robs his grandfather, Sir Bounteous Progress, of his wealth.

A Chaste Maid in the Cheapside, undoubtedly the best of Middleton's comedies, gives a broader picture of Jacobean life. "As a study in manners, in fact, the play is unsurpassed in Jacobean drama, except perhaps by *The Alchemist* and *Bartholomew Fair.*"[42] To give an illustration, the scene of the promoters highlights Middleton's powers of observation and his marvellous ability to mould contemporary rackets into his dramatic material.

As the promoters during Lent are greedily looking for meat and confiscating whatever they find, a man enters with a basket of meat concealed under his cloak. Immediately they seize the meat. But when the servant of Master Beggarland, who is free with his bribes, enters with a basket, the same promoters just let him go scot-free saying:

> Go, go, we see thee not; away keep close! (II, ii, 122)

Now enters a Country Girl concealing her illegitimate child in her basket. The promoters avariciously seize the basket, but only to be fooled. Probing the basket they first discover a fat loin of mutton and then the child to their painful surprise.

> Second Promoter. A Child!
> First Promoter. A pox of all dissembling cunning whores!
> Second Promoter. Here's an unlucky breakfast! . . .
> Villainous strange!
> Life, had she none to gull but poor promoters,
> That watch hard for a living? (II, ii, 158-64)

The scene brings out contemporary ways of making 'a living' by corrupt means. Thus, most of Middleton's comedies are thoroughly representative and prove that he is "a hearty observer of life at first hand."[43]

If Marston and Middleton present the ugly and least edifying elements in the society of their time, Dekker and Heywood portray citizen-life in its rosiest colours. They glorify the rising middle class and the lower classes. Naturally their plays deal with the ordinary lives of men and women with their favourite pastimes like hawking, hunting, dancing, singing and playing the game of cards after dinner. They also deal with their social barriers, emotional entanglements, marital harmony and superstitious beliefs.

'The Child of London,' Dekker writes especially of London and for the cockney people. With his hearty joy and easy-going cheerfulness, he finds mostly gentility among citizens. His masterpiece, *The Shoemaker's Holiday*, realistically presents the class distinctions of the age. In this play we have a thorough-going picture of the three classes—the landed aristocracy, the rich merchant class and the working labour class. It seeks to present the various conflicts of these three classes especially those arising from marriage alliances. Lacy, the nephew of the Earl of Lincoln, is in love with Rose, a citizen's daughter. But with their class-consciousness, neither Lacy's uncle nor Rose's father approves of the match. The Mayor, who "scorns to call Lacy son-in-law," tells the Earl:

> Poore Citizens must not with Courtiers wed,
> Who will in silkes, and gay apparell spend
> More in one yeare, than I am worth, by farre. (I, i, 12-14)

The Earl in turn tells his nephew not to cast an amorous eye

> Vpon so meane a project, as the love
> Of a gay wanton painted citizen (I, i, 76-78)

Symon Eyre also dissuades Rose from marrying Lacy:

> A courtier, wash, go by, stand not vpon pisherie pasherie: those silken fellowes are but painted Images, outsides, outsides, *Rose;* their inner linings are torne: no, my fine mouse, marry me with a Gentleman Grocer like my Lord Maior, your father, a Grocer is a sweete trade, Plums, Plums: had I a sonne or Daughter should marrie out of the generation and bloud of the shoe-makers, he should packe: what, the Gentle trade is a living for a man through Europe, through the world. (III, iii, 40-47)

The passage reveals how the shoemaker takes a legitimate pride in his profession and how strongly he feels the necessity and desirability of getting married in one's own class.

Although *The Shoemaker's Holiday* primarily "appealed to the pride of the citizen-craftsman in his craft and status," it is not altogether devoid of shrewd, caustic comments on social ambition, wealth and luxury."[44] For instance, when Margery, Eyre's wife, vociferates:

> I must enlarge my bumme, ha, ha, how shall I looke in a hoode I wonder? . . . It is verie hot, I must get me a fan or else a maske. . . . But, *Rafe*, get thee in, call for some meate and drinke, thou shalt find me worshipful towards thee. (III, ii, 33-34; 44; 99-101)

Dekker seems to laugh at her naive assumption of dignity.

Like Dekker, Heywood is concerned with presenting middle class life, its conventions, its beliefs, its pastimes and its various problems with sureness of touch. "With his tender charity and generous impulses he is able to understand the problems of life and present them realistically."[45] Heywood's plays of domestic life exquisitely portray the bourgeois elements in the Jacobean society with 'simplicity,' 'sympathetic humanity' and 'vivid realism.'[46]

Heywood's plays of London life reflect the prevailing attitudes, customs, conflicts and sentiments. They essentially appeal to national as well as local pride of the citizens. The first part of *Edward IV* gives us a clear picture of the siege of London by the rebel Falconbridge and his repulse by the citizens. The events of the play are located in quite familiar places – Mint, Cheapside, Lombard Street. Further, 'velvet coats,' 'gorgets,' and 'leading staves' the whole companies of mercers, grocers, drapers and the rest are vividly represented on the stage. Similarly in the second part of *If You Know Not Me, You Know Nobody*, we witness the planning, building and naming of the Royal Exchange.

In his *Fair Maid of the West*, the streets and inns are shown crowded with laughing gallants moving about in a rollicking mood. These tavern-scenes have been justly praised by critics for their superb realism.[47] These 'shining gallants' come only to court the tavern maid, Bess. She, no doubt, allows them to dote upon her but she knows where to draw the line, even if she is a maid in the tavern. Her lover Spencer says how

> She'll laugh, confer, keep company, discourse,
> And something more, kiss; but beyond that compass
> She no way can be drawn. (I, iii)

Even Goodlack who has a poor opinion of the tavern maids admits that

> 'Tis a virtue
> But seldom found in the taverns. (I, iii)

Thus the tavern scenes bring the first part of the play nearer to life, "a life that has been shared and experienced even by the commoners of that age with pride and satisfaction."[48] Then there are certain passages in the subplots of *A Woman Killed with Kindness* and *The English Traveller* which almost recreate the scenes of real life by their close, initmate touches and homely images. This kind of accuracy in detail seems to make the remote past tangible and familiar. The 'social significance' of Heywood's plays, thus, lies "in the kind of conduct they extol. Most of them contain examples of neighbourly dealing; debts are forgiven, the poor and unfortunate are relieved. 'Impersonal' economic processes, that is, are not accepted with complacency; they are seen in terms of human suffering and happiness."[49]

Massinger, like Ben Jonson, critically observes the significant social and economic activities of the age. Though his themes are often drawn from the Jonsonian field "there is fresh perception of a contemporary world, and the treatment shows that the tradition on which Jonson drew is active in Massinger."[50] In *The City Madam* and *A New Way to Pay Old Debts*, we have two realistic comedies dealing with contemporary London.

In the figures of the City Madam and her daughters on the one hand and in the figure of Luke Frugal on the other, the Jacobean social morality is 'vivified.' The City Madam, Lady Frugal, and her daughters, longing to "be ladified" exhibit throughout the play a purely material ambition. They simply scare away the suitors by making extravagant demands for luxury after marriage. Anne, for instance, from Sir Maurice demands:

> French and Italian cooks, musicians, songsters,
> And a chaplain that must preach to please my fancy:
> A friend at court to place me at a mask;
> The private box ta'en up at a new play,
> For me and my retinue; a fresh habit,
> Of a fashion never seen before, to draw
> The gallants' eyes, that sit on the stage, upon me;
> Some decayed lady for my parasite,
> To flatter me, and rail at other madams;
> And there ends my ambition. (II, ii)

Luke Frugal essentially represents the acquisitive attitude that was becoming common in Jacobean times. He has already bidden

> Religion, conscience, charity, farewell!
> To me you are words only, and no more;
> All human happiness consists in store. (IV, ii)

He exults over the treasures filling his room:

> In by-corners of
> This sacred room, silver in bags, heap'd up
> Like billets saw'd and ready for the fire
> Unworthy to hold fellowship with bright gold
> That flow'd about the room, conceal'd itself.
> There needs no artificial light; the splendour
> Makes a perpetual day there, night and darkness
> By that still-burning lamp for ever banis'd! (III, iii)

The passage invariably reminds us of Volpone's address to gold. Also, he resembles Sir Epicure Mammon in his infinite avarice driven home to us when he says:

> Increase of wealth
> Is the rich man's ambition, and mine
> Shall know no bounds. (IV, ii)

A New Way to Pay Old Debts, like *The City Madam*, is a comedy of London manners representing as it does the new wealthy class that threatened the privileges of the gentry. If Sir John Luke of *The City Madam* represents the thriving merchant class, Sir Giles Overreach stands for the new aristocracy of wealth. Being conscious of his enormous wealth, he appeals to his depressed daughter:

> In birth! why art thou not my daughter,
> The blest child of my industry and wealth?. . .
> Be thou no enemy to thyself; my wealth
> Shall weigh his titles down, and make you equals. (III, ii)

So he plans to marry her to a nobleman and thus triumph over the aristocracy:

> And therefore, I'll not have a chambermaid

That tie her shoes, or meaner office
But such whose fathers were right worshipfull.
'Tis a rich man's pride; there having ever been
More than a feud, a strange antipathy
Between us and true gentry. (II, i)

Massinger's two plays witness to the vital social and economic conflicts of the day.

Thus, the contemporary writers of comedy have, in their own way, reflected various aspects of the times in their plays. However successful these playwrights hâve been in their attempt to hold a mirror to the times, their picture of the contemporary life seems to fall short of a comprehensive whole, as it is likely to be self-conscious, or restricted by other factors, or coloured by romance.

It is to Jonson, then that we have to turn in order to have the image of "the very age and body of the time his form and pressure." For, more than any of his contemporaries he seemed to have had that ability of vigorous intellectual grasp to hold the pageant of life steadily and the capacity for detachment to reproduce the same in his plays with fidelity. In his comedies we gain a vivid impression and a comprehensive image of Elizabethan and Jacobean life.

In his earnest object to show an "image of the times," Jonson pictures such outstanding phases of contemporary life as the problem of dramatic art – its playwrights, players and theatre-goers – the court life, the interrelationship of classes, the tendencies of the non-dramatic poetry then appearing and, above all, the character and significance of everyday life.

Jonson gives us a peep, as it were, into the theatrical world of his time in his Prefaces, Prologues, Inductions and throughout the plays themselves. He shows us what the contemporary stage was like. It was the time of rival companies[51] and rival playhouses[52] when writing for the stage was a means of livelihood. And competition was so keen that the pleasure of the audience was the first care of the playwrights. While propounding his theories of dramatic technique Jonson traces these aspects of the contemporary drama, pointing out its flagrant violation of realism and dramatic Unities and romantic excesses. Besides, stage tricks such as acrobatics, juggling and conjuring were prevalent on the Elizabethan stage.[53] Jonson gives a sample of these in the mountebank scene in *Volpone* (II, v).

Jonson lets us know the condition of the playwrights of the Elizabethan period. The average playwright was relatively an unimportant person. As the playwrights pandered to the demands of actors and audience without regard for the dignity of their calling, they could not command respect in society and the very profession of playmaking was considered to be disreputable. This is clearly brought out in the words of Ovid Senior who says:

> What? shall I have my sonne a stager now? an enghle for players? a gull? a rooke? a shotclogge? to make suppers, and bee laught at? PUBLIVS, I will set thee on the funerall pile, first.
> (*Poetaster*, I, ii, 15-18)

Jonson tells us something about the players of the time in general. The players had a good capacity for wine and capons and they were full of jests and inclined to have flamboyant manners. (*Bartholomew Fair*, V, iii, 5-85) These were what were called the 'common players' who were looked down upon. Jonson shows this through the contemptuous words of Tucca who refers to them as

> honest gent'manlike scoundrels, and suspected to ha' some wit, as well as your *poets*; both at drinking, and breaking of iests: and are companions for gallants. (*Poetaster*, III, iv, 152-55)

Jonson shows us what the theatre-going public of the time was like. The Elizabethan audience attended the theatre mostly as a fashion and to pass the time.[54] Among the audience, apart from the groundlings, were found such representative types as the curled, tobacco-smoking gallant who attended the play merely as a matter of fashion, (*The Case is Altered*, II, vii, 46-47) the man from the country who came to London "once in fiue yeeres at a parliament time or so," (*Poetaster*, III, iii, 188-90) the swaggering captain who would see a play if it were "a good bawdie one." (*The Staple of News*, 'The Indvction,' ll. 8-13) Jonson also reveals the audiences of the Elizabethan private theatres who "consisted mainly of courtiers, gentlemen of the Inns of Court, wits, and women of fashion, together with such hangers-on as gamblers, soldiers, prostitutes, and would-be gallants."[55] He shows how particularly the "women of fashion" claimed to be the "persons of quality" and came to the theatre "to see, and to be seene," expecting every play to "be a merry one." (*The Staple of News*, 'The Indvction,' ll. 9-13) The Elizabethan audience also included such peculiar persons as came

> to see, who weares the new sute to day? whose clothes are best penn'd, what euer the part be? which *Actor* has the best legge and foote? What *king* playes without cuffes? and his *Queene* without

gloues? who rides post in stockings? and daunces in bootes?
(*The Staple of News*, 'The Indvction,' ll. 39-43)

The passage illustrates how fantastic the tastes of some of the audience had been. However, the chief offenders among the audience were the empty-witted fashionable gallant

Who (to be thought one of the iudicious)
Sits with his armes thus wreath'd, his hat pull'd here,
Cryes meaw, and nods, then shakes his empty head,
Will shew more seueral motions in his face,
Then the new *London, Rome,* or *Niniueh*
And, (now and then) breakes a dry bisquet iest, . . .
He steeps in his owne laughter.
(*Every Man Out of His Humour*, Grex, ll. 160-62)

Lastly Jonson presents in his plays the puritan opposition to the theatre[56] of the times particularly through the typical puritan Rabbi Zeal-of-the-land Busy who denounces the puppet play crying:

Downe with *Dagon*, Downe with *Dagon*; . . . I wil remoue *Dagon* there, I say, that *Idoll*, that heathenish *Idoll*, that remaines (as I may say) a beame . . . in the eye of the brethren; a very great beame, an exceeding great beame; such as are your *Stage-players, Rimers,* and *Morrise-dancers*, who haue walked hand in hand, in contempt of the Brethren, and the *Cause*; and beene borne out by instruments, of no meane countenance. (*Bartholomew Fair*, V, v, 1-13)

Jonson reproduces the fashions and practices of the non-dramatic poetry of the time. Though Jonson was primarily interested in the drama, he was quite alive to the state and future of English non-dramatic poetry in those years that lay between Spenser and Milton. For, poetry in Jonson's time had become a fashionable trick of the successful courtier.[57] Jonson presents the amateur versifiers at court in the two coxcombs – Matthew and Fastidius Briske. Matthew boasts before Stephen:

I am melancholy my selfe diuers times, Sir, and then doe I no more but take pen, and paper presently, and ouerflow you halfe a score, or a dozen of sonnets, at a sitting.
(*Every Man in His Humour*, III, i, 90-93)

If the fit of melancholy fails to inspire to produce poetry, the courtier must necessarily

> hearken out a *veine*, and buy: prouided you pay for the silence, as for the worke. Then you may securely call it your owne.
> (*Cynthia's Revels*, III, i, 63-64)

This shows the extent to which courtiers of the day freely indulged in plagiarism.

The contemporary court life is also well reflected. Jonson says how the court was "a bountifull and brave spring; and waterest all the noble plants of this island" in which

> the whole Kingdome dresseth it selfe, and is ambitious to vse thee as her glasse. (*Cynthia's Revels*, The Court, ll. 7-8)

Nonetheless, he is not blind to the superficialities of the court life. It was fashionable in the court to affect scholarship, poetry and histrionic talent. There are many instances in Jonson's plays where a courtier steals verses from some obscure poet or scholar in order to win his lady's favour. Conversation had become a matter of fashion at court. The conversation was well-larded with foreign phrases and affected an interest in the public issues of the day. Jonson through Crites regrets the waste of energy and brains of the courtiers in the pursuit of "these outward and effeminate shades."

Touching the world of scholarship of the times, Jonson, while showing the great scholars, exposes the pseudo-scholars. Matthew in *Every Man in His Humour* is a typical pseudo-scholar of the day. In order to show off his scholarship, he always carries Kyd's *Spanish Tragedy* in his hands. To him source-hunting is an end by itself. To Bobadill's question as to whose verse he read to him, Matthew readily bluffs:

> This, Sir? a toy o'mine owne, in my nonage: the infancy of my *Muses*! (I, v, 72-73)

Clove and Orange in *Every Man Out of His Humour* are great pretenders to scholarship. At the arrival of Sogliardo and others Clove tells Orange:

> pr'y thee let's talke fustian a little and gull 'hem: make 'hem beleeue we are great schollers. (III, iv, 7-8)

We can easily trace in Jonson's plays the seamy side of the glory and splendour of the Golden Age of the Renaissance. Jonson might be thought of as the Marlowe of low-life of Renaissance England. He paints the ludicrous underside of the great heroes of the past in the characters of his middle comedies. Marlowe's *Tamburlaine*, the world-conqueror, is never larger to Jonson than a Sejanus or a Volpone. Faustus simply shrinks in Jonson's hands to Subtle, Mephistophilis to Face, and Helen of Troy to Dol Common. The vast world of Tamburlaine or of Faustus is in Jonson's drama narrowed down to a bedchamber or to a London house during the plague or to Smithfield during Bartholomew Fair.

Besides holding the mirror up to the stage, the non-dramatic poetry, the court, the scholarship of the times and the spirit of the Renaissance, Jonson gives a comprehensive picture of the daily life as he found it within as well as without the doors of London. As F.R. Leavis points out "Jonson was as robustly interested in men and manners and his own talk as in literature and the poetic art."[58] Jonson closely observed the minutest things with zest and zeal and transcribed his objective observations into his plays with great fidelity. This does not necessarily mean that Jonson brings in details for their own sake or just to enable himself to practise his theory of offering "an image of the times." His artistic economy and brilliant dramatic talent would never allow him to do so. All the details he brings in invariably serve some artistic purpose or other. Sometimes they serve as a setting to interpret a particular character or to extenuate a foible and at other times to show the distinction between various characters.

Jonson represents the contemporary habits of daily life – eating, smoking, singing, reading, dressing, duelling and gambling. Kinds of food in Jonson's time were prescribed rather by fashion than by personal taste. The social aspirant of the day necessarily

> learne to make strange sauces, to eat *aenchouies, maccaroni, bo oli, fagioli,* and *ca iare*. (*Cynthia's Revels*, II, iii, 105-6)

Then, the fashionable dinner must needs be served in silver dishes and eaten with elaborate nicety. For instance, the doting Fallance admires the courtier's table manners:

> O fine courtier! . . . how vpright hee sits at the table! how daintily he carves! how sweetly he talkes, and tels newes of this lord, and of that lady! how cleanely he wipes his spoone, at euery spoonfull of any whit-meat he eates, and what a neat case of pick-tooths he carries about him, still! (*Every Man Out of His Humour*, IV, 34-40)

The passage exquisitely sums up the dining manners of the courtiers of the time.

The varieties of tobacco and the elaborate devices for lighting which are found in Drugger's shop show what a fashion smoking had become.[59] We are shown how Bobadill uses seven pounds of tobacco in a week and discourses volubly on diffferent brands. (II, v, 71-72) When Fastidius Briske wants to call on Saviolina at the court he finds a pipe of tobacco a social asset. He eagerly asks Cinedo:

> Is my tobacco readie, boy?. . . This tobacco is not dryed, boy, or else the pipe's defective. (*Ibid*., III, ix, 36-39)

The people of the time, evinced a great deal of interest in reading.[60] But the books, barring the serious scholars, one read were often a matter of fashion. Matthew visits Bobadill with an approved volume of *The Spanish Tragedy* and at the slightest provocation begins to read a few passages. Fungoso would like to "lie abed and reade the *Arcadia*," till his tailor finishes his suit. We find a great book-lover in Dauphine who enjoys his bachelor retirement and reading to such an extent that Truewit warns him saying:

> You must leaue to liue i'your chamber then a month together vpon AMADIS *de Gaule* or *Don QUIXOTE*. (*Epicoene*, IV, i, 55-57)

The Elizabethans took a keen interest in music[61] – sacred and secular, vocal and instrumental. Jonson's plays abound in allusions to music, and songs.[62] In *Every Man Out of His Humour* a 'viol de gamba' hangs on the walls of Madame Saviolina's court apartments. When Fastidius Briske comes there to woo her, he takes the instrument down and plays upon it a soothing accompaniment to a tough conversation. When Deliro's wife is at odds with him, he steps into the street and returns with a band of musicians to play and restore her good humour. In *Cynthia's Revels* Amorphus, the would-be courtier, composes an ode upon his lady's glove and sets it to his "most affected instrument, the lyra" and says:

> Why, doe you not obserue how excellently the dittie is affected in euerie place? that I doe not marrie a word of short quantitie to a long note? nor an ascending sillable to a descending tone?
> (*Cynthia's Revels*, IV, iii, 327-30)

This shows how at times even poetry followed the pattern of music.

The Elizabethans were fond of fashionable costumes.[63] Portia's remarks upon one of her suitors hits off happily the fashion of the day:

> how oddly he is suited! I think he bought his doublet in Italy, his round hose in France, his bonnet in Germany, and his behaviour every where. (*The Merchant of Venice*, I, ii, 78-81)

The two gulls in *Every Man in His Humour*, Matthew and Stephen, excellently illustrate this aspect. From them we learn that the stiffened ruff was the most important fashion and that the dress of a gentleman was considered incomplete if he did not wear a rapier or a sword.

This leads us to the fact that the people were also fond of fencing and duelling.[64] There was a whole literature of fencing and duelling. Every gentleman was expected to be well-versed in the science of fencing. Bobadill claims to "have absolute knowledge" and "very rare, and un-in-one-breath-utterable skill" in the art of fencing. Subtle makes a table with mathematical demonstrations relating to the art of quarrels. We find Matthew and Kastril learning lessons in fencing from Bobadill and Subtle respectively.

The Elizabethans were also given to gambling that was prevalent in England right from the Middle Ages.[65] Jonson shows this wide-spread evil practice. In *The Alchemist* there are references to gambling houses such as 'the Dagger' and 'Madam Augusta's' and also to the well-known gamblers of the day like 'dead Holland' and 'living Isaac.' The play presents three gamblers Dapper, Surly and Kastril. Kastril is fascinated by the idea of having a 'familiar spirit' to have success assured at gambling.

Jonson gives as intimate a picture of the outdoor life as of the indoor. As we know from the contemporary writers like Dekker, the London streets were full of jostle and noise.[66] Jonson represents this hubbub in lively detail. In *The Silent Woman*, Morose, the gentleman that loves no noise, lives in a street, "so narrow at both ends, that it will receive no coaches, nor carts, nor any of other common noises." (I, i, 167-69) Managing to keep himself away from the usual disturbing cries of vendors he has been "upon various treaties with the fish wives and orange women" to make them not to cry near his house. Still he is harassed by the "chimney sweepers, brommen, costermongers and brasiers" who will not so easily agree to silence. Besides, there were the boisterous street entertainers like

> a Beare-ward . . . with the dogs of some foure parishes . . . and a Fencer marching to his prize. (I, i, 173-78)

Jonson lets us know some of the outdoor diversions of the time. Hunting, fowling, tennis, riding, betting on races and bowling were the prominent fashionable outdoor pastimes.[67] Stephen studies the sciences of hawking and hunting which he says "are studied more than the Greek, or the Latin." To a question—"What should a man doe?"—Clerimont answers giving the things wherein fashionable young men exercise themselves:

> Harken after the next horse-race, or hunting-match; lay wagers, praise *Puppy*, or *Pepper-corne*, *white-foote*, *Franklin*; swear vpon *White-maynes* partie. (*The Silent Woman*, I, i, 35-37)

In *Cynthia's Revels* we learn of horse-riding and playing tennis. Mercury tells Cupid how Hedon

> courts ladies with how many great horse he hath rid that morning . . . he dares tell 'hem, how many shirts he has sweat at *tennis* that weeke, but wisely conceales so many dozen of bals hee is on the score. (II, i, 63-69)

Then, the narrow, crowded streets were full of catchpenny entertainments taking place at the same time when people were rushing to the theatres to see plays. Trained animals such as monkeys, elephants, camels and especially bears were made use of on the Elizabethan stage[68] and the names of the trainers of these animals were as widely known as the names of great actors and playwrights. The people took great interest in these shows. Waspe tells how

> Yesterday i' the afternoone, we walk'd *London*, to shew the City . . . and where hee (Cokes) spi'd a *Parrat*, or a *Monkey*, there hee was pitch'd with all the littl(e) long-coats about him, male and female, no getting him away! (*Bartholomew Fair*, I, iv, 107-16)

Excluding the theatre, the most elaborate entertainment for the Elizabethan people was the puppet-show or 'motion.' The motions could be seen at Fleet-bridge. The whole manner of presentation is set forth in *Bartholomew Fair*. The performance is announced by a banner. The rate of admission is on a sliding scale. Lanthorne tells Filcher:

> And there come any Gentlefolks, take two pence a piece. (V, i, 21-22)

The puppets are kept in a basket and the showman manipulates them quite dexterously and also talks for them.

Jonson projects effectively the dominant issues – economic, social and moral – of the Jacobean world. The economic instability of the times resulted in the mushroom growth of monopolies, patents and projects. The nefarious activities of the projectors and monopolists had increased most alarmingly by the middle of the reign of James I.[69] Jonson displays these activities in *The Devil is an Ass* (1616). He presents the contemporary projectors in Meercraft who projects various ways – "by suits, by marriages and by undertakings" – to enrich men and make them great. Jonson shows how the avaricious projector lures a series of greedy fools into his net through his promises of patents.

Far-reaching social changes came about in the wake of the economic upheaval. With the rise of the gentry, people grew enamoured of being considered gentlemen in society. Stubbes tells us how every man was

> crying with open mouth, I am a gentleman, I am worshipful, I am Honorable, I am Noble.[70]

Jonson's plays abound in instances of this craze for gentry. The word 'gentleman' recurs throughout *Every Man in His Humour*. Bobadill constantly swears: "as I am a gentleman." However, it is in Sogliardo that Jonson presents the most typical aspirant to gentlemanship. Sogliardo is so enamoured of the name of 'gentleman' that "he will have it, though he buys it." He takes "a most gentleman-like resolution":

> I haue land and money, my friends left me well, and I will be a Gentleman, whatsoeuer it cost me.
>
> (*Every Man Out of His Humour*, I, ii, 2-3)

The age Jonson lived in was essentially superstitious. The people believed in such pseudo-sciences as alchemy, astrology, palmistry, witchcraft and necromancy. Jonson reproduces this crudely superstitious character of his age. Subtle and Face represent the typical alchemists of the times. Sir Epicure Mammon has such an unshaken faith in alchemy that he fondly proclaims:

> This night, I'll change
> All, that is mettall, in my house, to gold.
>
> (*The Alchemist*, II, i, 29-30)

Dapper would have 'a familiar' to help him win cups at horse-races and make him a successful gambler. Drugger would have ill-days crossed out of his almanack and also have magic signs to attract customers to his shop. Dame Pliant would be told of her fortune. The puritans, Ananias and Tribulation, pay a handsome amount of money to procure 'the philosopher's stone' which is to perform wonders.

People in Jonson's time were greatly fascinated by the published pamphlets of all sorts of news least bothering themselves whether or not the news was authentic. This contemporary craze for current news is clearly brought out by Jonson in *The Staple of News*. Thomas, the barber, who has a pretty talent in spreading gossip, tells Pennyboy Junior of a newly erected Staple of News:

> Where all the newes of all sorts shall be brought,
> And there be examin'd, and then registered,
> And so be issu'd vnder the Seale of the *Office*,
> As *Staple Newes*; no other newes be current. (I, ii, 33-36)

And we find at the Staple Registrar and clerks examining and filling all sorts of news –

> *Authenticali*, and *Apocryphall* . . . *Barbers newes* . . . *Taylors Newes, Porters,* and *Watermens newes* . . . *vacation newes, Terme-newes,* and *Christmas-newes* . . . *Reformed newes, Protestant newes,* and *Pontificiall newes*. (I, v, 8-15)

Thus, Jonson comprehends in his characteristic 'image of the times' most of the findings of all contemporary exploration, most of the forms of life to be found in Elizabethan and Jacobean London, and reflects their background, the people's habits and processes, their daily life, particularly the eccentricities and the peculiarities of their gesture and speech. Apart from the idealists and saintly figures, Jonson has ranged over the whole of the society from courtier to water-carrier and has set vividly before us a motley company of its types and has faithfully mirrored the variety of its fashions.

However full is this picture of life that Jonson presents, it has been often felt that Jonson's world, being exaggerated, is far removed from the world of our daily existence. J.C. Grierson, for instance, complains that Jonson "flew at comparatively small game" and in all his plays wasted his powers "on pigmies whom at the distance of three centuries we can hardly descry."[71] But the point is that, though the new comic world Jonson creates, particularly in his masterpieces, is not precisely our world, it is, nonetheless, closely related to our reality without being the same. In a similar manner "Jonson's world, while being exaggerated, is exaggerated in proper proportions, so that we see a magnified version of part of our daily experience, and we are startled by this new vision of the commonplace."[72]

This great phenomenon is accomplished by Jonson technically by 'stilisation' of and 'concentration' on the chosen medium. In full realisation of what he was doing, Jonson accepted a strict dramatic discipline and thereby achieved a trenchancy of comic language and a control of dramatic form. This artistic discipline results in the 'simplification' which "consists largely in reduction of detail. . . . This stripping is essential to the art, to which is also essential a flat distortion in the drawing. . . . The 'world' of Jonson is sufficiently large; it is a world of poetic imagination. . . . He did not get the third dimension, but he was not trying to get it."[73]

Also, Jonson's 'image of the times,' like that of the other Jacobean dramatists, is supposed to run the 'risk' that "the colours of what was once modern may fade in a few years, so that in the end nothing is left but an antiquarian interest."[74] Jonson's plays certainly escape this fate by virtue of their universality of appeal which has made them permanently available to us. Jonson confronts the principal aspects and developments of the time, we must bear in mind, only with the assurance of sharing with his audience and readers 'an inherited code of human experience.' As Salingar points out, "though Jonson's plays, more than their contemporaries, reshape it in 'the light of a particular vision,' the code was common as well as personal. Writing such as his—'not because of what it describes, but because of what it embodies'—provides the best means of understanding the human problems of its time; and hence, a means of understanding our own.[75] Plays like *Volpone* and *The Alchemist*, for instance, will continue to be contemporary so long as greed and lust remain human vices. They are particularly relevant to the present age in which life has been turned into something resembling a 'usurer's paradise.' *The Alchemist* "is fundamentally concerned with the nature of man; alchemy is only its subject matter. It never will lose meaning, even in a golden atomic age, as long as men ludicrously try to get something for nothing."[76] Also, for commercial purposes modern techniques of advertisement indecorously exploit classical myths,[77] just as Volpone calls on the Greek pantheon to seduce a reluctant wife. Meercraft's device, in *The Devil is an Ass*, of offering his dupe, Fitzdottrel, a choice of fantastic get-rich-quick schemes is also almost completely intelligible in our own time, since it is the exact equivalent of persuading modern investors to put their money into dud companies or non-existent gold-mines. Again, as in Jonson's world, in our own times too religion is worldly and business hypocritical. Then, we still have with us our Bobadills and Busys, our Matthews and Stephens, our Fungosos and Sogliardos, our Mammons and Voltores, our Dappers and Druggers and even our Corvinos and

Corbaccios. Besides, we still have our quacks and quackeries, our tricksters and gulls. Jonson can yet help us in taking a knowing laugh.

No doubt, some topical concerns of the early seventeenth century such as the debate between an orthodox catholicism and an evolving protestantism and some staple trends of the Jacobean society like the mushroom growth of monopolies, patents and projects, the rising capitalism and puritanism and particularly the prevalence of superstitious beliefs seemed less than vital issues to the centuries that followed.

Yet, from the perspective of the twentieth century we realise that what the Jacobeans discussed is what we are discussing still. Their subjects are ours and they remain a vital voice even in our own lives today. On various levels—philosophical, psychological, political, social and religious—the Jacobeans touched upon such abiding issues as man in the universe, why man does what he does, orthodoxy versus liberalism and relativism, social order versus individual need, that we still must discuss, still must argue out. It is in this sense the Jacobean and Caroline dramatists are modern. They are relevant to our present condition and speak to the predicament we are involved in today. Hence, it is a tribute to Jonson's keen mind and sound judgment that his scale of values is not unacceptable today. Just as Shakespeare is 'timeless and universal,' so, perhaps, Jonson can be. Jonson's plays, like all powerful dramatic symbols, remain alive or gain new life once they are experienced aesthetically.

NOTES

1. *Every Man Out of His Humour*, III, vi, 206-7. H.L. Snuggs, however, thinks that Jonson, for his definition of comedy, is indebted to the Fourth Book of Minturno's *De Poets* rather than to Cicero. See "The Source of Jonson's Definition of Comedy," *MLN*, LXV (Nov. 1950), pp. 543-44.
2. "The Poetics," *Literary Criticism: Plato to Dryden*, ed. Allan H. Gilbert, p. 74.
3. "Poetica," *Ibid.*, p. 224.
4. *The Boke named the Gouernour*, ed. H.H.S. Croft, vol. I, p. 124.
5. "The Schoolmaster," *English Works*, ed. W.A. Wright, p. 266.
6. "Apology for Poetry," *Elizabethan Critical Essays*, ed. Gregory Smith, vol. I, p. 176.
7. Lodge, "A Defence of Poetrie," *Ibid.*, p. 81. Heywood, *An Apology for Actors*, Sig. Fly.
8. Malone Society Reprint (1909), ll. 2015-17.

9. 'To the General Reader,' *Sophonisbe, The Plays*, ed. H.H. Wood, vol. II, p. 5.
10. John Russell Brown, *Shakespeare's Plays in Performance*, p. 33.
11. M.C. Bradbrook, *The Growth and Structure of Elizabethan Comedy*, p. 109.
12. J.R. Brown, "On the Acting of Shakespeare's Plays," *The Seventeenth Century State: A Collection of Critical Essays*, ed. G.E. Bentley, p. 53.
13. E.C. Dunn, *Ben Jonson's Art* (Northampton: Mass., Smith College, 1925), p. xiii.
14. "In Elizabethan painting there was a curiosity known as the 'prespective picture' which seen from a particular angle would display objects which, if the picture were directly faced, would be too distorted to be recognized." (M.C. Bradbrook, p. 109)
15. See A.V. Judges, ed. *The Elizabethan Underworld.*
16. A.B. Grosart, ed., *Life and Complete Works of Robert Greene*, vol. I, pp. 132-33.
17. *Ibid.*, p. 7.
18. See *Ibid.*, 'The Epistle,' pp. 197-201.
19. *Ibid.*, vol. X, p. 276.
20. See F.W. Chandler, *The Literature of Roguery*, (London: 1909), vol. I.
21. *The Works of Thomas Nashe*, ed. R.B. McKerrow, vol. II, p. 211.
22. Brian Gibbons, *Jacobean City Comedy*, p. 216. See also L.C. Knights, "Elizabethan Prose," *Drama and Society in the Age of Jonson*, pp. 301-2.
23. *The Works of Thomas Nashe*, vol. II, p. 229.
24. Dekker, "The Belman of London," *Non-Dramatic Works*, vol. III, p. 168.
25. L.C. Knights, p. 229.
26. Dekker, "The Seven Deadly Sins of London," *Non-Dramatic Works*, vol. II, p. 64.
27. Brian Gibbons, *Jacobean City Comedy*, p. 217.
28. "The London of Queen Elizabeth, by its size, wealth and power, was the most formidable unit in the Kingdom." G.M. Trevelyan, *English Social History* (London, 1942), p. 142.
29. "London, absorbing more and more of the home and foreign commerce of the country at the expense of many smaller towns, was already a portent for size in England and even in Europe." *Loc. cit.*
30. See L.C. Knights, pp. 78- 81.
31. "This was indeed the golden age of the Inns, when all was pulsating with vitality and *joie de vivre*." A.L. Rowse, *The England of Elizabeth*, p. 522.

32. Herford and Simpson, vol. I, p. 9.
33. J. Spedding, ed., *Works of Francis Bacon*, vol. VIII, p. 109.
34. Aubrey, *Brief Lives*, ed. Clark, vol. II, p. 182.
35. "Never can there have been more class-consciousness, one feels in any age." A.L. Rowse, p. 245.
36. "The exact division among the collaborators is not easy to determine, but the coherence and firmness of the structure, particularly in the denouement, seem due to Jonson." A.H. Thorndike, *English Comedy* (New York, 1929), p. 149.
37. Brian Gibbons, p. 23.
38. T.S. Eliot, *Elizabethan Dramatists*, p. 92.
39. K.M. Lynch, *The Social Mode of Restoration Comedy*, p. 25.
40. R.H. Barker, *Thomas Middleton* (London: O.U.P., 1958), p. 52.
41. Brian Gibbons, p. 168.
42. *Ibid.*, p. 78.
43. K.M. Lynch, p. 25.
44. L.C. Knights, pp. 236-39.
45. M.V. Rama Sarma, *Heywood: A Prose Shakespeare*, p. 31.
46. See M. Velte, *The Bourgeois Elements in the Dramas of Thomas Heywood*, p. 140.
47. See for instance, Symonds, ed., *Plays of Heywood*, 'Introduction,' p. xiv.
48. M.V. Rama Sarma, pp. 45-46.
49. L.C. Knights, p. 255.
50. *Ibid.*, p. 273.
51. The two leading companies were the Lord Chamberlain's company (1596-97) and the Lord Admiral's Company (1600). Other companies were the Earl of Worcester's Company (1604), the Duke of York's Company (1610), the first Lady Elizabeth's Company (1611), the Children of the Revels' Company (1629). "In the Tudor period, in addition to the professional Companies, the schools, the Inns of Court and the Universities had been important theatrical centres." F.S. Boas, pp. 11-12.
52. The leading playhouses were the Globe on the Bankside, the Blackfriars theatre on the north side of the Thames, the Fortune of the north-west of the City, the Curtain in Shoreditch, the Red Bull playhouse in Clerkenwell, the Cockpit in Drury Lane, the Hope on Bankside, and the Salisbury Court Playhouse in Whitefriars.
53. See "Juggling Tricks and Conjury on the English Stage before 1642," *MP*, XXIV (1926-27), pp. 269-84.
54. See Dover Wilson, *Life in Shakespeare's England* (Pelican Books, 1944), p. 215.

55. William A. Armstrong, "The Audience of the Elizabethan Private Theatres," *RES*, X (1959), pp. 233-49.
56. "From the erection of the theatres in 1576 to their suppression at the outbreak of the Civil War, the Puritan party waged an unceasing warfare against the state." Dover Wilson, p. 227.
57. Poets were engaged in "seeking less to please the public than to attract the notice of the Court . . . or of some lord of fashion when poetry was fashionable." (G.M. Trevelyan, *England Under the Stuarts*, p. 51).
58. F.R. Leavis, "English Poetry in the Seventeenth Century," *Scrutiny*, IV (Dec. 1935), p. 244.
59. "The habit of taking tobacco in long clay pipes was very general by the time the Queen died." (G.M. Trevelyan, *English Social History*, p. 200)
60. "As the public today consumes newspapers . . . so the Elizabethan man in the street bought and read broadsides and pamphlets that related sensational events, strange wonders, the untimely ends of criminals, and the frailties of human kind." (Louis B. Wright, *Middle-Class Culture in Elizabethan England*, p. 419)
61. See John Buxton, *Elizabethan Taste* (London, 1963), pp. 172-73.
62. There are 26 songs scattered through his plays besides numerous references to music. See Edwin S. Lindsey, "The Music in Ben Jonson's Plays," *MLN*, XLIV (1929), pp. 86-92.
63. "'Fashions from proud Italy' and France were always being imitated . . . costly trinkets of all sorts were worn by men as much as by women." (G.M. Trevelyan, *English Social History*, p. 159)
64. "Clashing of swords was then daily music in every street." (Dover Wilson, p. 128)
65. See G.M. Trevelyan, *English Social History*, p. 88.
66. "In every street, carts and coaches make such a thundering as if the world ran upon wheels. . . . Besides, jammers are beating in one place, tubs hooping in another, pots clinking in a third, water-tankards running at tilt in a fourth." (Dover Wilson, p. 125)
67. See D.H. Madden, *The Diary of Master William Silence: A Study of Shakespeare and of Elizabethan Sport* (1897, rep. 1969)
68. See Louis B. Wright, "Animal Actors on the English Stage before 1642," *PMLA*, XLII (1927), pp. 656-69.
69. See L.C. Knights, p. 211.
70. *Anatomy of Abuses*, ed. Purnivall, p. 29.
71. J.C. Grierson, *The First Half of the Seventeenth Century*, p. 102.
72. David Cook, ed., *Volpone*, 'Introduction,' p. 25.
73. T.S. Eliot, *Elizabethan Dramatists*, p. 81.

74. Marchette Chute, *Ben Jonson of Westminster* (New York: Dutton, 1953), p. 186.
75. L.G. Salingar, "Review" of *Drama and Society in the Age of Jonson, Scrutiny*, VI (1937-38), p. 119.
76. Edward B. Partridge, p. 238.
77. "The great god Mercury has become the name of an automobile. Adonis and Atlas have degenerated into trade-names. Venus . . . is now used to sell brassieres; and Medusa (with more appropriateness) to sell cement." (*Ibid.*,pp. 236-37)

Profit and Delight

The function of the English drama was traditionally didactic. Drama, after all, was brought into being only because it seemed, more than any other existing genre, an effective method of preaching to the people. The "ostensible purpose of dramatic production remained didactic to the end of the Medieval drama. Now the end of the Medieval drama almost coincided with the culmination of the Renaissance drama."[1]

The authors of the allegorical plays dedicate their works to the exaltation of virtue and the suppression of vice. Ulpian Fulwel, for example, exclaims in the preface to his play, *Like Wil to Like* (1568), that the reader may see therein, as in a glass,

> The advancement of virtue, of the vice the decay:
> To what ruin ruffians and roisters are brought.[2]

Tancred and Gismunda is prefaced by a similar statement:

> herein they all agree, commending virtue, detesting vice, and lively deciphering their overthrow that supress not their unruly affections.[3]

Edwards intoduces his play *Damon and Pythias* with a didactic statement:

> In comedies the greatest skill is this, rightly to teach
> All things to the quick. . . .[4]

The moral function of art, specially of the comic art, is inherent in all Renaissance critical doctrine. The entire fabric of Sidney's *Apology for Poetry* is strewn with didacticism.[5] Spenser, in his discussion of poetic composition, allows a high place for the didactic value of poetry.[6] Nashe states that poetry is

> a more hidden and diuine kinde of Philosophy, enwrapped in blind

> Fables and darke stories, wherein the principles of more excellent Arts and morall precepts of manners, illustrated with diuerse examples of other Kingdomes and Countries, are contained.[7]

Then, Gascoigne in *Certayne Notes of Instruction concerning the Making of Verse or Ryme in English,*[8] Webbe in *A Discourse of Englishe Poetrie,*[9] and Puttenham in *The Arte of English Poesie,*[10] stress the conventional theory that poetry should necessarily profit mankind.

The main forces tending to thrust the Elizabethan dramatist towards the didactic were not only the allegorical tendencies during the Mediaeval and Renaissance literary men, mentioned above, but also the Puritan attacks on the theatre. From the early Christian period to the Renaissance, a hostile attitude toward plays and players continued through the Church. And by the last quarter of the sixteenth century, the denunciation reached a climax.[11] The theatre was said to be a school of abuse and bawdry, the veritable nest of the devil. Plays were severely attacked on the ground that they taught and encouraged vice and sedition. They were also held responsible for spreading plagues and for robberies, seduction and murders. In a word, the plays were said to be the source of all evil.

Consequent on all these forces and influences, dramatist after dramatist insists that his drama, whether comedy or tragedy, is an indictment of vice and an attempt to improve society. Chapman, for instance, points out that

> material instruction, elegant and sententious excitation to virtue, and deflection from her contrary (are the) soul, limbs, and limits of an authentical tragedy.[12]

Similarly Heywood pleads that comedies

> discourse of Pantaloones, Vsurers that have vnthrifty sonnes, which both the fathers and sonnes may behold to their instruction; sometimes of Courtesans, to diuulge their subtelties and snares, in which yong men may be intangled, shewing them the meanes to auoyd them.[13]

Massinger, defending comedy on moral grounds, says how plays

> Decipher to the life what honours wait
> On good and glorious acitons, and the shame
> That treads upon the heels of vice.[14]

But the Elizabethan and Jacobean dramatists were also subjected to a strong antidote for a strict moral theory. Their plays had to be brought on the boards, and the Elizabethan audience were very vehement in their likes and dislikes. They, in turn, liked romantic improbability, disguises, battles, sword play, broad farce and ribald jokes, quick wit-battles, and even demanded blood, revenge and ghosts on the stage. Although the dramatists were by no means pleased by the demands of the audience, in their professional interest they had to reckon with them. To give an example, in Chapman's *Revenge of Bussy D'Ambois*, the Guise states the ideal end of tragedy:

> I would have these things
> Brought upon stages, to let mighty misers
> See all their grave and serious miseries play'd
> As once they were in Athens and old Rome. (I, i, 319-22)

But Clerimont quickly reminds the Guise of the demands of the audience:

> Nay, we must now having nothing brought on stages
> But puppetry, and pied ridiculous antics:
> Men thither come to laugh, and feed foot-fat,
> Check at all goodness there. (I, i, 323-26)

The Elizabethan dramatists could, however, read Horace's famous couplet,

> aut prodesse volunt aut delectare poetae
> aut simul et iuccunda et idonea dicere vitae (*Ars Poetica*, ll. 333-34)

and the Renaissance commentaries on it, which gave them the right to include material in their works for didactic as well as aesthetic purposes.

The Renaissance critical theory never forgot the injunction of Horace, which decreed that the poet was to provide moral instruction in a pleasing manner. Although Sidney considered the business of comedy to be a presentation of the common errors of life in a ridiculous and scornful manner, he allowed a place to laughter coupled with delight.[15] Nashe is only echoing the conventional thought of his age when he says:

> In playes, all coosonages, all cunning drifts ouer guylded with outward holinesse . . . are most liuely anatomiz'd.[16]

Thus, the dramatists are to teach, but they are also to delight, since whatever they may have to say of profit will be more palatable, if it is turned out in a fictional guise—from which an audience can derive pleasure.

The Horatian critical dictum which holds it to be the poet's duty to instruct and to entertain at one and the same time is evident in the theory and practice of Elizabethan and Jacobean dramatists. Marlowe shows himself characteristically at the meeting point of Mediaeval and Renaissance values. In his tragedies he shows how inordinate aspiration leads perversely to triviality. As W. Moelwyn Merchant rightly points out, "Marlowe is never more in accord with the orthodoxy of his intellectual origins than when he explores the patterns of sin and punishment in the cosmic order and to this pattern the plays all return at their conclusion."17

Shakespeare's plays, it is true, do not formulate a judgment. Nevertheless a judgment is implicit. Although his comedies are rather concerned with ideals, with wooing and wedding than with day-to-day affairs of London life, Shakespeare seeks to affirm in them a generous, true and ordered mode of existence. We respond to their harmony, integrity, humour and beauty, and in thus responding we affirm ourselves. "In such an affirmation," as J.R. Brown points out, "there is a judgment upon life, a judgment which is only implicit but which may receive a wider hearing than the reproofs of a satirist or the precepts of a moralist. To such plays we may return again and again with profit and delight."[18]

Heywood's comedies and tragedies easily lend themselves to moral and aesthetic interpretation. Dekker's plays give evidence of being modelled on moral and didactic theories. When Massinger in *The City Madam* ridicules the vain efforts of the ladies of Sir John Frugal's family to ape the style of the gentry "he is at one and the same time, setting before us an amusing piece of satiric portraiture, and making a perfectly serious social and moral criticism."[19] However, it is to Jonson that we have to turn not only for a more comprehensive treatment of the didactic theory but also to find unity of didactic theory and practice in a greater measure.

That Jonson was not content with his early attempts to combine didactic and comic elements is evident from the change of his dramatic technique in every one of his first five comedies. From the composition of *The Case is Altered* (1597) to the completion of *Volpone* (1605) Jonson's comedies, we may say, are experimental. In no single comedy before *Volpone* is Jonson able to achieve his object of the fusion of the didactic and the comic. Either the satiric and didactic material is overshadowed by the Comic as in *The Case is Altered*, or the didactic material overshadows and almost obscures the comic material as in *Every Man Out of His Humour.*

Of Jonson's early plays only *A Tale of a Tub* and *The Case is Altered* are extant. *A Tale of a Tub*, unacknowledged by Jonson, was written without any didactic or satiric content.[20] It is in *The Case is Altered* that Jonson made an effort to divert his comedy towards didactic ends. Nevertheless, it is primarily a romantic comedy and the didactic content is quite subsidiary. The exposure of the follies of the gallants, Onion and Juniper, is, no doubt, laughable but it lacks any great didactic value. If the satire is embedded in the boisterous exuberance in which the play is steeped, it is lost in light and funny conversation. Avarice, embodied in Jaques de Price is, no doubt, an excellent vice for moralistic treatment. But there is little stress on the social effects of his avarice. Moreover, most of the scenes in which the miser appears are more comic than didactic. On the whole, the atmosphere of the play lacks moral consciousness.[21]

In *Every Man in His Humour* Jonson begins to combine a considerable amount of satire with his comedy. He attacks the false social values by which the fashionable and would-be-fashionable gallants regualte their conduct. Through Matthew, Stephen, and Bobadill he parodies the elaborate terminology associated with fencing (I, iii, 184-229; II, iii, 123-53), hawking (I, i, 28-56), quarrelling (I, i, 86-110; III, ii, 107-15; iv, 145-59). He ridicules the poor literary taste of pretenders to fashion (I, iii, 66-70; 125-52; III, iv, 22-102). Thus the action of the play is designed to exhibit the fatuities, the folllies, the obsessions, the pretensions, and the absurdities of the different characters. The more serious threats to society—the breakdown in communication between generations (Knowells) and between husband and wife (Kitelys)—are eventually dissipated through the timely intervention of Justice Clement. And though the play "concludes amid reconciliation, rejoicing, and communal festivities, there remains the realization that were it not for the fateful, ordering presence of Doctor Clement, the follies would have continued and developed into serious social problems."[22]

However, at least half of the play is concerned with nonsatiric matter,[23] and even the satire the play contains is light as most of the material on the follies of the gallants is comic. The oaths of Bobadill, the swordplay of Matthew and Bobadill (I, iii, 195-229), and the argument over the virtues and evils of tobacco (III, ii, 107-16)—all this is essentially a theatrical stuff, causing a great deal of amusement to the audience. Jonson, however, has given so much of importance to wit and humour in *Every Man in His Humour* that his didactic purpose is pushed to the background. This he may well have realised, perhaps, to his great dissatisfaction.

The result is a radical change of technique in the immediately following play, *Every Man Out of His Humour*. The satiric and didactic material does no longer take a secondary place in this play which is moralistic to the core. The moral purpose is to make men "fit for fair societies" by giving them "pills to purge" them of their shallowness and of their false social values.

The didactic material is embodied in the main characters – Fastidius Briske, Fungoso, and Sogliardo. Fastidius, who is an adept in the art of speaking always of his friendships with the great, is purged of his folly when he is confronted with the severe punishment of confinement in a debtors' prison. He then cries "O, heaven." Fungoso, who is a blind imitator of Fastidius, is finally cured of his delusions and resolves never to imitate

> any more gallants either in purse, or apparel, but as shall become a gentleman, for good carriage, or so. (V, ix, 3-5)

Sogliardo, who is prepared to buy the name of a gentleman, is finally exposed as

> A swine without a head, without braine, wit, any thing, indeed, ramping to gentilitie. (III, iv, 65-66)

and is snatched out of his folly.

It is now manifest that Jonson's primary purpose in the creation of these characters is didactic rather than dramatic. Their portrayal is expository rather than theatrical. The shallow characters talk of their follies or display them rather than enact them. On the whole, the play is overweighted by matter. Jonson's dramatic sense is almost overshadowed by his intense desire to include didactic satire in the play.

In *Cynthia's Revels* again the didactic element overpowers the comic purpose. The play is at once a document of Jonson's intellectual idealism and a proof of his thoroughgoing scorn for the rampant follies of the court life. The "purpose" of the play is

> to correct,
> And punish, with our laughter, this nights sport
> Which our court-*Dors* so heartily intend:
> And by that worthy scorne, to make them know
> How farre beneath the dignitie of man
> Their serious, and most practis'd actions are (V, i, 17-22)

To execute his purpose Jonson again changes his dramatic technique, choosing a mythical framewrok thereby representing the conflict between good and evil.[24] Flawless Cynthia, virtuous Arete and Crites, the champion of wisdom and virtue – all Jonson's representatives of moral excellence – embody good. The corrupt, shallow, vain and silly courtiers – Amorphus, Anaides, Hedon and Asotus – and their ladies – Argurion, Philautia, Phantaste, and Moria – represent evil. Building masque-like scenes, played by the antithetical characters, Jonson contrasts the good and bad elements in court society. Crites and Arete serve as foils to the false courtiers as well as to their ladies who talk of nothing more serious than their clothes, cosmetics and pages.

Jonson succeeds exceedingly well in his endeavour

> to inflict iust paines
> On their prodigious follies. . . (V, i, 10-11)

The courtiers and their ladies are at last rid of their follies and are summoned to dry their

> weeping eyes,
> And to the well of knowledge haste;
> Where purged of your maladies,
> You may of sweeter waters taste:
> And, with refined voice, report
> The grace of CYNTHIA, and her court. ('Palinode,' ll. 35-40)

All the persons who have bathed in the fountain of self-love find, in the end, restoration in the well of knowledge.

In *Poetaster*[25] Jonson bends the historical matter of the Augustan age into a stout framework for his didactic and comic purposes. As the title implies, "the play is primarily a dramatic defense of poetry, a theatrical and effectively written 'ars poetica.'"[26] The moral purpose is to vindicate the true poets and to expose poetasters. As in *Cynthia's Revels*, Jonson here balances good characters – Horace, Virgil and the Emperor – with bad ones – Crispinus and Demetrius – and includes sententious speeches in order to emphasize the moral.

The entire action of the play is arranged in such a fashion as to lead to the arraignment of the poetasters for having

> most ignorantly, foolishly, and (more like your selues) maliciously, gone about to depraue, and calumniate the person and writings of QVINTVS HORACIVS FLACCVS . . . *poet*, and *priest*, to the

Muses. (V, iii, 224-28)

Crispinus is relieved of the 'Crudities' in his poetic diction by means of pills administered to him by Horace. Finally, the Poetaster and his helpmate are bound over by an "oath of good behaviour." Jonson ultimately shows how

> Vertue, without presumption, place may take
> Aboue best Kings, whom onely she should make. (V, ii, 26-27)

But the serious substance of the play is interspersed with a great deal of comic element. By now Jonson seems to have realized the necessity for more comic material. Hence the inclusion of burlesque, farce, parody and dramatic enactments of follies in this comedy. These comic and theatrical devices manifest themselves mostly around Captain Tucca, Crispinus, Albius, Chloe and Lupus. Several of the comic scenes are adroitly managed with extreme cleverness and vivacity. Particularly Chloe's entertaining of the scene in which an honest citizen's ambitious wife is eager for the fashions of the court are very amusing. But the most amusing character in the comedy is Tucca – a special type of the military bully distinct both from Bobadill and Falstaff. Also, the trial scene is quite funny as Crispinus with difficulty regurgitates words like "oblatrant," "furibund" and "prorumped."

It is in *Volpone* that Jonson demonstrated his didactic and comic techniques in their maturity. The experimental devices of the previous 'comical satires' are here eschewed. There is no chorus, Asper or Crites, here to explain the didactic function. The satire is implicit. The morality is pervasive but the moral accent is never distinctly or separately heard. It only qualifies the value of every note.

Jonson's moral purpose in *Volpone* is

> to informe yong-men to all good disciplines, inflame growne-men to all great vertues, keepe old-men in their best and supreme state.
> (Dedication, ll. 24-26)

With his earnest purpose "to informe men in the best reason of liuing," Jonson builds the play on the power of wealth and its repercussions. Almost every scene is so designed as to exhibit the repercussions of wealth, the insolence which it breeds and the infamies which are committed for excessive love of it. In short, *Volpone* is a powerful picture of moral depravity of the age.

Volpone is the embodiment of lust for sensual pleasures. Wealth is his instrument. The legacy hunters – Voltore, Corbaccio and Carvino, the birds of prey – are motivated entirely by greed. Blinded by inordinate avarice for wealth, Corvino condescends to procure his own innocent wife, Corbaccio disinherits his own son by declaring him to be a bastard and Voltore perjures himself twice in the open court. "Society may depend upon its Moscas to outwit its Corbaccios, its Voltores, and its Corvinos, but it can only wait for the Moscas and the Volpones to betray themselves."[27] The denouement is brought about through Mosca's own greed. Volpone, Mosca and the three legacy hunters are duly punished. Celia who is resistant to vice and Bonario who rescues Celia are saved. Though for the time being these two virtuous characters suffer, ultimately they are rewarded and vice is worsted. The play closes on a didactic note:

> Let all, that see these vices thus rewarded,
> Take heart, and loue to study 'hem. Mischiefes feed
> Like beasts, till they be fat, and then they bleed. (V, xii, 149-51)

Volpone provides as much delight as profit. Nevertheless, it is often said to be too forbidding a play to provide any amusement. "If Jonson ever sports here," we are told, "it is in the sombre and lurid fashion of his own 'sporting Kyd.' . . . The air is heavy and fetid with moral disease."[28] "The satirical intensity," says Gregory Smith, "rarely, if ever, permits that laughter at vice."[29] We cannot possibly fall in line with these views. Because, we know that Jonson meant *Volpone* to be a merry comedy. The last lines of his Prologue announce his goal:

> All gall, and compresse, from his inke he drayneth,
> Onely, a little salt remayneth;
> Wherewith, he'll rub your cheeks, til (red with laughter)
> They shall looke fresh, a weeke after. (ll. 33-36)

And there is every reason to suppose that Dryden would have included *Volpone* when he wrote: "To make men appear pleasantly ridiculous on the stage was his talent. . . . That Ben Jonson's plays were pleasant, he must want reason who denies."[30]

Volpone is not, in any case, a too forbidding play. It does provide plenty of fun, mirth and innocent laughter. The play bubbles over with what may be called sardonic humour. Almost every scene is larded with dramatic poetry that is constantly imaginative, comic, and exciting. The comic phase of *Volpone* has not received the due attention because laughter is so integral a part of the terrible portrayal of greed that the reader is likely to overlook the variety of theatrical and ironic laughter.

Also, the comic material of *Volpone* is such that it requires visual representation on the stage for its fullest expression and appeal.

The play is replete with a variety of comic scenes. Apart from the comic treatment of the gulls, "the gigs of Nano, Castrone and Androgyno, the mountebank scenes, and the action of Sir Politique and Lady Would-be consume some 900 lines out of 2400, or almost 38% of the first four acts."[31] The scenes in which the legacy hunters appear to make their respective offerings to the magnifico and discover how bad his health is, are full of good theatrical stuff. Voltore's pompous affability and self-complacent credulity render his folly laughable. Assured by Mosca that he is the sole heir to Volpone's property, he bursts out in childish glee:

> Happy, happy, me!
> By what good chance, sweet MOSCA?
> MOS. Your desert, Sir;
> I know no second cause.
> VOLT. Thy modestie
> Is loth to know it; well, we shall requite it. (I, iii, 47-49)

Corbaccio is very funny. Reassured by Mosca of his succession to Volpone's riches, he croaks his joy at the imminence of Volpone's death and his prospective wealth. We cannot but laugh when such an old creature says:

> I may ha' my youth restor'd to me, why not? (I, iv, 129)

Next comes the "witty merchant" Corvino. It is amusing to watch Mosca overcome Corvino's prudence and spur him into shouting stupid insults into Volpone's ear.

Then, the fantastic creatures—Nano, Androgyno and Castrone, whom Volpone maintains for his amusement make a good deal of comic appeal. The mountebank scene in which Volpone with "a starched beard" and "an old tilt-feather" sells patent medicine is out and out comic. Above all, the voluptuous visions which Volpone paints before the eyes of the distracted Celia are a provocation to the senses. Then, the last scene in which Voltore falls down on the floor pretending that he is possessed by a devil under the delusion that he will surely, in this manner, win Volpone's favour, is quite hilarious. All this suggests that the effect of the play is far from that of tragic foreboding.

However, *Volpone* marks a crucial phase of Jonson's development as a comic dramatist. The success of *Volpone* seems to have alleviated

Jonson's bitterness over the failure of *Sejanus* and the three unsuccessful attempts to bring about a harmonious fusion of 'profit and delight.' Naturally his mood is relaxed. Besides, as his powers of realistic depiction have come into full play, his loudly proclaimed moral purposes are subdued. He now seems to concur with Shakespeare and Donne that good and evil, in this world, are matters of opinion. So to Jonson, mankind is subdivided, it now seems, not into good and bad men but into rogues and fools. Consequently, he seems to feel that his role as a comic playwright is not to judge but to observe. Therefore we may say with Harry Levin that after *Volpone* "Jonson's genius underwent a metempsychosis of its own and, having died with a stern satirist, was reborn in a genial observer."[32]

After *Volpone* Jonson reverts to the light-hearted gaiety of *Every Man in His Humour* in *Epicoene.*[33] The play is "the most genial of the works of Jonson, the freak of a happy mood, written with a lighter pen and looser spirit, allowing his theme to develop of its own motion."[34] A different kind of comedy from the preceding plays, *Epicoene* flashes with an intense lustre.

The plot devices of the play are in tune with Jonson's assertions in the prologue. The plot follows with a wonderful union of the inevitable and the unforeseen. Jonson here presents "a man who is no man who marries a woman who is no woman."[35] The play grows more and more amusing as we pass from Act to Act. The high comedy of the collegiate ladies, the low comedy of the captain and Mrs. Otter, the braggart knights and the Latinest barber are all masterly strokes of comic genius. Such a play naturally stirs genial mirth in an ever increasing degree. The manners and the conversation particularly of the young men – Clerimont, Dauphine and Truewit – are more entertaining than it is common with Jonson. Hence, it is not hyperbolical to say that "*Epicoene* will keep the reader or the spectator for whole scenes together in an inward riot or an open passion of subdued or unexpressed laughter."[36]

However, it is difficult to agree with Swinburne that "in *Epicoene* we have pure farce without a trace of moral tone."[37] The moral tone of *Epicoene* is, no doubt, looser and more ambiguous than that of any other of his comedies, but Jonson has certainly not abandoned his moral purpose. Below the farcical surface action of the play can be found the serious themes of courtly affectation, unnatural sexuality and pretence to authority and literary achievement. There is abundant satire against the manners and affectations of the day. The fool, Sir John Daw, aspiring to be taken for a gentleman of the town, is a typical fool of fashion of the day.

In *Epicoene* we have a long attack on women. The collegiate ladies with their matchless mixture of pretension and profligacy, hypocrisy and pedantry are made the butt of ridicule. Also, the vices of women in general are denounced when Truewit elaborates and particularizes on all classes and types of women:

> O, a woman is, then, like a delicate garden; nor, is there one kind of it: she may varie, euery houre; take often counsell of her glasse, and choose the best. If shee haue good eares, shew 'hem; good haire, lay it out; good legs, weare short cloathes; a good hand, discouer it often; practise any art, to mend breath, cleanse teeth, repaire eye-browes, paint, and profess it. (I, i, 104-11)

Jonson, in this manner, "blazes away at the targets set up by countless misogynistic writers from classical times onwards: the lustfulness of women, their extravagance, their passion for clothes, their obsession with their own appearance, their desire to dominate men, and especially to tyrannise over their husbands, their unfaithfulness and deceit, and above all, of course, their incessant chattering and noise."[38]

The conclusion of the play furnishes no punishments. Jonson seems to suffer his fools rather easily by allowing their pretensions to social, sexual, and literary achievement to go too largely unpunished. He now chooses the indirect path to satire—"the mock encomium and the paradoxical action of self-exposing folly."[39] Perhaps, the most interesting aspect of paradox is Jonson's mock celebration of folly. The gulls revel in absurdity and the wittier and more articulate characters praise folly in a way that ironically undercuts its glories.

The Alchemist is built on the double theme of lust and greed. The profession of alchemy at once notorious and obscure with its mountebank practices and its mystic pretensions, the most picturesque of social pestilences, was a matter best fitted to furnish forth the cosmos of Jonsonian typical comedy. The purpose of the play is the shaming of a variety of gulls victimized by the charlatan philosophy of the day, thereby hoping to "better men." The confederate swindlers, Subtle, Face and Dol Common bait and dupe Dapper, Drugger and Sir Epicure Mammon. The mere expectation of plentiful gold and the very sight of a lady enraptures Sir Epicure. Dapper and Drugger are lured by the prospects of easy money. Tribulation and Ananias, the hypocritical puritans, are overjoyed at the prospect of possessing gold. But, by dazzling their victims with a show of infinite riches and by exploiting their greed, the three partners cheat the gulls of their money. Jonson thus shows how the desire to become suddenly rich brings people into the sharper's clutches. While exposing a contemporary phase of imposture and its corresponding credulity Jonson, in *The Alchemist*, paints a picture which remains true to the permanent facts of human roguery and weakness.

Though soaked in satire, *The Alchemist* is not without its comic purpose. Just as the satiric is ingeniously woven into the purely comic world of *Epicoene,* the comic is adroitly introduced into the satiric world of *The Alchemist*, testifying to the fact that

> When the wholesome remedies are sweet,
> . . . in their working, gaine, and profit meet. ('Prologve,' ll. 15-16)

As Anne Barton rightly observes, *The Alchemist* is "The funniest play Jonson ever wrote, the most cunning in its marriage of erudition with brilliant theatricality."[40] It stands out from the rest of his work for the number of bizarre and hilarious stage situations it invents. We thoroughly enjoy the dramatic situations in which Dapper is blindfolded being pinched by Face and Subtle and Surly is trapped in his Spanish disguise. The audience also derive pleasure in the simulated prostration of the two charlatans, Subtle and Face, when the laboratory blows up off-stage, their real panic when Lovewit unexpectedly returns from his hop-fields or the innocent salutations of Ananias just at the moment when that household has exploded into a pitched battle.

In this essentially artistic play, the comic is ingrained in the very ingenuity of the plot, the liveliness of the action and the delightful delineation of manners: The satire unfailingly flavours the fun without destroying it. Laughter and delight are wrought into the composition of Dol, Face and Subtle, but the satiric, ironic quality is also there. They are shown on more than one level, as rogues, as insects or animals, and as higher beings, that they and others think they are. The simultaneous existence of multiple levels "helps create some of the humour and much of the irony which gather about a whore who thinks of herself as a 'republiqe,' a quack who will 'thunder' a man in pieces, and a pander who wears a uniform and calls himself 'Captaine.'"[41] Hence it is as difficult to isolate the comic and the didactic in these characters as in that of the wife of Bath or in that of the boisterous rogues in *The Beggar's Opera.* Thus, *The Alchemist* yields a world of profit and delight.

In *The Devil is an Ass,* after a gap of nine years, Jonson adopts the old devil lore for his didactic and comic purposes. The play is an attempt to heal the social and psychological evils attendant on a belief in witchcraft. Jonson's satirical exposure of the simulation of being possessed unequivocally lends itself to reformatory purpose, weakening the belief of the audience in supernatural occurrences. Jonson ultimately succeeds in bringing about a realization that every knave is not to be credited with supernatural powers.

The ridicule and farce with which the fake possession is infested would certainly act as a corrective to any court and as an eye-opener to any lawyer like Eitherside in the play who is inclined to credit such far-fetched evidence. The play built on the vices of the citizens of London concludes conveying a moral lesson to all of them:

> It is not manly to take ioy, or pride
> In humane errours (wee doe all ill things,
> They doe 'hem worst that loue 'hem and dwell there,
> Till the plague comes) The few that haue the seeds
> Of goodnesse left, will sooner make their way
> To a true life, by shame, then punishment. (V, viii, 169-74)

Jonson makes use of the old devil-lore to achieve comic effects also.[42] The witches embodyng Jonson's allegory serve well to heighten the pictorial effect of the play. Besides, the comedy is full of humour. Particularly the character of Fitzdottrel, provokes laughter throughout. Though perfectly gulled he refuses to believe that he has been so. On the other hand he glories in his credulity:

> Let me alone, I would enjoy my selfe,
> And be the *Duke* o' *Drown'd-Land*, you ha' made me.
> (IV, vii, 82-83)

Furthermore, Meercraft, with his fantastic schemes for making twelve thousand pounds by a new method of dressing dogskins, twenty thousand by a new system of bottling ale, and an untold sum of money by making wine of raisins and another by serving the whole state with tooth-picks, rouses laughter profusely. Above all, Pug provides a lot of entertainment from his entrance to earth to his exit with his prayers and pleadings in his state of affliction:

> O, call me home againe, deare *Chiefe,* and put me
> To yoaking foxes, milking of Hee-goates,
> Pounding of water in a morter, lauing
> The sea dry with a nut-shell, gathering all
> The leaues are falne this *Autumne*, drawing farts
> Out of dead bodies, making ropes of sand,
> Catching the windes together in a net,
> Mustering of ants, and numbering atomes; all
> That hell, and you thought exquisite torments, rather

Then stay me here, a thought more: (v, ii, 1-10)

As Pug is thus imploring his master to relieve him from the agony of earth and take him back to "home againe" the audience laugh irresistibly.

The didactic purpose of *The Staple of News* is to present at once the use and abuse of money. It is not as though Jonson had a contempt for money. He had contempt only for its blind worshippers. As an intellectual he believed in the right use of money and he tries to teach this to an unheeding age – the

> . . . guilty race of men, that dare to stand
> No breath of truth: (V, vi, 3-4)

The main subject of the play is an allegory upon the use and abuse of wealth in which Pennyboys serve and worship Lady Pecunia Do-all, who is the personification of wealth as a motive force in human affairs. The names of the characters themselves indicate the didactic foundation of the play. If Pennyboy Senior is a thoroughgoing spendthrift, Pennyboy Canter is out and out covetous and usurious. Pennyboy Junior, who acts as Jonson's surrogate, is a moderator. He preaches moderation and sometimes even goes to the extent of advocating a Stoic way of life. Through him Jonson proclaims the intended moral of the piece:

> The vse of things is all, and not the *Store*;
> Surfet, and fulnesse, haue kill'd more then *famine*.
> The Sparrow, with his little plumage, flyes,
> While the proud Peacocke, ouer-charg'd with pennes,
> Is faine to sweepe the ground, with his growne traine,
> And load of feathers. (V, vi, 26-31)

Furthermore, at the close of the play Jonson teaches all

> The golden meane: the *Prodigall* how to liue,
> The *sordid*, and the *couetous*, how to dye:
> That with sound mind; this, safe frugality. (V, vi, 64-66)

Thus the play ends with a variation of the traditional 'Plaudite' of comedy. The audience is asked not only for applause but to partake the newly-formed and reformed society. Jonson's ideal society, for a moment, is realised. Having learned to shun the extremities of self-indulgence and abnegation, the characters give promise of rational, temperate lives and decorous behaviour.

While there is a good deal of 'profit' from all sides of the play, we are far from being deprived of 'delight.' Jonson's Horatian promise is never forgotten. The moral allegory of the play is harmoniously combined in "a festive comedy written to celebrate life in general and the pre-Lenten carnival season in particular."[43] *The Staple of News*, like *Twelfth Night* and the court masques, is a festive celebration.

Jonson sets the holiday-mood of the play from the outset. Mirth leads the Gossips on to the stage and announces her hope that the "Play will be a merry one!" (The Indvction, ll. 13-14) As the play proper starts, we find Pennyboy Junior in a holiday mood. Being his twenty-first birthday, it is a festive occasion. For a while he has a universal wish fulfilment. Then, we have a professional supporter of festivity in Lickfinger, the cook, whose vocation is to cater to the desires of festive celebrants. Because the season is carnival, there is much talk of good food—fish, poultry, custards, pies, relishes and sauces—in the play. The move to festivity reaches a climax when Pennyboy Senior declares a year and a day of Jubilee for Pecunia's ladies.

Besides, dealing with the ridiculous office of the staple, the secondary plot of the play offers excellent fun. It delightfully depicts the mob's madness for published pamphlets of news with "no syllable of truth in them." We naturally laugh at such silly longing for false news. Perhaps, never before has such an admirable fun been made of the 'humours' of a newspaper office.

The purpose of *The New Inn* has been thoroughly mistaken. The theme of the play is not a romantic rhapsody, as has been thought by some critics,[44] but an ironic illustration of the disparity between appearance and reality. The central episodes of the play are the discourses on love and valour that Lovell delivers to Lady Frampul in the presence of the entire company. These episodes are generally interpreted as serious romantic exposition of Platonic love and Aristotelian valour.[45] As Douglas Duncan has pointed out "though love and valour have been nominally romantic subjects, the treatment has been consistently either satiric or didactic."[46] One can perceive that there is something absurd in Lovell's situation. While so solemnly delivering a highly Platonic discourse on disinterested and perfect love (III, ii, 91-112) he himself is consumed with passion for Lady Frampul. In other words, he is unable to act in accordance with the theory of love he propounds. Again delivering on the one side a highly articulate discourse on valour (IV, iv, 37-101) he coolly takes to his bed on the otherside, in an agony of unrequited love. Also the reactions of Lady Frampul are "ludicrously hyperbolical." The scenes thus show the inconsistency between appearance and reality.

The same is true of the characters themselves. As has already been indicated, Lovell appears to be in complete command of his faculties, but in reality he is not. Pru becomes sovereign of the festivities in the inn but in reality she is Lady Frampul's maid. The Host appears to be a professional inn-keeper, but in reality he is not. The nurse appears to be an Irish beggar, but she is not. Frank appears to be a boy but in reality it is a girl. In this manner, nothing is what it appears to be.

However, having "meant to please" all Jonson has presented in this play

> things fit,
> In all the numbers, both of sense, and wit, ('Epilogue,' 5-6)

The jovial host who

> must ha' iouiall guests to driue my ploughs,
> And whistling boyes to bring my haruest home, (I, i, 22-23)

and whose philosophy of life is:

> Be iouiall first, and drinke, and dance, and drinke . . .
> *Be merry, and drinke Sherry;* (I, ii, 14-29)

is a source of great amusement to the audience throughout the play.

The comic purpose is further served by the low comedy supplied by Fly, Bat Burst, Sir Glorious Tipto and others. Particularly the vulgarities of Fly and Tipto who would

> rather choose to thirst: (for wine) and will thirst euer,
> Then leaue that creame of nations, vn-cry'd vp. (IV, 2, 25-26)

keep the audience continually amused. Added to this, the quite useless intermezzo of Stuff, the tailor, and Pinnacia, his "richly habited" wife would entertain the audience well. Jonson has, thus, succeeded

> To giue the *king*, and *Queene*, and Court delight:
> (Second 'Epilogue,' l. 4)

The Magnetic Lady is the continuation and the conclusion of the series of Jonson's comedies. With love-intrigue as the central motive the play yields enough of entertainment. Placentia, the marriageable young niece of the magnetic lady, constituting the 'centre attractive' of the play, draws to her a diversity of guests of different 'humours.' The plan is delightfully carried out to the amusement of the audience.

Although thorougly amusing, the play has its own didactic end. The purpose is to bring about the reconciliation of the individual humour to its original tenor as well as of the group to a reasonable and comfortable relationship. The avaricious characters—Sir Moth Interest, Mistress Polish, Mr. Bias, Mrs. Keepe, Mother Claire, Parson Palate, Doctor Rut, Tim Item, Silkworm, Practice—are attacked through their ridiculous follies—the fantastic tricks, the jealousies of rival suitors, the plots and the counterplots of domestic factions, the opinionatedness of guardians and the crafts of the nurses. At last, after "the amends," all are reconciled to truth and peace is drawn on

> This new discovery, which endeth all
> In reconcilement. (V, x, 133-34)

Thus the didactic purpose of the play is well served.

To sum up, with a growing sense of urgency to include in his comedy the philosophic material which should eternize it, Jonson switched over from the easy-moving, and light-hearted plays—*The Case is Altered* and *Every Man in His Humour*—to *Every Man Out of His Humour* and *Cynthia's Revels* for a better integration of character and action with the moral purpose, and succeeded only partially. But with *Poetaster,* to some degree, and with *Volpone*, *Epicoene*, *The Alchemist* and *Bartholomew Fair* consummately, he outgrew the heavy sententiousness of his "Comicall Satyres." Jonson's diminishing emphasis on punishment of folly is clearly discerned in his mature plays except, of course, in *Volpone*. For, as moral attitudes become more closely integrated with artistic forms in these plays, "punishment serves increasingly as emotional resolution rather than as the execution of strict justice."[47] This is the finally arrived method of Jonson, the serious moral realist and the comic artist.

Thus, Jonson succeeded well in his dogged determination to make comedy convey serious thought as well as serious laughter thereby achieving a harmonious fusion of "profit and delight." Comedy in his hands becomes a perfect communication between the author and the audience. Jonson, like Shaw later on, seeks to teach through pleasurable means right values of life. But, in doing so, he is not concerned with narrow morality or petty rules of conduct. It is not as though he was a doughty champion of didacticism. He is by no means a conventional moralist. The material of his plays is derived not from any abstract heights of theology but from the matter which interests him personally. Also, his treatment of good and evil and of social and economic problems in his plays is based not so much on the ethics of his own and preceding ages as on what he himself considers to be good and evil. Moreover, his failure, to mete out poetic justice to the miser in *The Case is Altered*, to censure the rogues in *Every Man in His Humour* and in *The Alchemist*, to give anything but sympathetic portrayals of low-life characters in *Bartholomew Fair*, and to preach sermons on drunkenness is enough to indicate that he is more interested in achieving dramatic effects than in punishing the evil. It is now clear that Jonson's is essentially a comic dramatist using the didactic theory for literary and dramatic purposes.

NOTES

1. David Klein, *Literary Criticism from the Elizabethan Dramatists*, p. 3.
2. Dodsley, *Select Collection of Old English Plays*, ed. W.C. Hazlitt, vol. III, p. 307.
3. *Ibid.*, vol. VII, p. 15.
4. *The Dramatic Writings of Richard Edwards, Thomas Norton, and Thomas Sackville*, ed. John S. Farmer, pp. 3-4.
5. *Elizabethan Critical Essays*, ed. Gregory Smith, vol. I, pp. 152-55, 158-64, 171, 190-93.
6. "Letter to Sir Walter Raleigh," Prefixed to *The Faerie Queene, Works*, ed. E.A. Greenlaw, C.G. Osgood, and F.M. Padelford, vol. I, pp. 167-70.
7. "The Anatomie of Absurditie," *Works*, ed. R.B. McKerrow, vol. I, p. 26.
8. *Complete Works*, ed. John Cunliffe, vol. I, p. 470.
9. *Elizabethan Critical Essays*, vol. I, pp. 250-51.
10. *Ibid.*, vol. II, p. 25.
11. See E.K. Chambers, *The Mediaeval Stage*, vol. I, pp. 8-12. and *The Elizabethan Stage*, vol. III, pp. 185-86; Gregory Smith, *Elizabethan Critical Essays*, Introduction, vol. I, pp. xxi-xxxi; Elbert N.S. Thompson, *The Controversy between the Puritans and the Stage* (Yale Studies in English, No. 20).
12. *Bussy D'Ambois*, 'Dedication,' ll. 18-20.
13. *An Apology for Actors*, Sig. F4r.
14. *Plays,* ed. William Gifford and Francis Cunningham, I, i, p. 194.
15. "An Aplogy for Poetry," *Elizabethan Critical Essays*, vol. I, pp. 199-201.
16. "Pierce Penilesse his Supplication to the Diuell," *Works*, ed. McKerrow, vol. I, pp. 213-14.

17. W. Moelwyn Merchant, "Marlowe the Orthodox," *Christopher Marlowe* (Mermaid Critical Commentaries), ed. Brian Morris, p. 192.
18. John Russell Brown, *Shakespeare and his Comedies*, p. 205.
19. Cyrus Hoy, ed., *The City Madam,* 'Introduction,' p. xiv.
20. *A Tale of a Tub,* originally written in 1596-97, was revised and licensed only on May 7, 1633. It is when Jonson finally revised the comedy that he inserted satiric material. This is made clear from the allusions in the play to Inigo Jones.
21. It is not for nothing that Jonson discarded *The Case is Altered* altogether later. The seeds of his discard undoubtedly lay in his lack of enthusiasm for romantic comedy as a medium for didactic material.
22. Lawrence L. Levin, "Clement Justice in *Every Man in His Humour,*" *SEL*, XII (Spring 1972), p. 307.
23. See Elisabeth Woodbridge's chart of the amount of space devoted to humorous characters in *Every Man in His Humour*, which gives an estimate of the satiric material. (*Studies in Jonson's Comedy,* pp. 51-53).
24. Herford and Simpson think that Jonson got the idea of mythical framework from Aristophanes's *The Birds* and *The Clouds* (vol. I, p. 399). But nothing prevents us from considering that Jonson got the idea as well from Lyly's *Endymion* which he was certainly acquainted with.
25. *Poetaster* is often dismissed merely as a document in the War of the Theatres. David Daiches, for instance, thinks that the play is "a vindication of Jonson's own positon against his enemies." (*A Critical History of English Literature*, p. 315) This is not quite true inasmuch as Jonson is really contrasting poetasters with poets. Once we ignore the stage quarrel we can appreciate the play as Jonson's attempt to combine philosophical material on good poets with satire on bad poets.
26. E.W. Talbert, "The Purpose and Technique of Jonson's *Poetaster,*" *SP*, XLII (1945), p. 226.
27. W. Speed Hill, "Biography, Autobiography, and *Volpone*," *SEL*, XII (Spring 1972), p. 328.
28. Herford and Simpson, vol. II, p. 55.
29. Gregory Smith, *Ben Jonson* (London: Macmillan, 1919), p. 110.
30. *Essays of John Dryden,* ed. W.P. Ker, vol. I, pp. 138-39.
31. Ralph Nash, "The Comic Intent of *Volpone*," *SP*, XLIV (Jan. 1947), p. 38.
32. Herry Levin, "Jonson's Metempsychosis," *PQ*, XXII (July 1943), p. 239.

33. Also, *Epicoene* resembles *Every Man in His Humour* in that Dauphine, Clerimont and True-Wit, though more polished and sophisticated, are gallants of the same type as Knowell and Wellbred; Daw and La-Foole are improved versions of Stephen and Matthew and Captain and Mrs. Otter play another variation on the theme of marital warfare which in different ways Kitely and Mrs. Kitely, and Cob and Mrs. Cob represented.
34. John Palmer, *Ben Jonson*, p. 176.
35. J.J. Enck, *Ben Jonson and the Comic Truth*, p. 149.
36. Elisabeth Woodbridge, *Studies in Jonson's Comedy*, p. 30.
37. A.C. Swinburne, *A Study of Ben Jonson*, p. 53.
38. J.B. Bamborough, *Ben Jonson*, p. 94.
39. William W.E. Slights, "*Epicoene* and the Prose Paradox," *PQ*, XLIX (April 1970), p. 187.
40. Anne Barton, p. 142.
41. Edward B. Partridge, p. 120.
42. Jonson made considerable use of devil-lore in his masques particularly in *The Masque of Queens*, drawn from the Classical and Mediaeval periods as well as from the supernatural occurrences of his own day.
43. D.R. Kifer, "*The Staple of News*: Jonson's Festive Comedy," *SEL*, XII (Spring 1972), p. 337. The play is closely tied to the season by a number of specific references to Shrovetide and Lent—Induction, ll. 11-12 and 62-65; Intermean, II, l. 63; III, ii, 83-84; V, v, 35.
44. See F.S. Boas, p. 127; G.B. Tennant, ed., *The New Inn* (Yale Studies in English), p. xxxi.
45. See Herford and Simpson, vol. II, pp. 196-97.
46. Douglas Duncan, "A Guide to *The New Inn*," *EC*, XX (July 1970), p. 32.
47. William W.E. Slights, p. 187.

Sport with Human Follies

If Jonsonian comedy is to be realistic, 'familiarly allied to the time,' and moral, provoking intelligent laughter, then it is almost inevitable that it should be satirical. Moreover, there was an established historical connection between satire and comedy. It was generally accepted in the Renaissance that comedy had its origins in the ancient Greek 'satyr plays'[1] in which the dramatists

> presented the lives of Satyers, so that they might wisely, under the abuse of that name, discover the follies of many theyr foolish fellow citesens.[2]

"This proto-comedy," as J.B. Bamborough points out, "was believed to have developed in time into the 'Old Comedy' of Aristophanes, which had a more direct moral intent and ridiculed named offenders against the canons of Society, and this in turn became the 'New Comedy' in which actual persons were no longer represented on the stage but general follies were attacked in their typical guises."[3]

Therefore, in keeping with his didactic attitude, Jonson was determined to 'sport with humane follies' in his characteristic comedy. Furthermore, he was assured by the Renaissance theories of 'Vetus Comoedia' that in doing so "he was returning lost social functions to the place of their origin, the stage, and revivifying moribund dramatic values."[4] On top of that, the age was ready for satire and Jonson "readily rolled forward gloriously on the crest of the wave."[5]

Satire, of course, was no new thing to the English drama nor to the popular stage of the time. From the beginning playwrights had been conscious of satire and it abounded in the Moralities and the Interludes. To cite but a few instances, Barclay in his Prologue to *The Ship of Fools* (1509) says:

> The present Booke have been nat inconvenyently the Satyr (that is to say) the representation of foulyshness.

In his Dedication of *The Steele Glas* (1576) George Gascoigne explains how

> From layes of Love to Satyres sadde and sage,
> Our poet turns, the travaile of his time.

Coming to Jonson's own times, Marston in *The Scourge of Villainy* says:

> From out the sadness of my discontent,
> Hating my wonted jocund merriment
> Only to give dull time a swifter wing
> Thus scoring scorn, of idiot fools I sing[6]

Thus the early writers as well as Jonson's own contemporaries repeatedly asserted that their purpose in writing plays was serious and their methods restrained.

All the same, none of these writers seems to have conceived satire as exclusively applicable to any one literary form as Jonson did. We may say that "no English dramatist had yet attempted comedy on the basis of so severe an interpretation of its scope as a picture of follies and foibles."[7] For, to Jonson the end and aim in comedy was ridicule of folly and every form of pretension, affectation, and the exhibition of the comic hideousness of lust, avarice and dishonesty.

But, at the same time, Jonson is not a formal satirist. He is essentially a comic artist. The English writers of formal satire – Lodge, Hall, Guilpin and Marston[8] – who expressed themselves with increasing fervour and boldness from 1593 to 1599 invariably assumed the role of reformer. They conceived their business to be not such the derision of folly as the exposure of vice. As Campbell points out these formal satirists "worked themselves up into a state of vociferous indignation; their voices became strident and their lash played upon the prisoners of evil with cruel abandon."[9] Hall strikes the note which all of those formal satirists repeat, when he pronounces:

> The 'satyre' should be like the porcupine,
> That shoots sharp quilles out in each angry line,
> And wounds the blushing cheeke, and fiery eye,
> Of him that heares and readeth guiltily.[10]

Guilpin exclaims the same when he says that the writers of satire

> are Antidotes to pestilentiall sinnes,

They heale with lashing, seare luxuriousnes,
They are philosophicke true Cantharides
To vanities dead flesh.[11]

Also, the formal satirists were essentially imitators of Latin literature. Although their corrective zeal was stimulated by the contemporary social and economic abuses, most of the objects against which they directed their satire were drawn from the pages of the Latin satirists—Horace, Lucilius, Juvenal, Persius and Lucullus. In the words of Alden, "without exception (save in the case of alchemy and one or two others) the vices and follies in these satires are those of classical satire."[12]

Even in presenting follies and abuses the formal satirists followed the classical models and methods. Accordingly they presented sin and folly as traits of clearly conceived individuals thereby creating only semi-dramatic figures. For instance, Marston, in *The Scourge of Villainy*, after exhibiting a pseudo gallant who is all face and clothes, summarily dismisses him:

Is this a man? Nay, an incarnate devil,
That struts in vice and glorieth in evil.[13]

Having cultivated themselves on these lines, the formal satirists, naturally enough, had no use for good-humoured laughter. Instead, they developed a feeling of discontent with the human situation and fostered that "Timon-like cynicism."

Jonson emerges as a different satirist altogether, though he too, to some extent, seems to have been influenced by the methods and models of the Latin satirists in his early stage, particularly in his 'Comical satires.' The things he satirizes are those follies that touch him individually. His task, therefore, is to shed comic laughter on follies he deems inimical not so much to the social structure of the actual world as to his own personal standards.

To Jonson's aim of satire, 'humour' affords an admirable weapon. Jonson sets his net wide enough to entrap all classes and types of men from the courtier to the water-carrier for the purposes of satirical ridicule. He minutely observes human follies and presents them with a vivid force which drives the ridicule home. He, however, bids us not so much to scorn and loathe the follies he sports with as to laugh at them.

In his earlier plays Jonson's satire is employed mainly against individual vices and affectations. In *Every Man in His Humour* he has conceived "a kind of domestic panorama showing typical practitioners of recognizable follies, presenting an engaging picture of the relatively harmless side of human folly and absurdity."[14] The play is a display of the relatively pleasant foibles which contribute to the comic way of the world.

Jonson holds up to ridicule the jealousy of Kitely, the choleric humour of the boastful swaggerer – Bobadill, the melancholic humour of the town gull – Matthew, and the affectations of the fashionable pastimes of hawking and hunting of Stephen, the country gull. But the final deflation and correction of the follies ridiculed are brought about in a manner quite different from that of the formal satirists. The agent of correction is Clement who "combines the roles of poet, priest, educator, and justice to arrive at judicious decisions."[15] Hence, no salutary rebuke is made, no words of withering scorn uttered. After getting Cob and Tib reconciled to each other, Clement gently proceeds to the rest:

> Come, I coniure the rest, to put off all discontent. You Mr. DOWNE-RIGHT, your anger; youmaster KNO'WELL, your cares; master KITELY and his wife, their iealousie. (V, v, 69-72)

Thus, an atmosphere of gaiety is established in which the 'humour' characters recognize their follies and give them up. No doubt, Brainworm has the true satirist's bent, but the Justice appropriately tempers satire with clemency especially when he finally concludes:

> 'Tis well, 'tis well; The night wee 'll dedicate to friendship, loue, and laughter. (V, v, 84-85)

But Jonson's satiric attitude is certainly accentuated in his next play *Every Man Out of His Humour.* Evidently there is a sudden and radical change[16] from the preceding easy-going domestic comedy of manners to the scathing satire of the present play. Asper, the author's spokesman, tells us that here we are to be confronted with follies that are devastating in their effect on the body politic and must therefore be extirpated. ('Grex,' ll. 3-26)

Asper, a harsh and pitiless judge of whatever is vicious or ridiculous, assumes the guise of Macilente and strikes at the follies and vices of the characters who have succeeded in gaining worldly goods and favours. Delirio, the idolising husband, Puntarvolo, the mad quixotic gentleman, Sordido, the miserly father and an assiduous peruser of almanacks who thinks of hanging himself in order to prove the prophets wrong – are all thoroughly ridiculed and finally jolted out of their humours.

Jonson's satirical lash is, however, centred upon false social standards typified in Fastidius Briske, Fungoso and Sogliardo. Fastidius always boasts of his friendships with lords and ladies. He assures Carlo Buffone that he is "haunted at the court" and at his "lodging, with your refin'd choise spirits." (II,i, 83-84) He vociferates that Signior Illustre, Count Frugale, and Signior Luculente vie with each other for his favour when he goes to the court. (II, iii, 181-86) He further boasts how he dallied with countess and how another lady sent her coach twice to his lodgings. Then he proudly displays his lady's 'garter,' in which he has hung his 'dagger.' (II, vi, 19-27) But all his vanities are pricked and exposed as Macilente, coming from the court, reports the true state of affairs:

> Alas, the poore *Phantasticke*! hee's scarce known
> To any lady there: and those that know him,
> Know him the simplest man of all they know. (II, iii, 189-91)

Fungoso, notorious for his "volley of othes," is a pathetic imitator and shadow of Fastidius Briske. His goal of life is to copy the clothes of Fastidius. He lies to his father to secure money and finally resorts to imploring the old man for clothes to set him up in fashion. (II, iii, 149-54) Finally he is rid of his folly when he is left in an inn to pay the bill with his empty pockets.

Sogliardo is enamoured of the name of a gentleman. To be considered a gentleman is the be-all and end-all to him. Hence, on the advice of Buffone, he attempts to turn four or five hundred acres of land into two or three trunks of apparel, (I, ii, 40-42) to run into debt, (I, ii, 110-14) to keep a large train of followers, (I, ii, 129-38) to affect an intimacy with the great, (I, ii, 71-78; III, iv, 104-7) to learn to take tobacco in the most artistic manner, (III, iii, 47-65) to study the fashion of quarrelling, (I, ii, 79-85) to purchase a coat of arms, (I, ii, 149-54) and to buy a handsome tomb to perpetuate his name. (II, i, 70-75) Thus Jonson ridicules the various fantastic ways one would adopt in order to be considered as a gentleman in society.

While continuing and expanding the techniques of *Every Man Out of His Humour,* Jonson introduces a new technique in *Cynthia's Revels* for his satirical purpose. He brings allegory and masque to the service of his comical satire thereby suggesting an idealised rather than violently satirical reformation of 'manners.' The idealistic point is brought out that vice is its own punishment:

> But there's not one of these, who are vnpain'd,
> Or by themselues vnpunished: for vice
> Is like a furie to the vicious minde,
> And turnes delight it selfe to punishment. (V, xi, 130-33)

Thus, in his second attempt to create effective dramatic satire, Jonson modifies his severity. He elevates harsh comical satire to a sort of court entertainment enriched with all the traditional peculiarities of the masque.

Cynthia's Revels attacks the vapidnes of court life. Jonson here ridicules the corrupt, shallow and silly values which the court and the higher ranks of society sometimes used for standards, through four vain courtiers and their stupid ladies. Amorphus, assured of his charm for the ladies, is affected in language and is always careful to emphasize his travels and his culture. (I, iv, II, iii; III, i, v) The shameless Anaides is made the butt of ridicule as proficient in all "the illeberall sciences, as cheating, drinking, swaggering, shoring and such like." (II, ii, 92-95) Hedon, the reveller, makes pretence to skill in the lighter arts of versifying and music and boasts of his powers on horseback and at tennis. (II, i, 48-69)

Coming to the ladies, Argurion, with her "most wandring and giddy disposition," runs "from gallant to gallant . . . most strangely, and seldome stayes with any" and she loves "a player well, and a *lawyer* infinitely; but your foole above all." (II, iii, 164-80) Moria, who thinks "her selfe wise against all the iudgements that come," is a "Lady made all of voice, and aire, talkes anything of anything." (II, iv, 13-15) Philautia who admires herself for all is "faire, and she knowes it . . . shee can dance, and she knowes that too: play at Shittle-cock, and that too: no quality shee has, but shee shall take a very particular knowledge of, and most lady-like commend it to you. . . . A most compleat lady in the opinion of some three, beside her-selfe." (II, iv, 37-47) Thus the satire falls upon the worthlessness of the courtiers and their ladies. However, the newly introduced mythology "serves to remove the satire from such direct and immediate application as to be disrespectful to the Queen, or even dangerous. At the same time it enables the poet to emphasize the chief fault of the courtiers, their self-love."[17]

Jonson makes his satire more dramatic and comic in *Poetaster* than in the two preceding plays though it is also termed a 'comicall satyre.' All the same, the significance of *Poetaster* as a work of art has been clouded, treated as it was, as a document in the 'War of the Theatres.'[18] It was regarded exclusively as a play devised to deride and humiliate Dekker and Marston in particular. Crispinus was immediately identified as Marston, Demetrius as Dekker and Horace as Jonson.[19]

But the business of the play, properly understood, is much more comprehensive than mere personal attack and passionate self-justification. For, Jonson had such a great respect for critical theory that he could not possibly distort the accetped forms of either satire or comedy in order to disgorge personal animosities or to produce an immediately effective stage play. So even the most fervid determination to lampoon his professional detractors could hardly have led him to ignore all the normal demands of an audience. Even if the play attacks Dekker and Marston, the attack is very far from being its main function, limited as it is to a handful of very amusing scenes.

Poetaster could be considered as fundamentally a social satire. As O.J. Campbell rightly observes "under cover of the historical fiction of Augustan Rome Jonson attacks the dissolute society of his own age."[20] He levels his satire against bad poets but through a symbolical picture of the relations between true poets and poetasters. Thus the mood of personal hostility is restrained and, what is more, generalized according to the accepted rules of civilized literary behaviour.

Consequent on this artistic restraint and generalized nature of the play, Crispinus and Demetrius become essentially types of intellectual incompetence and fraud, although they occasionally display the individual characteristics of Marston and Dekker. Jonson, in this manner, generalizes and objectifies his hostile attitude toward the world in which he lived and toward certain individuals with whom he was then quarrelling. *Poetaster* thus forms an ambitious attempt to produce an effective mixture of personal, ethical and social satire and to clarify the independence of the three modes of ridicule and correction. But Jonson succeeds only partially. He accomplishes no perfect fusion of the different elements. The requisite for such a fusion Jonson first shows in *Volpone.*

Broadened in scope and increased in intensity, Jonson's satire, in his middle and later plays, is employed chiefly against social vices. It is not that he neglected them altogether in his earlier plays. In those plays also he lashed out at the use of tobacco, the addiction to swearing, the belief in astrology and the fashionable pastimes like fencing, hawking and hunting. But the criticism of social vices has been indirect and quite incidental, the focus being on individual weaknesses and affectations. From *Volpone* onwards, however, Jonson directs his trenchant satire mostly toward the vices and evils that were eating into the vitals of the society of his day.

Avarice occurs with greater frequency than other vices, because, as it had been in Elizabethan England, it was the most virulent and protean of all social and moral vices so prevalent in the life which Jonson knew.[21] Besides, the mass of conventional material before Jonson was so great that he could not possibly ignore it.[22] He seems to have chosen avarice because it is highly flexible and theatrical. The usurer and miser serve as excellent comic butts. For, an avaricious man, whether he is a usurer or a miser, worships gold[23] and is a slave to money. (*A Trick to Catch the Old*

One, IV, v, 58-64) He is always afraid that some one will steal his money; so much so that he is troubled even in his sleep by dreams of loss of his wealth. (*The Merchant of Venice,* II, v, 18) The audience disliked both the usurer and miser and were delighted to have them gulled.[24] Moreover, satiric comedy such as Jonson's needs fools and Jonson seems to have been quite aware of the ease with which avarice makes fools of men.

Jonson, however, uses material connected with avarice strictly as a comic dramatist with a didactic purpose. He does not attempt any study of the highly complex economic problems caused by avarice. He is interested only in depicting the ugliness of avarice in many of its manifestations. The protean vice is clearly demonstrated in Jonson's varied presentations of avaricious characters. Avarice is also treated as a major theme in several of his comedies.

Jonson's treatment of avarice in his early plays like *The Case is Altered* and *Every Man Out of His Humour* is, however, conventional and he fails to show a very clear or vigorous picture of the ugly face of the vice. In these plays little more is done with the misers, Jaques de Prie and Sordido, than to make them play the role of comic butts. But this relatively poor presentation of avarice is only an evidence of the struggle Jonson had, to perfect his satiric techniques.

Jonson's satiric technique is mature by the time he comes to compose *Volpone*. Avarice appears here in all its ugliest forms. The legacy-hunters—Voltore, Corbaccio and Corvino—the birds of prey, are all motivated entirely by greed. Blinded by their inordinate greed they plot the most inhuman deeds in order to secure Volpone's property. Corvino condescends to prostitute his innocent wife to Volpone; Corbaccio disinherits his good son by declaring him to be a bastard and Voltore shamelessly perjures himself twice in the open court to win the favour of Volpone. The parasite, Mosca himself, is motivated primarily by avarice and the vice brings about his downfall.

In *The Alchemist* avarice is not only combined with other follies but is related to particular forms of chicanery prevalent in Jacobean London. The three rogues—Subtle, Face and Dol Common—are motivated largely by avarice and they organize the elaborate hoax of the alchemical laboratory in order to amass money. The dupes come to the shop to secure astrological and alchemical assistance because they are avaricious to the core. Dapper, the lawyer's clerk, arrives in search of a 'familiar,' a 'flye' which will enable him to win in his gambling. Drugger, the shopkeeper, as avid in his greed as Dapper, comes to the laboratory to find out how best he could lure the customers "by necromancie" to his shop. Sir Epicure Mammon comes for the philosopher's stone which will enable him to acquire wealth beyond the dreams of an emperor.

In *Bartholomew Fair* several of the visitors to the Fair, particularly Quarlous, are avaricious. Although Quarlous ridicules Winwife's idea of marrying the widow Purecraft, pointing out all the evils in marrying an old woman for her money, (I, iii, 57-103) he at last decides to marry the widow himself thinking aloud:

> Why should not I marry this sixe thousand pound, now I think on't? and a good trade too, that shee has beside, ha? . . . It is money that I want, why should I not marry the money, when 'tis offer'd mee? . . . I am resolu'd! I were truly mad, an' I would not! (V, ii, 75-86)

Avarice manifests itself in association with one of the economic evils of London in *The Devil is an Ass* as in *The Alchemist.* Meercraft, the avaricious projector, is a swindler who lures a series of greedy fools into his net through his promises of patents and monopolies. His greed is brought to the limelight when he fondly resolves to have money at any rate:

> I'll haue her! Raise wooll vpon egge-shells,
> Sir, and make grasse grow out o marro-bones,
> To make her come. (II i, 8-10)

Meercraft is ready to propose anything which will enable him to squeeze money from people. His projects are many. He has a scheme for "the recovery of drown'd land"—all the submerged land in England which would cost "eyghteen millions." He has other schemes like getting nine thousand pounds from the king's glover for tanned dogs' skins and "two and twenty thousand pounds" from a scheme to bottle ale and a great deal of gain from the production of raisin wine.

Avarice in *The Staple of News* too is linked with a swindling operation of Jonson's own day. The satire is levelled against the avarice and knavery of the swindlers who organise the news bureau as well as the avarice and the miserliness of the usurer, Uncle Peni-Boy.

The motivating force in *The Magnetic Lady,* Jonson's last comedy, is also avarice. Most of the characters—Sir Moth Interest, the usurer, Mistress Polish, Mr. Bias, Mrs. Keepe, the nurse, Mother Claire, the midwife Parson Palate, Doctor Rut, Tim Item, the apothecary, Sir Diaphanous Silkworm, the courtier, and Practise, the lawyer are avaricious. Their behaviour is chiefly regulated by this trait and they are satirised through the ridiculous follies attendant upon avarice.

Thus, Jonson makes the best dramatic use of avarice utilising it in almost every possible form. He uses avarice as substantial matter which can be cast into a wide variety of comic moulds. It is tightly interwoven with elements of plot and comedy.

Lechery is a vice sufficiently prevalent in any age to engage the attention of satirists or moralists. The Jacobean dramatists use lechery for characterisation as well as for motivation of plots. In the Jacobean satiric comedy lechery is chiefly associated with the gallants. Barnard and Bowdler in Heywood's *The Fair Maid of the Exchange* and Lipsalve and-Gudgeon in Middleton's *The Family of Love* are motivated by their lust. Calrindore, Perigot, and Novall in Massinger's *The Parliament of Love* regard adultery as a game. Matheo, the gallant in Dekker's *The Honest Whore* is lascivious to the core. Marston's satire in *The Fawne* is focused on the lascivious conduct of the courtiers–Sir Amoroso Debile-Dosso, Herod Frappatore, and Nimphadoro.

Jonson, in his satirical treatment of lechery, does not follow the usual pattern of the Latin and Jacobean comedy. He carefully restrains himself on the subject, because his attitude toward lechery is not puritanical.[25] Besides, Jonson is a comic dramatist and the comic conception of lust is usually amoral and concerned with manners rather than ethics. Naturally enough, Jonson's plays neither champion chastity nor countenance gross sensuality.

Jonson generally treats lust as a social folly. The light amorousness of Fallace and Fastidius Briske in *Every Man Out of His Humour* makes lust appear to be a probable folly rather than a despicable moral crime. Fallace's thoughts dwell amorously upon the frivolous gallant. She sighs:

> O, how happy is that lady aboue other ladies, that enioyes so absolute a gentleman to her seruant! A countesse giue him her hand to kisse? ah, foolish countesse! hee's a man worthy . . . to kisse the lips of an empresse. (II, vi, 117-21)

In the end, when her husband actually discovers her kissing Fastidius, she feels that she is only disgraced and Fastidius can only murmur of "the wrinkled fortunes of this poore spinster." (V, xi, 32)

Hedon, Amorphus and Asotus in *Cynthia's Revels* are interested in amorous dalliance rather than in visits to the brothel. They appear in scene after scene in which they are concerned with courtship. (I, iv, v; II, ii, iii; III, i, ii, v; IV, ii, iii, v; V, ii)

The lust of Chloe and captain Tucca in *Poetaster* is also presented as a light social folly. Throughout the play, the audience feels that Chloe's desire for a lover is no more violent than her desire for a coach. Tucca's broad ribaldry and his use of the language of the brothel are comically treated as conventional traits in the braggart soldier of Italian and

English comedy.[26]

The Ladies Collegiates in *Epicoene* are, no doubt, satirised as lecherous but their lechery is treated only as a part of the less serious vices of sham, gullibility and stupidity. (IV, iii; V, ii) Wittipol in *The Devil is an Ass* appears to be a lecherous gallant as he woos Mistress Fitzdottrel in several scenes (I, vi; II, vi) but in the denouement he relinquishes his desire for the lady and assures her that he "can love goodnes . . . more/Then . . . *Beauty.*" (IV, vi, 37-38)

However, in two of his plays—*Volpone* and *The Alchemist*—Jonson treats lust not as a social folly but as a breach of the moral code. Volpone's lechery appears with terrifying concentration in his sudden passion for Celia, the virtuous wife of Corvino. No sooner does Mosca describe Celia to Volpone than the magnifico regrets why he "had not known this before" and longs to see her "though but at windore." (I, v, 107-27) When Corvino, tricked by Mosca's scheme, brings Celia to Volpone's chamber even before the appointed time, Mosca says in an aside:

> did ere man haste so, for his hornes?
> A courtier would not ply it so, for a place. (III, vii, 4-5)

When Celia is left alone in the inner room with Volpone, he is moved into voluptuous raptures and sings:

> Come, my CELIA, let vs proue,
> While we can, the sports of loue; . . .
> Sunnes, that set, may rise againe:
> But if, once, we lose this light,
> 'Tis with vs perpetuall night. (III, vii, 165-73)

After tempting Celia in vain with his treasures, Volpone paints before her eyes the splendour of the passion he has to offer. He says that her

> bathes shall be the iuyce of iuly-flowers,
> Spirit of roses, and of violets,
> The milke of vnicornes, and panthers breath
> Gather'd in bagges, and mixt with *certan* wines. (III, vii, 213-16)

In *The Alchemist*, unlike *Volpone*, lust is treated in a markedly light manner. We find lust in its ordinary, animal manifestations in Dol Common, Face and Subtle. The three schemers in the alchemist's shop regard their illicit sexual relations as the natural order of things. (I, i, 176-79)

The two rogues regard Dol's prostitution as an asset. Having lured Surly, disguised as a Spanish nobleman, to the house Face gleefully tells Subtle that a "noble Count" is coming

> to make his battry
> Vpon our DOL, our Castle, our *cinque*-Port,
> Our *Douer* pire, our what thou wilt. (III, iii, 10-19)

Furthermore, both the rogues, Subtle and Face, want to possess the "soft and buxome widdow," Dame Pliant, who "melts like a Myrobalame!" (IV, ii, 42) They agree to draw lots to decide as to who shall marry her. "You'll ha' the first kisse," says Face, in annoyance, "'cause I am not readie." "Yes," agrees Subtle smugly, "and perhaps hit you through both the 'nostrils." (IV, ii, 40-41) Finally. Face agrees to take the whore off Subtle's hands "with all her faults." (IV, iii, 90)

The common lechery of Dol, Face and Subtle is contrasted with lust overblown and rotten in Sir Epicure Mammon. From the time he appears on the stage, Sir Epicure displays an absurdly libidinous disposition. The moment he comes to know that the philosopher's stone is almost completed he plans to buy first and foremost sexual gratification. He longs

> To haue a list of wiues, and concubines,
> Equall with SOLOMON; who had the *stone*
> Alike, with me: and I will make me, a back
> With the *elixir*, that shall be as tough
> As HERCVLES, to encounter fiftie a night....
> I will haue all my beds, blowne vp; not stuft:
> Downe is too hard. And then, mine oual roome,
> Fill'd with such pictures, as TIBERIVS tooke
> From ELEPHANTIS: and dull ARETINE
> But coldly imitated. Then, my glasses,
> Cut in more subtill angles, to disperse,
> And multiply the figures, as I walke
> Naked betweene my *succubae*. (II, ii, 35-48)

The lechery of Sir Epicure is thus reduced to an absurdity. The emotion which it rouses is merely contemptuous amusement.

Thus, Jonson's portrayals of lust show us a wide variety of the weakening, the degrading, and the ugly aspects of the vice. He treats lust essentially as a comic dramatist without an exaggerated sense of the moral values involved in the action.

Jonson chose drunkenness for his satirical treatment not merely because it was a vice prevalent in the Jacobean London[27] but because the drunkard on the stage is basically comic, acting as he does automatically.[28] Besides, the drunken man is grotesque in his deviation from the normal thereby becoming "immortal in the realm of laughter."[29]

In the satirical treatment of drunkenness, the Jacobean dramatists are rather sententious. Chapman, Marston, Dekker, Heywood, Middleton and Massinger include in their comedies moral speeches on the evils of drink. In Chapman's *May-Day* Lodovico discovering Aurelio in a drunken state says:

> What a loathsome creature man is, being drunk! Is it not pity to see a man of good hope . . . quite drowned, in a quart part.
>
> (I, i, 197-203)

There is quite an ironic speech on drunkenness in Marston's *The Fawne*:

> Drunkenness brings all out, for it brings all the drink out of the point, all the wit out of the pate, and all the money out of the purse.
>
> (V, i, 176-80)

Middleton in his *A Trick to Catch the Old One* rebukes the drunkard, Dampit:

> here, he lies, like a noisome dunghill, full of the poison of his drunken blasphemies. (IV, v, 52-53)

But Jonson's attitude toward drinking is different.[30] Unlike many other Jacobean dramatists, Jonson is unusually tolerant in his portrayals of the drunkard in his comedies. He makes no obvious attempts to turn drinking scenes into sermons. The portrayal of Buffone's drinking bout with himself in *Every Man Out of His Humour* (V, iv, 44-90) offers a good example. As he drinks toasts to himself with the affected declarations and gestures, the satire falls upon affectation and grossness rather than upon drink. Even when Jonson designates drunkenness as a vice in a character, as in the case of Anaides in *Cynthia's Revels,* (II, ii, 92) he does little more than ridicule it with other vices in a delineation of a gallant. Juniper's drunkenness in *The Case is Altered* is employed mainly for its low-comedy effect.

Thus Jonson preaches no sermons such as are delivered by Chapman and Marston. He includes no moral asides in the drinking scenes scattered through his plays. His use of drunkenness, then, appears to correspond with his personal attitude. We may say that to Jonson drunkenness is a vice only insofar as it makes a man a fool, and as it is an index of wastefulness and affectation.

Jonson's satire is directed against other contemporary vices like fraudulent demoniac possession and faked necromancy[31] connected with witchcraft. The devil, of course, was outmoded on the stage, but he was comic and familiar, and therefore was a good subject for laughter.

In Fitzdottrel's first soliloquy in *The Devil is an Ass* (I, ii, 1-53) Jonson satirises the work of actual conjurers in and around London with whom he was absolutely out of patience. He exposes the process of false demoniac possession through Meercraft's description of the simplicity of the game to Fitzdottrel. Meercraft urges how

> It is the easiest thing . . . to be done.
> As plaine, as fizzling: roule but wi' your eyes,
> And foame at th' mouth. A little castle-soape
> Will do't, to rub your lips: and then a nutshell,
> With toe, and touch-wood in it to spit fire. (V, iii, 1-5)

We have in *Volpone* and *The Devil is an Ass* two most positive exposures of the tricks and habits of false demoniac possession. On the instigation of Volpone, Voltore, the lawyer, pretending to be possessed with the devil, falls on the floor in the court. Volpone highlights the scene with his convincing remarks:

> See, see, see, see!
> He vomits crooked pinnes! his eyes are set,
> Like a dead hares, hung in a poulters shop!
> His mouth's running away! doe you see, signior?
> Now, 'tis in his belly . . .
> 'T will out, 'twill out; stand cleere. See, where it flies!
> In shape of a blew toad, with a battes wings! (V, xii, 24-28, 30-31)

In *The Devil is an Ass* Jonson exposes the ease with which court and public alike could be deceived by false demoniac possession. Fitzdottrel with the intention of escaping "the imputation of being cuckold" (V, v, 38-53) is tricked by Meercraft, the projector, into false demoniac possession. Fitzdottrel, with a false belly, a soap in the mouth to foam and sentences of Spanish and Greek on tongue, demonstrates the gamut of possible tricks of demoniac possession before the lawyer, Sir Poule Eitherside, who comes to the conclusion that the exhibitions are 'palpable.' But overcome by the sudden revelation that Pug, whom he has been entertaining as his servant is in reality one of the imps of Satan,

Fitzdottrel discloses the devices he has been using to impose upon the credulous spectators and the law:

> Sir, I am not bewitch'd, nor have a *Diuell*: . . .
>   I will tell truth,
> And shame the Fiend. See, here, Sir, are my bellowes,
> And my false belly, and my *Mouse*, and all
> That should ha' come forth! (V, viii, 138-45)

Thus, Jonson uses devil-lore to strengthen his satire on the viciousness of London life and to help him achieve comic and theatrical effects, as he does in his masques, particularly in *The Masque of Queens.*

Jonson lashes out at one of the persistent social pests of the age—Puritanism.[32] He thought the Puritans a menace to church and state. Besides, to him as to any other dramatist of the time, the Puritans personified the attack on the theatre. Hence, his tone is slightly acid whenever he mentions the Puritans. Nonetheless, Jonson's treatment of the Puritans is broadly comic and satiric rather than doctrinaire. His satire on the Puritans represents his fully developed satiric technique.

The Jacobean dramatists generally associated with the Puritan vices like avarice (*Sir Giles Goosecap*, II, i, 262-65), gluttony (*The Malcontent*, V, iii, 145), lust (*The Family of Love*, I, iii, 161-70), and drunkenness (*A Chaste Maid in Cheapside*, III, ii, 88-89, 161-68), and their baseness was always covered with hypocritical piety. But Jonson focuses his satire on their hypocrisy, the most comic of all. With his mature satiric technique Jonson uses hypocrisy to develop his characters and his plots and builds satire and comedy from it. It is to make them more disgusting that he uses the sub-vices of avarice and gluttony. And he ingeniously forces artistic elements like parody, repetition, contrast and incongruity to serve the purpose of satire and laughter.

We cannot possibly agree with W. David Kay that "no play of Jonson before *The Alchemist* contains satire on Puritans."[33] In *Volpone* Jonson ridicules the Puritans as notorious for gluttony, priggishness and prudery. While discussing Pythagoras' doctrine of the transformation of souls, Androgyno relates to Nano that the soul when it left the mule went

> Into a very strange beast, by some writers cal'd an asse;
> By others, a precise, pure, illuminate brother,
> Of those deuoure flesh, and sometimes one another:
> And will drop you forth a libell, or a sanctified lie,
> Betwixt euery spoonefull of a natiuitie-pie. (I, ii, 42-46)

Here Jonson satirises the Puritans as great eaters of meat as well as eaters of one another in the metaphorical sense of being fanatical. Their claim to inner illumination is also mocked at.

In *Epicoene*, again quite incidentally, Jonson shows how the Puritan sect was a social pest. Truewit, in his attempt to dissuade Morose from marrying, paints before him the dangers of matrimony with a Puritan wife, warning how Morose will be obliged to

> feast all the silenc'd brethren, once in three daies; salute the sisters; entertaine the whole family, or wood of 'hem; and heare long-winded exercises, singings and catechisings, which you are not giuen to, and yet must giue for: to please the zealous matron your wife, who, for the holy cause, will cosen you ouer and aboue.
>
> (II, ii, 80-85)

It is in *The Alchemist* that Jonson finds the best opportunity to satirize the Puritans. Here he ridicules them as moral humbugs and hypocrites preaching what they themselves do not practise. The two Puritan brethren of Amsterdam, Tribulation Wholesome and Ananias come under heavy fire. Tribulation wants to establish the Puritan morality by means of immorality, bribing the civil magistrate with "aurum potabile." Ananias, who denounces Subtle as a heathen and his stone as a work of darkness, is overjoyed at the prospect of having gold.

Jonson seems to cover the multitude of vices which he wanted to attribute to the Puritans when he makes Subtle say that the Puritans, after receiving the philosopher's stone, will not need

> to winne widdowes
> To giue you legacies; or make zealous wiues
> To rob their husbands, for the *common cause:*
> Nor take the start of bonds, broke but one day,
> And say, *they were forfeited,* by *Prouidence.*
> Nor shall you need ore night to eate huge meales,
> To celebrate your next daies fast the better. . . .
> Nor cast
> Before your hungrie hearers, scrupulous bones,
> As whether a *Christian* may *hawke*, or hunt;
> Or whether, *Matrons*, *of the holy assembly*,
> May lay their haire out, or weare doublets:
> Or haue that idoll *Starch*, about their linnen. (III, ii, 69-82)

In this ironic catalogue of Puritan vices and offences Jonson's satiric lash is visible.

A close examination of the satiric material in Jonson's comedy would reveal that Jonson has attacked more social evils than any other single Jacobean dramatist. We may say that there is hardly a folly, an affectation, or a fraud of his day which he does not satirize in his plays. Avarice, lechery, quackery connected with alchemy and astrology, fake demoniac possession, the danger of the projects of monopoly, hypocritical puritanism—all these are found more vigorously and thoroughly satirized in Jonson's plays than in those of any other major Jacobean dramatist.

It should, nevertheless, be borne in mind that Jonson is essentially a comic artist, not simply a satirist or a reformer. He is not a satirist in the sense Swift or Pope is. Nor his satire on social and economic problems is the conventional matter of Jacobean dramatic plots. It is evident from the study of the didactic and satiric content of his comedies that he endeavours to build his plots and characters out of the very material which he wants to attack. Thus he ingeniously works satire into the dialogue and the dialogue into the movement of the plot so much so that to remove the satire is to remove plot and character.

Jonson's unerring relentlessness, therefore, is born as much of his artistic integrity as of his intellectual uprightness. His censorship is certainly more judicious than strictly moral. He is mainly concerned with follies and vices that are intellectually unacceptable rather than morally deplorable. Jonson seems to be one with Bernard Shaw when the latter, in his defence of *Mrs. Warren's Profession*, says: "I have spared no pains to make known that my plays are built to induce, not voluptuous reverie but intellectual interest, not romantic rhapsody but human concern."[34]

Also, Jonson's treatment of human follies and vices is theatrical rather than sociological. As a dramatic artist he seems to be more interested in the dramatic use and comic effect to which a vice or folly can be put than in the mere correction of evil. Hence he is essentially a comic dramatist who bends his energies even to the creation of satire. As T.S. Eliot reiterates, "satire like Jonson's is great in the end not by hitting off its object, but by creating it."[35] This point calls attention to the uniqueness of Jonson's comic world, by virtue of which he transcends the limits of space and time, and has that element of 'permanent modernity.' So it is not as though "in selecting 'humours' as his prime target he was condemning himself inevitably to a degree of ephemeral triviality."[36] The kind of individual and social behaviour Jonson satirized is still the product of genuine and recurrent aspects of human nature.

NOTES

1. See Ejner J. Jensen, "The Wit of Renaissance Satire," *PQ*, 51 (April 1972), pp. 394-409.
2. Thomas Lodge, "Defence of Poetrie," *Elizabethan Critical Essays*, ed. Gregory Smith, vol. I, p. 80.
3. J.B. Bamborough, *Ben Jonson*, pp. 26-27.
4. O.J. Campbell, *Comicall Satyre and Shakespeare's "Troilus and Cressida,"* p. 54.
5. Allardyce Nicoll, *World Drama*, p. 288.
6. *The Works of John Marston*, ed. A.H. Bullen, vol. III, p. 367.
7. *Ben Jonson*, ed. Brinsley Nicholson and C.H. Herford (Mermaid Series), 'Introduction,' p. xviii.
8. See Francis Meres, "Palladis Tamia," *Elizabethan Critical Essays,* ed. Gregory Smith, vol. II, p. 320.
9. O.J. Campbell, p. 35.
10. Joseph Hall, "Virgidemiarum, Sixe Bookes," *The Three Last Bookes of Byting Satyres*, Lib. 5, Satire 3, Sig. F3v.
11. Edward Guilpin, "Skialetheia or, A Shadow of Truth," *Certain Epigrams and Satyres*, Sig. C.V.
12. R.M. Alden, *The Rise of Formal Satire,* p. 123.
13. *The Works of John Marston*, vol. III, p. 345.
14. C.G. Thayer, *Ben Jonson: Studies in the Plays*, p. 28.
15. L.L. Levin, "Clement Justice in *Every Man in His Humour,*" *SEL*, XII (Spring 1972), p. 306.

    Clement may be taken as a prototype for central figures in the next three plays. For the purpose of the anatomizing of vice Clement is replaced by the multiple perspective of Asper-Macilente and Cordatus in *Every Man Out of His Humour*, Crites in *Cynthia's Revels,* and by Horace in *Poetaster* who are related to Clement in their interest in poetry, proper education and the correction of various social abuses.
16. This radical change in Jonson's satiric attitude is connected by critics like O.J. Campbell (pp. 54-134) with the restraining order launched by the Archbishop of Canterbury and the Bishop of London on June 1, 1599 against satirists. ("A Transcript of the Registers of the Company of Stationers of London," ed. Edward Arber [1876], vol. III, p. 316) Other critics have assumed that Jonson was motivated by a personal resentment at not being sufficiently appreciated as a playwright. But a much simpler and more

reasonable answer could be that Jonson, perhaps, wanted to explore in this play the possibility of applying to stage some of the techniques of pure satire. Jonson seems to adopt the methods of satiric verse to drama. The relative plotlessness of *Every Man Out of His Humour* offers a good proof to the point.

17. Allan H. Gilbert, "The Function of the Masques in *Cynthia's Revels*," *PQ*, XXII (1943), p. 230.
18. See R.A. Small, *The Stage-Quarrel*, pp. 25-58; See also A. Davenport, "The Quarrel of the Satirists," *MLR*, XXXVII (1942), pp. 123-30.
19. See J.H. Penniman, *The War of the Theatres*, p. 76.
20. O.J. Campbell, p. 131.
21. The various problems of avarice involved in Tudor England such as the exorbitant rate of interest and the chicanery practised by money lenders are explained in R.H. Tawney's Introduction to Thomas Wilson's *Discourses Upon Usury*. Also, see C.T. Wright, "The Usurer's Sin in Elizabethan Literature," *SP*, XXXV (1938), pp. 178-94.
22. See C.T. Wright, pp. 176-97. The list of books denouncing usury are published in *NQ*, 5th Ser. X (1978), pp. 281, 341, 422; XI (1879), pp. 63, 163, 262, 361 and 466.
23. For example, Spenser's description of Avarice:

    For of his wicked pelfe his God he made,
    And vnto hell him selfe for money sold;
    Accursed vsurie was all his trade . . .
    (*The Faerie Queene*, Bk. I, Canto IV, ll. 27-29)

24. See Arthur Bivens Stonex, "The Usurer in Elizabethan Drama," *PMLA*, XXXI (1916), pp. 190-210.
25. This is suggested to us by such details as Jonson's stories related to Drummond about his mistresses. See *Conversations*, ll. 287-94, 476-82.
26. See Daniel C. Boughner, "The Braggart in Italian Renaissance Comedy," *PMLA*, LVIII (9143), pp. 42-83.
27. In 1606 parliament passed "An Acte for represeinge the odious and loathsome synne of drunkenes." According to the law, the habit had "of late growen into common use within this Realme." (*Statues of the Realm*, 4 James I (1606-1607), C. 5, p. 1142)
28. Bergson points out that automatism is the basic source of laughter. (*Laughter: An Essay on the Meaning of the Comic*, pp. 146-47)
29. J.Y.T. Greig, *The Psychology of Laughter and Comedy*, pp. 112-15.
30. That Jonson was too convivial himself to deal in a militant or

moralistic way with drunkenness is clear from our knowledge of *Conversations.* (ll. 295-302) Moreover when Jonson was reconciled with the Church of England, to indicate his robust faith he "drank out all the full cup of wyn." (*Conversations*, ll. 314-16)

31. Despite the work of King James in detecting fraudulent practices in persons pretending to be possessed with the devil, impostures of various types of demoniac possession continued. (See G.L. Kittredge, *Witchcraft in Old and New England*, pp. 279, 316, 318-28).

    Greene's 'conny-catching' pamphlets, vividly portraying the London underworld rogueries, abound in practices of false demoniac possession. Then, we have Edgar in disguise in *King Lear* and Autolycus in *The Winter's Tale* who remind us of such practices.

32. Puritanism was an element in English social and religious life which was growing stronger during the reign of James. (See William Haller, *The Rise of Puritanism* (1570-1643); M.M. Knappen, *Tudor Puritanism: A Chapter in the History of Idealism.*
33. W. David Kay, "The Shaping of Ben Jonson's Career: A Re-examination of Facts and Problems," *MP*, 67 (Feb. 1970), p. 228.
34. *The Collected Works of Bernard Shaw*, ed. Ayot St. Lawrence, vol. VII, pp. 165-66.
35. T.S. Eliot, *Elizabethan Dramatists*, p. 80.
36. J.B. Bamborough, *Ben Jonson*, pp. 104-5.

Persons such as Comedy Would Choose

As Jonson based his theory of comedy on the precept and example of the comic writers of antiquity as interpreted by Renaissance critics, he was naturally influenced by them both in his conception and delineation of character. The doctrine of 'decorum,' preached by his favourite authors – Horace and Quintillian – and popularised by Sidney, coloured his conception and delineation of character. Decorum laid it down that characters in a drama should always act and speak 'in character.' In other words, the characters should behave as one would expect persons in their time of life and social position to behave. As Whetstone puts it:

> to worke a Commedie kindly (that is, according to its nature or 'kind'), grave old men should instruct, yonge men should show the imperfections of youth, Strumpets should be lascivious, Boyes unhappy, and Clownes should speake disorderlye.[1]

Besides, there was a further limitation summed up in a tag from Horace

> Seruetur ad imum, qualis ab incepto processerit, et sibi constet,

which Cordatus quotes in *Every Man Out of His Humour*. (V, v, 57-58) The Horatian tag in effect meant that "a dramatist had to establish his characters on or before their first entrance and then to see that they never subsequently did or said anything that contradicted their original presentation."[2] The concept of 'decorum,' thus, left no room for untypical behaviour, inconsistency in action, mixture of motive, or development of character. The characters, then, are to be fixed and unalterable ones.

It is not as though characters of this sort were thrust upon Jonson for his having committed himself to the 'Comedy of Humours.' He was ready to accept this limitation though not always bound by it. For, he himself "in make of mind, was, up to a certain point, naturally disposed to this typical and normal handling of character."[3] It is the playwright's instinct in him strengthened by reasoning and reflection that drove him towards this neat and tightly contained way of looking at and presenting character.

The 'humour' motive, however, helped Jonson in more than one way. First of all, it released him from the traditional categories of comic types, besides throwing the comedy of mere intrigue into the background once for all. Then, providing a bridge, as it were, between classical theory and modern life, the 'humour' motive "helped to render it possible for the master of satiric comedy, the doughty champion of classicism, and the most powerful of Elizabethan realists, to be united in the same man."[4]

All the same, too much stress should not be laid, as has sometimes been done, on the importance of 'humours' in Jonson's comedy. If he had, by any chance, limited himself to characters who were 'humours' in the strict and proper sense of the term, he would thus have had a very restricted cast indeed. Comparatively few of his characters will yield to 'humour' analysis, and his range is obviously much wider. The source of the comic which Jonson tapped in his comedies seems to be related, if not absolutely, to Meredith's explanation of the comic. According to Meredith, whenever men

> Wax out of proportion, overblown, affected, pretentious, bombastical, hypocritical, pedantic, fantastically delicate; whenever they are . . . self-deceived or hoodwinked, given to run riot in idolatries, drifting into vanities, congregating in absurdities, planning shortsightedly, plotting dementedly; whenever they are at variance with their professions, and violate the unwritten but perceptible laws binding them in consideration one to another; whenever they offend sound reason, fair justice; are false in humility or minded with conceit, individually, or in bulk,[5]

they are fit subjects for the satiro-comic spirit. These are also, in reality, the 'persons, such as (Jonson's) *Comoedie* would chuse' to portray.

Jonson starts with characters set, formed and fully defined at the very outset. His characters are, no doubt, taken from life, but once they enter his comedy they must necessarily leave behind them all their human inconsistencies and run to form. For, they are now in the hands of a master logician who would present them as 'studies in special types of behaviour.' Jonson catches them at a moment when they are most expressive for his purposes and invests them with all the details of dress, speech and action. "He seeks his effects by working from the outside, by picking out the contours of character in the changing limelight of circumstance."[6] And with his strict grasp of common circumstance and the immense resources of his thought and language, he is able to flash ray of light on each facet of the chosen character.

Before we proceed further, it is essential to remember that Jonson's method of characterisation is restricted and conditioned by certain factors. It is, of course, true that characterisation in Jonson is restricted less by the story than in the other Elizabethan dramatists. But, at the same time, it is conditioned more than that of others by Jonson's adherence to classical models and rules. Particularly his observance of the Unities has an important bearing on his characterisation. As the action of a comedy of his does not generally take more than twenty-four hours for its completion, Jonson is not in a position to represent many facets of a character's personality. So, his characters do not have the time to develop and grow and change.

However, it may be argued that Shakespeare in *The Tempest* and Dryden in *All for Love* show us several well-developed aspects of their characters, even while they closely observe the three Unities. But it may be pointed out that Shakespeare and Dryden did not aim at the kind of satire and realism favoured by Jonson. Besides, they revealed the past of their characters by means of reminiscences which would be quite out of place in the type of comedy attempted by Jonson.

Again, we should not lose sight of the fact that Jonson's acceptance of 'humours' as the basis of character-creation carries with it several obvious limitations. Its simple clear-cut theory of character naturally forbids any of that 'life-like complexity' which marks Shakespeare's full-blooded and dynamic characters. As the character is absolutely explained by his humour which is made known at his first appearance and, more often than not, by his name, it obviates all needs for a fine psychology. This phenomenon reacts in a serious way by preventing any self-development in the characters.

Also, the presentation of certain select 'humours' throughout a play invariably involves two risks in respect of characterisation—standardisation and exaggeration. It makes the characters become too rigid and uniform in habit, puppet-like after the fashion of the personages in the old Morality and thus dramatically unreal. It also involves the playwright in exaggeration if he would strive to escape from it. Furthermore, Jonson's insistence on the 'humours' is at cross purposes with his realistic intention. A 'humour' character is liable to be a caricature presented, not as a fully realized human being, but only as a fop, a jealous husband and an anxious father. As Anne Barton rightly points out, "especially after Shakespeare's way of handling character became established as an ideal, the supposed tyranny of 'humours' has served to blind readers to the subtlety and humanity of mature Jonsonian characterization."[7]

A clear and sympathetic understanding of these restrictions, limitations and risks and such other difficulties on the part of Jonson in his creation and portrayal of character is absolutely necessary for a correct and full appreciation of Jonson's art of comic characterisation. We must not, at any rate, belittle his brilliant achievement in characterisation. We must necessarily bear in mind that Jonson's alleged shortcomings in respect of characterisation are due to the restrictions imposed by his theory of comedy and his conception of the functions of a comic poet. Once we sympathetically take into consideration these restrictions and limitations by which Jonson was deliberately bound, his achievement in characterization would appear remarkable. Within his self-imposed limits, Jonson is able to hold the attention of the audience not only because his characters have sufficient vitality but also because they fulfil his aim of realism and moral elevation.

Yet, critics failing to understand Jonson's self-imposed system, have been constantly finding fault with him condemning his art of comic invention for many things he cannot help himself. The grounds of this criticism, however, lay undoubtedly in the unphilosophical habit of comparing Jonson's characters with the entirely different type of creations of Shakespeare or Beaumont and Fletcher.

It has often been felt that Jonson's characters are only English copies of Plautian or Terentian types, or that his gulls and misers, braggarts and rascally servants are a blind imitation of Latin comic characters. This is not true. Because, even if Jonson relies on the Renaissance 'decorum' for his conception of character "the genius of Jonson has intensified and individualised the portrayal of character beyond the limits of mere Horatian and Renaissance decorum."[8] There is a thorough-going transfusion of the comic spirit into the moulds of another race and time. And from their immediate contact with contemporary reality they derive gusto and exuberance. Jonson's men and women are essentially English men and women. For instance, Bobadill is not a mere soldier braggart of Plautine tradition. He stands out distinctly from the traditional types. With his up-to-date oaths, his skill in the tobacco art and in the latest duelling strokes and his haunting of the disreputable purlieus of London or the middle aisle of St. Pauls, he vividly expresses the Elizabethan species of the class.

Jonson's characters are often dismissed as mere personified abstractions. Coleridge affirms that they are "in the strictest sense of the term, abstractions."[9] But, to label Jonson's personages as mere personifications of a vice or a folly is to shut one's eyes to the nicety with which they are distinguished from other characters to which they bear a superficial likeness. What makes his characters appealing to us is his superb art of happily marking the different shades of the same colour thereby distinguishing the covetous from the covetous and the voluptuous from the voluptuous. Although "there is no room in his plays for sentiment, idyllic romance, or atmosphere, his types are far from being cut from one pattern."[10] Jonson quite ingeniously differentiates those of his figures which resemble each other most closely in type.

Just because Jonson, quite unlike other dramatists, makes matters easy to his hearers and readers alike, by way of clearly defining and minutely describing the characters he seeks to present, it is erroneous to think or say that he has done to more than define and describe. The living realism of his humour should not be ignored. What we, in this respect, should necessarily remember is that it is in the interests of dramatic clarity that Jonson seeks a simplification of the complexities of human nature and 'a common denominator for the diversity of mankind.' The dramatis personae is not an analysis and schematisation of human nature, but a rationalisation and simplification of human nature for the sake of his dramatic art.

Even if it comes to that, Jonson can be defended fully on the ground that modern psychology has shown us that ruling passions do exist and individuals in their grip do not change without a complete overhauling of their personalities.[11] Such neurotics are living parodies of average human emotions. Jonson seems to have foreshadowed, although he did not know the names for them, the maniac personalities, anal-erotics and types of conversion hysteria.

It is also complained that while Jonson is presenting striking types he fails to exhibit, in the action of his plays themselves, "the process of coming into being, the growth of character."[12] The charge seems inadmissible in that it cannot justly be levelled against a dramatist like Jonson who has committed himself to the classical unities which could hardly allow any kind of development. How can any character possibly grow and develop within eight or nine hours which his plays normally take for their action?

However, within the limits of the action Jonson appears to account for his characters admirably exhibiting them in operation. He enables us to notice the external features of any character as well as to understand the real nature of them. We are able to understand the best-drawn of them at all events through themselves.[13] However, what we must look for in Jonson's comedies, as in Moliére's, is a study not of character development but of characters which are already formed, or which are treated as if they were already formed. For instance, in portraying Morose, Jonson is not concerned to show how such a man came to harbour such an obsession of hatred of noise but how, given the fact of the obsession, he behaves in the grip of it.

Jonson has been reproached with a failure to create good and endearing characters. It is, of course, true that it is difficult to feel much affection for Jonson's characters. For, even Jonson's greatest creations like Volpone, Mosca, Subtle, Face, Sir Epicure Mammon are dramatizations of basic, unworthy human traits. But, this is the direct result of his decision to instruct by ridicule. It was but natural that Jonson's observation should turn rather to the uglier side of human nature than to the brighter. Depravity, failings, normal shortcomings attract his attention. He analyses them minutely and draws a striking picture of them. This makes his characters different from those of Shakespeare.

Jonson is attacked on the ground that he has created not characters but caricatures. "Jonson's characters," says Hazlitt, "are caricatures by dint of their very likeness, being extravagant tautologies of themselves."[14] But, we should remember that a flat distortion in the drawing of characters is quite essential to the art of a comic poet like Jonson. However, we may say that Jonson's comedies transcend caricature through their architectural beauty and poetry. To cite but one instance, Sir Epicure Mammon, though satirised as an embodiment of lust and greed, rises above the level of caricature by virtue of the poetic touch given to him. We tend to forget his 'humour' in his poetic rhapsodies. We find him tempt Dol Common painting a glorious picture before her:

> Wee'll therefore goe with all, my girle, and liue
> In a free state; where we will eate our mullets,
> Sous'd in high-countrey wines, sup phesants egges,
> And haue our cockles, boild in siluer shells,
> Our shrimps to swim againe, as when they liu'd,
> In a rare butter, made of dolphins milke,
> Whose creame do's looke like opalls: and, with these
> Delicate meats, set ourselves high for pleasure,
> And take vs downe againe, and then renew
> Our youth, and strength, with drinking the *elixir*,
> And so enioy a perpetuitie
> Of life, and lust. And, thou shalt ha' thy wardrobe,
> Richer then *Natures*, still, to change thy selfe,
> And vary oftener, for thy pride, then shee:
> Or *Art*, her wise, and almost-equall seruant. (IV, i, 155-69)

At any rate, Jonson's art of caricature, like Marlowe's, "is a great caricature, which is beautiful; and a great humour, which is serious."[15]

The most common charge that is levelled against Jonson is that his characters are not full-blooded, complete men and women but mechanical types especially when compared to those of Shakespeare. Hazlitt says, "Shakespeare's characters are men; Ben Jonson's are more like machines."[16] Coleridge concludes that "Ben's personae are too often not characters but derangements—the hopeless patients of a mad doctor rather."[17]

Our immediate answer could be that it was not in Jonson to body forth such figures as step out of the pages of Shakespeare and live with us as familiar acquaintances. It is neither his intention nor his endeavour to present full-blooded, life-like characters, or dynamic living individuals who can exist independent of their settings, but only 'persons' as are required by his characteristic comedy. There is no point, then, in condemning Jonson for what he never set out to do. We have, moreover, no right to demand of Jonson to give us complete human beings. Jonson, the satirist and the censor, did not require for his purposes the creation of complete men and women. We should also remember that where the main end is the satirical portraiture of social types, complete human beings demanding sympathy are out of place. However, Jonson's abundant wit and inventive resourcefulness succeeded to keep his characters human and interesting.

Another equally untenable charge levelled against Jonson is that he cannot invest even his female characters with the charm of Shakespearean romance. It is true that Jonson has not created charming women characters, not only in comparison to Shakespeare, but also in comparison to some of his own male characters. But the truth lies in the fact that Jonson does not require for his purposes the creation of charming women. We cannot expect from him a Portia, a Rosalind, a Viola, an Imogen, a Duchess of Malphi or even an Aspatia. Such women belong essentially to the romantic species and not to the satiric species which Jonson is chiefly concerned with. Hence the women characters, Kitelys, in *Every Man in His Humour* are insubstantial, created merely to fill two necessary parts. The court ladies in *Cynthia's Revels* as well as the Collegiate women in *Epicoene* simply serve the purpose of revealing the sad state of morals among the upper classes. Lady Politick Would-be is simply a chatter-box. Even Mrs. Fitzdottrel in *The Devil is an Ass* and Lady Frampul are dull and not quite convincing.

Nevertheless, we cannot possibly say that Jonson has 'scarcely one well-drawn female figure.' Jonson has to his credit at least two well-drawn women characters of excellence. Dol Common in *The Alchemist* is one of the most convincing women characters of Jonson. She is no common whore. She is a doll and common in the sense that she is a woman of the town, accessible to every one and prepared to play with every one. But, in fact, she is neither doll nor common. When she is instructed by Face to play the role of a stately lady before Sir Epicure Mammon, she says:

O, let me alone,
I'll not forget my race, I warrant you.
I'll keepe my distance, laugh, and talke aloud;
Haue all the tricks of a proud sciruy ladie,
And be as rude' as her woman. (II, iv, 7-11)

As the passage makes it clear she is a tactful woman. It is her adroit threat to leave the partnership:

S'death, you perpetuall curres,
Fall to your couples againe, and cossen kindly,
And heartily, and louingly, as you should,
And loose not the beginning of a *terme,*
Or, by this hand, I shall grow factious too,
And, take my part, and quit you. (I, i, 136-41)

that compels Face and Subtle to compose their quarrel. Again, she cheats Sir Epicure of his diamond ring and talks him out of his wits. She is a 'smock rampant' only at the beginning and briefly at the end of the play. Elsewhere "she is the Queen of Fairies, the mad sister of a lord, elegant enough in speech and manner . . . and able to spout theology out of Broughton."[18]

Then, we have in Ursula in *Bartholomew Fair* a very amusing woman character, indeed, a "female Falstaff." There are close echoes of the Falstaff sequences in the satiric descriptions of Ursula – 'a walking sow of tallow,' and 'an inspir'd vessell of kitchen-stuffe,' 'quagmire,' and 'a whole shire of butter.' She presides over the events of Bartholomew Fair with her greasy moon face like some disreputable minor deity. Like the wife of Bath, she has a high opinion of herself and describes herself modestly as

a plaine plumpe soft wench o' the Suburbs . . . iuicy and wholesome. (II, v, 83-84)

Ursula is a fat, old pig woman who sells hot roast pork sweating like Falstaff. She herself admits:

I am all fire and fat . . . I shall een melt away to the first woman, a ribbe againe, I am afraid. I doe water the ground in knots, as I goe, like a great Garden-pot. (II, ii, 50-52)

She is so fat that she overflows her chair which needs to be

> let out o' the sides, for me, that my hips might play? (II, ii, 64-65)

She smokes like a chimney, swears outrageously and is immensely proud of her booth. "With all her faults," as J.E.M. Latham suggests, "she has both warmth and kindness."[19] This is brought out especially when she welcomes Overdo to her booth and orders a six penny bottle of ale for him despite his disguise as Mad Arthur of Bradley. Such a character is certainly more than a type or 'humour.' She would be a worthy companion for Chaucer's wife of Bath and Shakespeare's Mistress Quickly.

It is, however, necessary to issue a word of caution in the study of Jonson's art of comic characterisation. The theory of 'humours,' as has already been suggested, should not be over-worked in the interpretation of Jonson's dramatic art. For, "Jonson's greatest achievements in characterization have nothing to do with the rigid patterns the commentators describe."[20] It is wrong to believe that all his characters are of the 'humours' type. It is not as though Jonson was incapable of creating lifelike characters. There are, at least, a few characters who evidently rise far above the 'humours' types by virtue of their being endowed with vigour, animation and an individuality of their own.

The immortal and inimitable Bobadill is the first and foremost of such living creations. He is far more than a mere type or 'humour.' For he is more self-expressive, more independent of the devices of setting on which the other personages rely as of necessity and a living creation like Shakespeare's. He is endowed with an individuality thanks to a freer allowance in the control of action and situation.

Like Falstaff Bobadill is exceedingly resourceful. There is in this fire-eater an unfailing submissiveness to reason. He lives in a mean lodging but excuses his residence on the ground that he loves

> a cleanely and quiet priuacy, aboue all the tumult, and roare of fortune. (I, v, 45-46)

Expecting much, he asks Matthew what money he has about him. When he learns that Matthew has only two shillings, Bobadill, instead of feeling depressed, says with perfect resignation:

> We will haue a bunch of redish, and salt, to tast our wine; and a pipe of *tobacco*, to close the orifice of the stomach. (I, v, 165-67)

When, in the midst of his boasts and fiery threats, Bobadill is caught by Down-right and trounced, he quite ingeniously defends himself saying that he was "bound to peace, by this good day" and also that he was

> strooke with a plannet thence, for I had no power to touch my weapon. (IV, vii, 141-42)

Bobadill amuses all the audience with his most fantastic scheme by which he and nineteen other choice spirits chosen by an instinct will in two hundred days kill forty thousand enemies of the queen in open fight "civilly by the sword" despatching them in batches of twenty. There is really life in this lean, hungry figure. Presenting, thus, a perfectly individualistic character Jonson rises above his usual method.

Jonson pours all his intellectual strength into the characters of Volpone and Mosca. They defy the application of the humour scheme. They rise far above the types. Secluded from the world, Volpone lives like a Roman among his creatures. Enjoying life with a gusto, Volpone is an epicurean. To him life is all fun and joy, and he wants to make the most of it. Therefore he expends all his mental powers on subtle schemes for making life a comedy. His passionate intensity is reminiscent of the great characters of Marlowe.

Volpone has been mistaken for an avaricious cheat. But Volpone cannot be charged with the vice that he himself ridicules and exposes in others. He is not blinded by the love of gold. He is not interested in the mere accumulation of wealth. As David Cook puts it, "the artist in him is stronger than the money-spinner."[21] This is clear from his own categorical declaration that he will 'glory'

> More in the cunning purchase of my wealth,
> Then in the glad possession; (I, i, 31-32)

Besides, greed makes a man circumspect. Volpone is shrewd enough in his own way but he is not circumspect. Otherwise he could not have been so reckless as to make Mosca his heir thereby throwing away his own wealth in pursuit of his game. This shows clearly how Volpone is not simply an embodiment of greed.

So, rather than giving us still another example of a greedy man in a play which already contains three of these, Jonson, we may say, is depicting in Volpone the real nature of evil. As Charles A. Hallett has pointed out "Jonson had various devil-traditions in mind when he was writing *Volpone* and he meant us to see Volpone, if not as Mammon himself, at least as a diabolical force, the essence of evil."[22] That Jonson meant us to take Volpone as an entirely terrestrial creature, with a Satanic approach to religion, is sufficiently indicated by the dual nature of Volpone as tempter in the first four acts and as tormentor in the final act of the play.

In Mosca Jonson paints a monumental portrait of the parasite. "He is no mere automation in a scheme of humours."[23] He is all deceit, craftiness, unscrupulousness, and double-crossing. In drawing this lively character, Jonson is indebted to the cunning parasites of the preceding English drama as well as to those of the Latin comedy.[24]

Mosca is no common trickster. He is a trimmer of infinite resources and "a dizzying mixture of chameleon adaptability and bottomless egotism."[25] Plausible and pliant, he comes very near Iago. He has the ability to deceive people and make each one think he is his friend while he is plotting against all of them, as Iago gulls Roderigo, Othello ad Cassio. He too receives such undeserved compliments as 'kind,' 'loving,' 'sweet,' 'excellent,' and 'grateful' Mosca—which suggest to us 'honest Iago.' Endowed with very sharp intelligence, Mosca knows the nature of his dupes thoroughly. When Volpone expresses his fear that the legacy-hunters may scent their trick, Mosca replies:

True, they will not see't.
Too much light blinds 'hem, I thinke. (V, ii, 22-23)

Thus, he guides Volpone through the dangerous and complicated circumstances of their common plots with the suppleness and quickness of a serpent. He is intelligent enough to plan and unscrupulous enough to execute any sort of devilry. Like Face, he is an ingenious contriver of situations, and like Iago he subtly spreads his net to entrap his victims, and if he is entrapped in his own net ultimately, it is because his master chooses to get him punished by ruining himself.

Like many other parasites, Mosca is a pander. But, his polished manner and subtle trickery make him superior to most other parasites. He is aware of his uniqueness as well as his superiority to the poor, hungry parasite. This is clearly brought out in his soliloquy. (III, i, 7-33)[26] He is not an ordinary hungry today but, as he himself boasts, a "fine, elegant rascal." As E.P. Vandiver has rightly pointed out Jonson has drawn in Mosca "the most outstanding of the so-called parasites in Elizabethan drama."[27]

The creation of Sir Epicure Mammon, again, is absolutely of the first class and no longer the mere vehicle of a 'humour.' He is an incarnation of a human temperament in which voluptuous and avaricious concupiscence is sublimed and idealised into something immortal. Sir Epicure may be a fool, yet he is an Elizathetan who is constantly preoccupied by dreams of magnificence and voluptuous desires. He "comes closer to Chaucer's January in the enthusiasm and extravagance of his self-deceit."[28] He is engrossed in the expectation of plentiful gold. The possession of the philosopher's stone, he thinks, will make him master of infinite wealth and he will pronounce to all his friends "the happy word, BE RICH." He further dreams that when his expectation of receiving the stone is fulfilled his "flatterers shall be the pure and gravest of divines," and his mere fools, "eloquent burgesses." His "foot-boy shall eat pheasant, Calver'd salmons, knots, god-wits, lampreys." As far as he himself is concerned he will have his shirts

> of taffata-sarsnet, soft, and light
> As cob-webs; and for all my other rayment,
> It shall be such, as might prouoke the *Persian*;
> Were he to teach the world riot, a new.
> My gloues of fishes, and birds'-skins, perfum'd
> With gummes of *paradise*, and eastern aire– (II, ii, 89-94)

Finally when "all the works are blown 'in fumo'" he persuades himself that he has been "justly punished" for his vice and lust and agrees to pay a hundred pounds as a token of penitence. He quits the scene almost with a stoic resignation:

> I will goe mount a turnep-cart, and preach
> The end o' the world, within these two months. (V, v, 81-82)

Bartholomew Cokes is one of Jonson's most enduring young characters drawn with amazing vigour, and put before us with extraordinary fidelity. He is a subtler and more imaginative study in fatuity than Stephen who is almost a caricature. He is presented as little more than a child. As a critic has recently pointed out in Bartholomew Cokes "Jonson was creating . . . a character to demonstrate the limitation of morality–some one outside the world of intelligence, as the name suggests, and outside the world of good and evil."[29]

The most regular visitor, he falls helplessly in love with the Fair. He calls it "my fair" because of his first name. He cannot buy just one ballad but "a whole bundle" because he collects the pictures on them and pastes them over the nursery chimney at home. Being interrupted by the gingerbread woman he proudly buys the whole of her basket. At last he finds himself perfectly in his element among the puppets when he says:

> I am in loue with the *Actors* already, and I'll be allyed to them presently. (V, iii, 131-32)

Cokes unfailingly reminds us of Sir Andrew Aguecheek. Epitomising, as it were, silly humanity itself, as Jonson views it in the *Discoveries,* (ll.

1437-44), Bartholomew Cokes is one of the most finished products of a simpleton.

Zeal-of-the-land Busy is another most convincing vital character Jonson gave to the stage. He is, again, no careful study of a humour dissected and anatomized, but a full-length portrait of the hypocritical puritan faithfully observed and presented with a careless vigour and animation. He is no vulgar impostor, no mere religious quacksalver of such a kind as supplies the common food for satire, but a hypocrite of the earnest kind, an "Ironside among the civilians." A sketch of sonorous hypocrisy and unconsumed greed, at once historically and universally just, Busy is a living character.

Longing for a roast pig, Busy comes to the Fair but he supplies himself with a noble reason for it saying:

> I'll eate exceedingly and prophesie; there may be a good vse made of it, too, now I thinke on 't: by the publike eating, of Swines flesh, to professe our hate, and loathing of *Iudaisme.* (I, vi, 93-96)

After eating two and a half servings of Ursula's roast pig and washing it down with "a bottle of painful ale" he starts condemning the Fair:

> Thou art the seate of the Beast, O *Smithfield*, . . .
> Idolatry peepeth out on euery side of thee. (III, vi, 44-46)

The snuffling glutton who begins by exciting our laughter finally ends his career in the stocks displaying a comic perversity of stoicism –

> I am glad to be thus separated from the *heathen* of the land, and put apart in the stocks, for the holy cause. (IV, vi, 86-87)

Thus, drawn with enormous vivacity and vigour of invention, Zeal-of-the-land Busy remains one of the liveliest and best hostile portraits of a Puritan in the English language.

Here, then, are characters who might be the envy of even the greatest masters of English drama – Bobadill, Volpone, Mosca, Sir Epicure Mammon, Bartholomew Cokes, Ursula and Rabbi Zeal-of-the-land Busy. No theory of 'humours' will account for them. Now it is evident that Jonson is also capable of producing immortal, individualised characters when the occasion demands. If such characters are less in number, it is because his main purpose is not to produce such characters but 'persons, such as (his) *Comoedie* would chuse.' And the kind of comedy he attempts, tends to choose, in order to achieve its end, mostly 'humours' types. Ben Jonson brilliantly succeeds in producing them.

Jonson's 'humours,' however, are not simply types in the sense Marston's or Moliére's are. They are simplified and somewhat distorted individuals with a typical mania. Their simplification does not, as is often assumed, consist in the dominance of a particular humour or monomania. The simplification, consists largely in reduction of detail and in the seizing of aspects relevant to the relief of an emotional impulse in order to make the character conform to a particular setting. This sort of 'stripping,' it should be noted, is essential to Jonson's dramatic art to which in turn a flat distortion in the drawing of character also becomes essential. Jonson's vitality and observant power endow his characters with life and make us believe in them. His characters are not 'a priori' from some abstract and ideal pattern. They are constructed, as it were from bits of real people. Also, Jonson habitually relates the quirks and oddities of behaviour he observes to underlying laws of human nature. As a result his characters have both an intellectual consistency and a universal significance. What is more, he "is able to add that extra of intensity which is the mark of the great creator."[30] We may conclude that Jonson's characters, on the whole, are as effective in their own way as those of Shakespeare, with this difference that "whereas in Shakespeare the effect is due to the way in which the characters *act upon* one other, in Jonson it is given by the way in which the characters *fit in* with each other."[31]

NOTES

1. "Dedication to *Promos and Cassandra,*" *Elizabethan Critical Essays*, ed. Gregory Smith, vol. I, p. 60.
2. J.B. Bamborough, *Ben Jonson*, p. 34.
3. Herford and Simpson, vol. I, p. 338.
4. *Ibid.*, p. 343.
5. George Meredith, *An Essay on Comedy and the Uses of the Comic Spirit*, pp. 89-90.
6. Gregory Smith, *Ben Jonson*, p. 88.
7. Anne Barton, p. x.
8. J.E. Spingarn, *Critical Essays of the Seventeenth Century*, vol. I, p. xv.
9. S.T. Coleridge, *The Complete Works of Coleridge*, ed. W.G.T. Shedd, vol. IV, p. 253.
10. H.R. Hays, "Satire and Identification: An Introduction to Ben Jonson," *KR*, XIX (1957), p. 275.

11. See C.G. Jung, "A Psychological Theory of Types," *Modern Man in Search of a Soul*, pp. 85-108.
Sandor Lorand. "Psychoanalysis and Literature," *Psychoanalysis Today*, pp. 371-80.
12. G. Freytag, *Technique of the Drama*, pp. 250-51.
13. Yet Jonson's undue indulgence in describing his personages even to an unwarrantable extent, and, what is more, his fondness for furnishing a sort of Theophrastic chorus for the readers' better guidance may have possibly misled critics to neglect the characters themselves.
14. Hazlitt, "Shakespeare and Ben Jonson," in *Lectures on the English Comic Writers*, ed. R.B. Johnson (Oxford: World's Classic edition, 1907), p. 49.
15. T.S. Eliot, *Elizabethan Dramatists*, p. 81.
16. Hazlitt, p. 48.
17. S.T. Coleridge, vol. IV, p. 187.
18. Rufus Putney, "Jonson's Poetic Comedy," *PQ*, XLI (Jan. 1962), p. 192.
19. J.E.M. Latham, "Form in *Bartholomew Fair*," *English*, XXI (Spring, 1972), p. 10.
20. D.H. Craig, ed., *Ben Jonson*: *The Critical Heritage* (Routledge, London and New York, 1990), p. 36.
21. David Cook, ed., *Volpone*, "Introduction," p. 31.
22. Charles A. Hallett, "The Satanic Nature of Volpone," *PQ*, XLIX (Jan. 1970), p. 52.
23. David Cook, p. 31.
24. See L.H. Holt, "Notes on Ben Jonson's *Volpone*," *MLN*, XX (1905), p. 165.
25. D.H. Craig, p. 36.
26. W.D. Briggs is of the opinion that this soliloquy is derived from Plutarch's "How to Tell a Flatterer from a Friend." (See "Source-Material for Jonson's Plays," *MLN*, XXXI (1916), p. 331.
27. E.P. Vandiver, Jr., "The Elizabethan Dramatic Parasite," *SP*, XXXII (July 1935), p. 427.
28. John C. McGalliard, "Chaucerian Comedy: The Merchant's Tale, Jonson, and Moliere," *PQ*, XXV (1946), p. 345.
29. J.E.M. Latham, p. 11.
30. H.R. Hays, p. 274.
31. T.S. Eliot, p. 74.

"A Particular Kind by Itself": Jonsonian Structure

The basic problem for anyone who writes within the dramatic form is, perhaps, the problem of finding proper structure for the play. For, "skill with a verse, insight into character, brilliant individual scenes—all these are likely to precede in the career of any playwright the final product toward which he aims: the structure in which language, character and action meet in unity."[1]

"Dramatic Unity," as Harold F. Brooks very rightly points out, "was as old in England as the great cyclic dramas. Latterly, some of their component plays, like the *Secunda Pastorum*, or groups of plays like the Passion group organised and largely re-written by the York 'Realist,' began to be developed as unified dramas on their own account; but even so, at least at York and Chester the cycle as a whole remained the full drama to which unity belonged."[2] Then, the Elizabethan dramatists in their endeavour to find proper structure searched for ways of achieving a careful design. For instance, "Shakespeare was constantly experimenting in order to find a comic form which would present several characters or groups of characters in relation and contrast with each other, and which would conclude in a scene which brought these various elements into some stable relationship."[3] Their problem was, thus, the achievement of unity out of diversity, because of their delight in variety and their intense expressiveness in multitudinous ways. Hence they tried a variety of forms such as syllogistic progression, qualitative progression, repetitive form, conventional form and particularly minor or incidental forms like metaphor, paradox, disclosure, reversal, contraction, expansion, bathos, apostrophe, series, chiasmus.[4] They did not always succeed in their attempt but when they did, it was never at the sacrifice of variety.

This is almost equally true of Jonson's drama. Becuase Jonson too loves variety as much as Shakespeare.[5] He likes abundance of words, characters and incidents. All the same, Jonson solves the problem of finding proper structure in a quite different way. If Shakespeare does it by inclusion and complex harmony, Jonson does it by exclusion and repetition. Again, whereas Shakespeare is fond of many themes and of modulations into many keys, Jonson is fond of one theme or two sharply contrasting themes but always in closely related keys.

This is because of the basic difference between the Shakespearean and Jonsonian comedy although both are highly complex. Jonson himself has described the difference in the conversation between the presenters, Mitis and Cordatus, in *Every Man Out of His Humour*:

> MIT. the argument of his *Comoedie* might haue beene of some other nature, as of a duke to be in loue with a countesse, and that countesse to be in loue with the dukes sonne, and the sonne to loue the ladies waiting maid: some such crosse wooing, with a clowne to their seruing-man, better then to be thus neere, and familiarly allied to the time.
>
> COR. You say well, but I would faine heare one of these *autumne*- judgements define once, *Quid sit Comoedia*? If he cannot, let him content himselfe with CICEROS definition (till hee haue strength to propose to himselfe a better) who would haue a *Comoedie* to be *Imitatio Vitae, Speculum consuetudinis*, *Imago Veritatis*; a thing throughout pleasant, and ridiculous, and accommodated to the correction of manners: (III, vi, 195-209)

The comedy described by Mitis has a romantic rather than a critical emphasis. Its principal characters are of blue blood; its theme is love and its aim is entertainment. But the comedy described by Cordatus in Ciceronion terms has a critical rather than a romantic emphasis. Its sphere of observation is the real life of ordinary men and women. Its attitude is satirical, its means pleasurable and its aim corrective. However, the essential difference between the two modes of English comedy—the Romantic and the Satiric—is not so much of realism as of attitude and tone.[6] The emphasis is on an altogether different set of human motives. The emphasis in Shakespearian comedy is on the poetic longings for love and adventure whereas in Jonsonian comedy it is on the grosser appetites for wealth and women. And the defining difference of tone is the difference between lyrical sentiment sympathetically expressed and critical satire unemotionally conveyed.[7]

With this difference in attitude and tone, Jonsonian comedy demands an altogether different structure from that of Shakespearian comedy. Satire has to be evolved from the very action. This is possible only when character, bred by a particular social scene, is conceived as the motivator of action. The intrigue must be more than a clever scheme for entertainment arbitrarily set in motion. It must be initiated by "traits of human nature liable to ridicule and must work itself out to the discomfiture of its initiator."[8] In short, dramatic action must be produced by the very satiric conception of human behaviour.

It is this kind of structure that Jonson seems to have aimed at, and having achieved it, he is greatly pleased. This is made clear from what Cordatus, representing Jonson, says in the induction to *Every Man Out of His Humour*:

> Faith Sir, I must refraine to iudge, only this I can say of it, 'tis strange, and of a particular kind by it selfe, somewhat like *Vetus Comoedia*'; a worke that hath bounteously pleased me.
>
> ('Grex,' ll. 230-33)

When Jonson thus said of the comedy he was working to develop that it was "of a particular kind by it selfe, somewhat like 'Vetus Comoedia'," he seems to have meant more than critics so far have given him credit for meaning.

Jonson's use of 'Vetus Comoedia' has generally been taken to be the 'New Comedy' of Terence. Jonson has almost always been discussed as if he belonged to the tradition of Menander, Plautus and Terence. Even most recently Daniel C. Boughner has stated[9] that Jonson organized the action of his plays in the quadripartite structure consisting of the 'Protasis,' the 'epitasis,' the 'catastasis' and the 'Catastrophe.'[10]

No doubt, Jonson defines the function of the 'Protasis' as

> a faire Presentment of your *Actors*. And a handsome promise of somewhat to come hereafter.
>
> (*The Magnetic Lady*, I, vii, 'Chorus,' ll. 3-4)

Then he warns the audience by means of the prompt Boy's expostulation to the censorious Damplay that it is not to

> looke . . . for conclusions in a *Protasis*? I thought the Law of *Comedy* has reserv'd ('hem) to the *Catastrophe*: and that the *Epitasis*, (as wee are taught) and the *Catastasis*, had beene interveening parts.
>
> (*Ibid*., ll. 8-11)

Nonetheless,, Jonson does not blindly adopt the quadripartite structure as it is. He gives it his own individual colour. He moulds it so as to suit the requisites of his comedy best by exploiting its flexibility with great audacity and ease. Jonson, in his dramatic practice, takes full advantage of the flexibility inherent in the four-part design and varies the length of the 'Protasis' according to the complexity of the action. Though in *Volpone* it coincides with Act I, in *Every Man in His Humour*, *Epicoene*, and *The Alchemist* it leaps across the act division to continue the dramatic movement into the beginning of Act II without pause. And it extends to the end of Act II in *The New Inn* in order to allow for the introduction of personages who make their first appearance only in Act II, scene 6. Furthermore, in *Every Man in His Humour* and *Epicoene* Jonson brings forward in the 'protasis' a series of themes or sub-actions which form the single action and which are developed separately till they converge at the 'Catastrophe.'

Madeleine Doran takes 'Vetus Comoedia' to be "the Old Comedy of Aristophanes as distinguished from the New Comedy of Menander."[11] Ray L. Heffner too thinks that we might gain more insight into Jonson's art "If we considered him instead in the quite different tradition of Old Comedy."[12] Jonson would seem to have recognized a dramatic kinship in Aristophanes' fundamentally satiric intention. This is indicated to us in the 'Apologetical Dialogue' appended to the Folio text of *Poetaster* where Jonson defends himself from the charge that all his writing is "mere railing" by an appeal to the authority both of Aristophanes and of the Roman satirists:

> Ha! If all the salt in the Old *Comedy*
> Should be so censur'd, or the sharper wit
> Of the bold *satyre*, termed scolding rage,
> What age could then compare with those, for buffons?
> What should be sayd of ARISTOPHANES?
> PERSIVS? or IUVENAL? Whose names we now
> So glorifie in schooles, at least pretend it.
>
> ('To The Reader,' ll. 186-92)

Jonson's method of concentration is certainly classical. Nevertheless Jonson seems to owe as much to the technique of the Morality play as to the New Comedy of Menander and the Old Comedy of Aristophanes. For, even though the allegorical habit of the Morality play "ceased in the eighties to be very common as a distinct form, its effect on the later drama, in the shaping both of attitude and of form was profound."[13] Baskervill suggests that Jonson might possibly be referring to the morality plays in 'Vetus Comoedia.'[14] Jonson himself uses the phrase 'Vetus Comoedia' with this sense in *Conversations with Drummond* (ll. 409-15) and L.C. Knights makes this identification categorically.[15] Most recently Alan Dessen also explains the unity of Jonson's plays as an adaptation of the technique of the Morality play.[16]

The tightly managed intrigue and the outward shape of the plot in the great comedies are, doubtless, like Latin and Italian comedy. Yet, the motivation of the intrigue in common human impulses of greed and folly makes these plays quite unlike Latin comedy. Especially in their moral-psychological combination of motives, Jonson's plays seem to us to have closer affinity with the tradition of the Morality play.

Whatever might be Jonson's sources—the New Comedy, the Old Comedy or the Morality play—he appears to have worked restlessly until he achieved an original dramatic form capable of conveying his satiric vision. And his art lies in his "manipulation of popular devices and classical tradition to his own purpose."[17]

Almost envying the licence and freedom enjoyed by the Ancients in handling the dramatic form Jonson refuses to

> bee tyed to those strict and regular formes, which the nicenesse of a few (who are nothing but forme) would thrust vpon vs.
>
> (*Every Man Out of His Humour,* Grex, ll. 268-70)

and says enthusiastically,

> I see not then, but we should enjoy the same licence, or free power, to illustrate and heighten our inuention as they did.
>
> (*Ibid.*, ll. 266-68)

With his firm belief that "wee have better meanes to pronounc . . . if wee will use, and apply, our owne experience . . . to all the obseruations of the *Ancients,*" (*Discoveries*, ll. 134-37) Jonson was determined to "make further discoveries of truth and fitness." (ll. 2101-03) One of the principal 'discoveries' he made is the organic form which has at its base a concern with physical as well as symbolic situation. And, however indebted Jonson was to the classical and Morality traditions, the form he finally achieved is distinctly his own—"a particular kind by it selfe."

Critics since the seventeenth century have agreed that Jonson is a master of comic structure. But there has been a good deal of disagreement concerning the precise kind of structure in which Jonson supremely excels. In discussing the structure of Jonsonian comedy we may speak of two schools of criticism—one focusing attention on the classical linear structure and the other on the thematic or symbolic structure.

The first school is represented by Dryden's famous comments in *An Essay on Dramatic Poesy* which has been duly supported by the Oxford editors of Jonson, and the second by Freda Townsend's stimulating study of Jonson's baroque technique in her *Apologie for Bartholomew Fayre:*

The Art of Jonson's Comedies which has been ably seconded by Ray L. Heffner, Jr.[18] and Edward Partridge.[19]

Dryden, to whom Jonson was pre-eminent among English dramatists by virtue of obeying the neo-classical rules of unity of time, place, and action, sees an essentially classical structure, with a logical order proceeding through a consistently rising action with the events of each act 'greater' than those of the preceding act. The 'examen of *The Silent Woman*' emphasizes that there is immense variety of character and incident but that "the action of the play is entirely one."[20]

Almost falling in line with Dryden, Herford and Simpson take the view that Jonson's structure, at its best, is the structure of Roman comedy, that is, singleness of action. They speak of the unity of action in *Every Man in His Humour* as being not simplicity, but the oneness of many parts. They think that the unity of the great plays like *Volpone* and *The Alchemist* "was won not by surrendering the multiplicity of minor actions so congenial to his Elizabethan passion for profusion, but by compelling them to become integral parts of the single all-embracing action."[21] Miss Doran may have kept in mind this notion of Jonson's structure when she comments on Jonson's "remorseless logic" in the unravelling of his plots. She says that he "creates a wholly logical world in which the interplay of the interest of his characters moves the plot towards a necessary conclusion."[22] Judging thus the form of Jonson's comedies from the classical point of view it is almost unanimously agreed that Jonson was a conscious artist guided in his drama by the models of Plautus and Terence.

But this picture of a regular, neo-classic Jonson, especially in the matter of plot structure, is disputed by the other school of critics of recent years. They find in Jonson what might be called a symbolic structure, a structure predicated on the use of central themes or symbols rather than line, as the ordering principle. Freda L. Townsend takes a strong objection to the view of Jonson's structure as singleness of plot. She argues quite persuasively that none of Jonson's great comedies has the unified action characteristic of Terentian comedy and enjoined by neo-classical precept. She finds a different kind of structure unifying the variety in Jonson. Granting that the matter in Jonson is as richly varied as that of Shakespeare or Beaumont and Fletcher or Middleton or Heywood she says, "yet variety does not mean forfeiture of order. 'The complex whole of the web asserts itself above everything else.' . . . The careful hand of the craftsman weaves together his many actions; characters appear and disappear according to a large plan which holds them all in order. Artistry is everywhere apparent—in execution of detail, in richness of effect, and, subtle unity."[23] Comparing Jonson's art with that of Ariosto and the baroque painters she sees *Bartholomew Fair* rather than

The Silent Woman as the culmination of his development away from a simply unified comedy toward one which involves the intricate interweaving of as many different interests as possible.

Ray L. Heffner thinks that we may gain more insight into Jonson's art if we consider him rather in the tradition of Aristophanes – of Old Comedy than in that of Menander, Plautus, and Terence – of New Comedy. He is of the opinion that in Jonson the comic structure is centred not on a plot but on the exploration of an "extravagant conceit." He says that in each of his major comedies Jonson "explores an idea or a cluster of related ideas through a variety of characters and actions. And the central expression of the unifying idea is usually not in a fully developed plot but in a fantastic comic conceit, an extravagant exaggeration of human folly, to which all of the more realistically conceived characters and incidents have reference," and concludes that "the essential unity of Jonson's comedy is thematic."[24]

Edward B. Partridge explains the structure and unity of Jonson's plays in terms of image clusters. He says that a certain unity is given to Jonson's play by the characteristically Jonsonian tone which is created partly by the imagery employed. He shows us how Jonson, by means of epithets, allusions, metaphors, and precisely chosen words, gives us "the proper comic perspective: cold, hard, and merciless, yet clear, free of cant, and massively controlled."[25]

This modern view of Jonson's technique is, perhaps, best summed up by T.S. Eliot when he says that the "immense dramatic constructive skill" that Jonson employs, "is not so much skill in plot as skill in doing without a plot," and concludes: "the plot does not hold the play together; what holds the play together is a unity of inspiration that radiates into plot and personages alike."[26]

These are the two fairly traditional ways of looking at the structure of Jonson's comedies, one of linear and the other the thematic or symbolic. Although Miss Townsend and Mr. Heffner seem pretty well convinced that their view is correct while Dryden's is not, that the structure is essentially baroque, not classic, we may take the stand that the views of the two schools of criticism are not mutually exclusive. There is no reason why in such a highly complex comedy as Jonson's there cannot be both a linear and a thematic or symbolic structure each complementing the other. A close study of Jonson's plots from this angle would show how their structure is at once linear and thematic – 'two levels of meaning carried on a single action,' if not in the early plays, which are experimental, at least from *Volpone* onwards.

Every Man in His Humour is built on a rapid Plautine intrigue. The plot is thin but perfectly original. The plot is a complex of several actions which are ingeniously tangled together. But beneath its apparent complexity the main threads of plot which hold the action together are simple. The first thread is the suspicion of elder Knowell that results in following his rakish son into town to check his wild doings and getting inveigled into a compromising situtation at Cob's house through the trickery of the servant, Brainworm. The second is the determination of the jealous husband, Kitely, to find his wife out and his ultimate awakening to the foolishness of his fears. The third is the thin love intrigue between young Knowell and Bridget. The three threads are interwoven mainly through the agency of the versatile Brainworm, each character being led to the Justice's house for the 'outing' of the 'humours' and the apportioning of rewards and penalties. The skilful manner in which the various threads are interwoven bears ample evidence of Jonson's constructive ingenuity.

All the same, the plot in itself has no sufficient strength to hold our interest. It has no central climax or turning point or any opposing force. While it continues, it does not proportionately develop. Nevertheless, *Every Man in His Humour* can be said to find its structural unity through the unity of tone based on a careful preservation of uniform tone in the comic element of the play. It should, however, be noted that the unity of tone is attained not in the original version but in the revised one. For, in its first version, young Lorenzo's passionate denunciation of the enemies of poetry as well as the savage punishments inflicated on the gulls towards the close greatly impaired the unity of comic tone. But, when Jonson revised the play he not only lightened the penalties of the fools but made a very significant excision by cutting Edward Knowell's eloquent defence of poetry thereby preserving the comic tone of the play. Though the play is not radically reshaped in the latter version the whole effect is quite different because of the two principal changes brought about. Thus after a stringent revision, *Every Man in His Humour* is left as a piece of pure comedy. This forms unmistakably a clear index to Jonson's development in his endeavour to achieve structural unity in his drama.

There is little or no plot in *Every Man Out of His Humour*. The action of the play itself is slight and quite meagre but seems to be sufficient for its purpose. The episodic plot is made up of characters—the would-be gallants, Fastidius Briske, Fungoso and Sogliardo, a ridiculous wife of a citizen, Fallace, a shallow court lady, Saviolina, a fantastic knight, Puntarvalo, and others—whose false social and intellectual standards are held up to ridicule. Jonson starts with these eccentric people for each of whom he has planned a little plot that will first show him off and then break up his characteristic habit of mind. Strutting on the stage, each one exhibits in his conduct the falsity and worthlessness of his social and intellectual standards. While the commentators, Mitis and Cordatus, ridicule him his discomfiture is brought about, and he is dismissed from the play. Thus the unity is brought about not only by bringing together a great variety of characters but by contriving to apply to one and all of them the same kind of purge.

Nevertheless, however well Jonson avails himself of the opportunities which drama offers for elaboration of the characters and for expansion of the action, one cannot but admit that he is somehow not able to disguise the mechanical way in which he assembles the characters and marshals them through and out of the play in a kind of single file. Besides, the arbitrariness of entrances and exits and the repeated exposing of humours contribute to the feeling of immobility in the action.

That Jonson was apparently well aware of the dramatic shortcoming of his experiment in *Every Man in His Humour,* although he never admitted any feeling of disappointment, is indicated in a new set of dramatic techniques he adopts for his next play, *Cynthia's Revels.* Now he tries a new type of construction for his plot, by joining Greek myth to contemporary and courtly issues. He chooses a mythical framework in which all the scenes embodying the material he wishes to satirise—the corrupt and shallow, the ridiculous and silly values the Court and the higher ranks of society sometimes use for standards—are symbolically unified into a coherent whole.

But the use of the classsic myth in *Cynthia's Revels* is said to have got in the way of its "action as a coherent whole."[27] Even the sympathetic critics like O.J. Campbell think that the mythological elements are at best "an attractive decorative novelty."[28] These views seem to ignore the fact that the Renaissance, like the Middle Ages, was prone to consider classical mythology as allegory concealing the wisdom of the ancients.[29] Familiar with conventional moral interpretations of classical myth, Jonson uses the Echo and Narcissus myths only in order to reflect the ethical maxims he attempts to inculcate. As E.W. Talbert rightly believes, the moral expositions of mythology in many speeches (I, ii, 25-53; 80-100; xi, 14-17; 18-26) "unify the mythological elements Jonson uses"[30] closely related as they are to the moral he purports to convey.

Approached as a hastily constructed document in the 'War of the Theatres,'[31] *Poetaster* has inevitably seemed to lack coherence and to be a mere collection of disjointed elements. Herford and Simpson say: "in respect of dramatic technique the *Poetaster* marks no advance whatever on its predecessors. The plot is little more than a hurried amalgam of more or less effective motives; and its technique . . . is a loose mixture of different technical methods for the most part already employed in one or another of the previous comedies."[32] But it would be rather strange if Jonson in his third effort to compose his new form of 'Comicall satyre' achieved no closer dramatic unity than that credited to him by critics. *Poetaster* is certainly more dramatic than its predecessors. The swiftness of its execution[33] has greatly tempered the over-elaboration which plays havoc with *Every Man Out of His Humour* and *Cynthia's Revels.*

Discarding the completely undramatic scenes of *Every Man Out of His Humour* and the allegory and masque-like staging of *Cynthia's Revels,* Jonson, in *Poetaster*, bends the historical matter of the Augustan age into a stout framework for action. The material turned into a drama is not a story, not even a plot in the conventional sense of the word, but a series of related ideas that go to make up an 'ars poetica.' So, the unity established for the play lies "less in a closely-knit, simply moving action than in a succession of intellectual attitudes that were adjacent in the minds that determined the nature of Renaissance culture."[34]

The play centres in the little group of rival dramatists who plot and persecute under the transparent masks of Crispinus, Demetrius and Horace. Jonson develops the comedy, in the main, by running the gamut of the poetasters from the clumsy Albius to the malicious Lupus, by manipulating the situations upon the stage in such a way that his butts exhibit their folly for laughter. The play shows no "disorderly composition." On the other hand, it clearly reveals, when it is read as a defense of poetry, "the careful and original 'inventio' that Jonson exercised in developing his own particular humanistic variations upon Renaissance thought and portraiture."[35]

Examined thus, the 'Comical Satires' are not really defective in structure as they are generally thought to be. Jonson's satiric bent, as has been shown, makes its way into a specific kind of structure in these plays, the characters being set up and moved about in accord with a preliminary frame of mind which has prejudged them. In each of these three plays there are, no doubt, brilliant dramatic moments and episodes but in general the critical interest[36] has usurped the dramatic. Then, it seems that Jonson in these essentially satirical plays is temporarily distracted from his real course of development ushered in *Every Man in His Humour.* Nonetheless, the 'Comical Satires' are highly developmental and also interesting inasmuch as they show Jonson's search for an adequate dramatic structure which is at once thematic and linear.

The early Plautine comedies, *The Case is Altered* and *Every Man in His Humour*, followed by the static critical plays of the 'War of the Theatres,' were thus in the nature of experiments. Jonson, however, found his true form with *Volpone*. Discarding the experimental devices of *Every Man Out of His Humour*, *Cynthia's Revels* and *Poetaster, Volpone* has no chorus, no commentators, no historical story to confuse the issue, no antithetical allegory and no rigid framework taken from Latin comedy.

It looks as though Jonson, with his experience and maturity now attained after a considerable period of deliberate and self-conscious development, chose to be less cosmic than his predecessors and less quantitative and more selective and exhaustive. The following major comedies unequivocally reveal Jonson's impressive mastery of the art of limiting and of completeness within those limits. The resulting form of the plays in his middle period from 1605-14 is curiously tight.

For the first time in *Volpone* since *Every Man in His Humour* our interest is attracted to the play instead of being directed outward from it to a generalized society. The plot of *Volpone* carries an interest in itself rather than being simply an excuse for the playwright's comments. The plot centres rather than radiates our interest so that the attention is constantly focused on the aesthetic experience even while variations are played upon the central theme of avarice.

Furthermore, it is in *Volpone* for the first time we are restricted largely to a single house permeated with the personality of a single individual who acts consistently as a "magnetic centre" attracting others to him. The structure of the play consists in the growth of Volpone's and Mosca's triumphs in gulling through variation of tricks within the set environment, the legacy hunters – Voltore, Corvino, Corbaccio, and Lady Politic Would-be. And Jonson successfully manages to relate character and environment in such a way that the two interact and interdetermine the structure of the play. Thus, we have in *Volpone* the unity of theme expressed, through unity of environment as determined by the magnetic centre.

All the same, the structure of *Volpone* is supposed to have been greatly marred by the lack of overt connection of the sub-plot with the main plot. The sub-plot which centres round Sir Politic Would-be, Lady Would-be and Peregrine has generally been dismissed by critics as irrelevant and discordant, loosening the fabric of the play. Even the most sympathetic admirers of Jonson have not been able to account satisfactorily for the presence of the three characters except by styling them a kind of comic relief to offset the 'sustained gloom' of the main action of the play.[37] They approached the problem exclusively in terms of physical action. But it is on the thematic level that their presence can be justified and their actions integrated with the main plot.

The thematic structure of the play finds its way through the author's use of the beast fable or bird lore.[38] If Volpone is the fox, Mosca the fly, Voltore the vulture, Corvino the raven, Corbaccio the crow, Sir Politic is the chattering poll parrot and his wife a deadlier specimen of the same species and Peregrine is the pilgrim falcon. Like parrots the Would-bes not only chatter but mimic. With Sir Politic, an effort to Italianize himself takes the form of his obsession with plots, secrets of state and Machiavellian intrigue. Lady Would-be apes the local styles in dress, cosmetics and reading. Peregrine, like the mythical hawk,[39] pursues the truth, striking at the ignorance of Sir Politic.

The Would-bes are also related to the main plot in another way. While imitating their environment they quite unwittingly travesty the actions of the characters of the main plot thereby caricaturing them.[40] Sir Politic Would-be functions as a comic distortion of Volpone. As his very name implies he is the would-be politician, the unsuccessful enterpriser whereas Volpone is the real politician, the successful enterpriser. Sir Politic, like Volpone, nurses his get-rich-quick schemes. But none of these ever progresses beyond the talking stage while every one of Volpone's schemes comes out quite successful loading his coffers with treasures. Again, while confiding to Peregrine that his money-making projects need only the assistance of one trusty henchman in order to be put into instant execution, Sir Politic is evidently hinting that Peregrine, by undertaking that assignment, should play Mosca to his Volpone. The antics of Lady Would-be caricature the more sinister gestures of Corvino, Voltore and Corbaccio. She is jealous like Corvino. She is as meaninglessly and perversely erudite as Voltore. And like Corbaccio, she makes compromising proposals to Mosca. Furthermore, Lady Would-be stands an ironic contrast to Celia just as Sir Politic does to Volpone. She is strident and parrot-like while Celia is meek and decorous. Thus the sub-plot of Sir Politic and Lady Would-be which seems at first to have little connection with the main plot turns out, on closer scrutiny, to be an ironic echo of the main plot. It certainly adds a fresh dimension and a profounder insight to the play.

However, when Jonson came to *Epicoene* he appears to have abandoned the conventional double plot in favour of proliferation of character, event and talk, in order to concentrate on a narrower range of possibilities.[41] Composing within more highly integrated scenes, and calling attention to the qualitative gradation of tone and meaning, he places stricter limits on time, place and event. He limits the potential formal constituents. The older quantitative method of achieving copiousness is thus displaced by a more selective variety and contrast, gradations within strict limits. The emphasis now falls upon a seeking out of all things within a limited subject, as means of achieving fullness.

The trick of Jonson's method of achieving such fullness lies, according to L.A. Beaurline, in his "mastery of variations within limits: he makes the episode seem absolutely exhausting, completely degrading, massively thorough. The full strength of Jonson's illusion lies, however, in the tissue of the plot. If progresses in a compact series, by ringing the changes, by turn and counterturn, creating the impression that all the possibilities are being wrung out of the scene."[42] Such seems to be the aesthetic of completeness or plenitude within arbitrary limits set on the material. And a consideration of this sort of impulse toward a kind of controlled completeness brings us, perhaps, closer to Jonson's characteristic design.

Epicoene, a delight of the Restoration stage and the 'critical darling of Dryden,' exemplifies Jonson's endeavour to attain to a further closeness of construction. Characterised by brilliance of structure and psychological deftness, both linear and thematic, the play's argument is completely self-contained. There is, in *Epicoene*, the beautifully-ordered plot structure which Dryden most enthusiastically describes and there is also the symbolic structure well described by Heffner and Partridge.

Epicoene accomplishes what it sets out to do with an absolute minimum of extraneous material. Jonson works out variations on a plot which has at its core a relatively simple, coherent story. Morose, a hater of noise, marries in order to disinherit his hated nephew, but the nephew, Dauphine, outwits him. The securing of Morose's estate is the central aim of the whole. Around this thread Jonson arranges characters, episodes, and recurrent motifs which are connected to it and to each other according to the total design of the play.

But, it seems to be much more accurate to consider *Epicoene* as consisting not of a Terentian plot held together by the 'noble intrigue' depending upon the delayed completion of a single, well-defined objective as Dryden analyzes it, but of a welter of characters and episodes whirling within a central theme. Because, there are points at which our attention gets radiated rather than focused. First of all, the settling of Morose's estate on Dauphine is not the ostensible aim of the action after Act III. Again the La Foole-Daw gulling which provides the matter for part of Act IV seems to come dangerously close to being simply a stopgap in the action. Even the Ladies Collegiates, for that matter, tend somewhat to develop an interest of their own. It is really the unit of theme which holds these links in the chain in position.

The thematic structure of the play will be clear when we know that the title, *Epicoene*, is applicable to much more than the central twist of the plot. As Partridge points out "nearly every one in the play is epicene in character in some way."[43] The Collegiate Ladies "with most masculine or rather hermaphroditicall authoritie" (I, i, 80) are too bold to be feminine. They appear so far from the feminine that Morose cries out: "O, mankind generation." (V, iv, 22) Mistress Otter who "falls upon" her husband, Captain Otter, and "beats him" is certainly masculine. The epicene natures of the women in the play naturally extinguish the masculine natures of men. Captain Otter becomes epicene as Mistress Otter becomes Captain Otter himself. Morose, in order to get rid of his wife, shows his willingness to become a eunuch. He tells the Ladies:

> I am no man, ladies . . . Vtterly vn-abled in nature, by reason of *frigidity*, to performe the duties, or any the least office of a husband.
> (V, iv, 44-47)

Also, La Foole speaking, as he always does, in an effeminate manner appears to be more feminine than masculine. Thus *Epicoene* can be said to find its thematic unity in the epicene nature of its characters.

The Alchemist offers, perhaps, the clearest example of Jonson's artifice of controlled completeness with a restricted field, a set number of characters and some simple principles for a "confidence game." The plot is of the simplest, observing all the Unities, especially the Unity of 'place' with even greater strictness than in *Epicoene*. Like *Volpone*, *The Alchemist* "is built on the double theme of lust and greed, and the whole play is constructed so as to isolate and magnify the central theme. The extraordinary complications of the plot all centre on Subtle and Face, and all work to one end. The play is completely self-consistent."[44] The dramatic action of the play thus evolves from the very satiric conception of human behaviour.

Carried on with unabating vigour from the opening, the action of *The Alchemist* is varied but compact. There is a sparkling variety of interest but all the interests, pointing in one direction, are but parts of a dominant whole. There is a tremendous variety in characterisation also, but every character is an integral part of the whole, contributing its own share to the development of action.

The plot is built forming a compact series, with repeated turns and counterturns with successively greater crises, and more and more people crowding on-stage.[45] The whole fabric, building climax on climax, is so plausibly presented that we forget its departures from the possibilities of life. Such art is "the epitome of Jonson's skill – to vary, to press a matter to its greatest potential, to please us at the same time that we stand admiring the subtle means by which our feelings are manipulated."[46]

All the same, the artistic beauty of the plot of *The Alchemist* is said to be marred by the inartistic ending of the play. When Lovewit, who entirely disappears from our interest during the course of the action, crops up conveniently towards the close at a climacteric moment in the action, probability is said to be stretched to the breaking point. Lovewit's appearance at the end is thus supposed to be not necessitated. W.A. Bacon complains that "the ending in this sense is not determined by the interaction of character and environment, but by an accident not strictly relevant to the environment."[47] Thus, the ending is supposed to break the logic of the design of the play.

But it should be remembered that Lovewit's return is prepared for at the beginning of the play itself. And it is essential that this should be almost, perhaps quite, forgotten before he actually does return, as the structure of the play depends partly upon successive crises in the unstable alliance of Subtle, Face and Dol. Also, we may say with Madeleine Doran that "in this world of human baseness and its consequences, accident is allowed, to be sure, in a not illiberal use of coincidence, but it becomes simply part of the data which the intriguer manipulates. It is the accident of the fly entering the spider's web." We should bear in mind that it is also by sheer accident that Drugger, Dapper, Kastril, and his sister all arrive at the Alchemist's laboratory on the very morning that Mammon and the Puritans are pressing for "projection." But, Face only weaves these lesser dupes into his scheme with brilliant improvisation. In the same way Face uses the unlucky arrival of his master on the same day to save his own face. Unable to hush up all that has taken place in the house, Face is compelled to confess everything. He readily begs his master's pardon and offers him the hand of a rich young widow, Dame Pliant and gets his pardon and a reward too. Thus Lovewit's unexpected arrival is used by Face to save his own face as he has done in the case of the other characters. That Jonson himself believed this to be in the fitness of things is indicated when Face addressing the audience says that though

> My part a little fell in this last *Scene*,
> Yet 'twas *decorum*. (V, v, 158-59)

If *The Alchemist*, thus, has the "rising" and "vertical" structure described by Dryden and Ellis-Fermor respectively, it also has the thematic structure. As alchemy works well as a metaphor for art, *The Alchemist* can be taken as not only about London confidence games but also about the relationship between art and nature, which by implication will refer to the relationship between the comic artist and the audience, as indicated in Subtle's speech:

> Beside, who doth not see, in daily practice,
> Art can beget bees, hornets, beetles, waspes,
> Out of the carcasses, and dung of creatures;
> Yea, scorpions, of an herbe, being ritely plac'd. (II, iii, 171-74)

The "art" which Subtle specifies is apparently comic art. So Subtle can be regarded as the symbolic comic artist-alchemist who (like Jonson, the comic artist himself) strips nature of its superficialities and impurities and reduces it to its quintessence all within the context of the purest comedy. The representatives of the major social classes of Jacobean England – Dapper, Drugger, Sir Epicure – who appear in the play to be exposed by the alchemist, Subtle, also appear in the theatre to be reformed by the arch-alchemist, Jonson. Thus alchemy as a metaphor for comic art unifies the whole action of the play into a thematic whole.

It is generally felt that in his last plays – *The Devil is an Ass* (1616), *The Staple of News* (1626), *The New Inn* (1629) and *The Magnetic Lady* (1632) – Jonson's constructive powers decrease. One of the main charges levelled against these last plays is that they lack unity. It is true that these plays lack the unifying force of a central satiric motive, such as is exhibited in *Volpone* and *The Alchemist.* They may not conform to the pattern of the linear-thematic structure which has so brilliantly characterized the middle comedies. Nevertheless, a certain unity is given to these plays by the characteristically Jonsonian tone which is created partly by the imagery.[48]

Somehow, Jonson's plots have not been properly understood nor appreciated by some critics. "It would be difficult," observes William Archer, "to find worse-constructed plays outside of Jonosn's works."[49] "Jonsons's plots," complains Edmund Wilson, "are incoherent and clumsy."[50] Nothing could be more fallacious than this short-sighted view, which is totally blind to Jonson's 'dramatic design' of each play as a whole. These critics do not appear to have realised that different types of drama require different kinds of dramatic unity.[51] The fallacy, however, rests on the common notion that the plot of a comedy ought to be the same kind as that of a tragedy. As L.J. Potts points out "when people speak of a plot, they usually have in mind a logical sequence of significant events, like the events that lead from the return of Oedipus to his native country up to the death of his wife and his own blindness, or from Macbeth's military successes to his murder of Duncan and on to his own death."[52] It is with this erroneous notion in mind that critics like Archer and Wilson have found fault with Jonson's plots. They seem to be unaware of the fact that comedy in general and the Jonsonian comedy in particular at once justifies and demands a different structure – 'a particular kind by it selfe.'

NOTES

1. Wallace A. Bacon, "The Magnetic Field: The Structure of Jonson's Comedies," *HLQ*, XIX (1955-56), p. 122.
2. Harold F. Brooks, "Marlowe and Early Shakespeare," *Christopher Marlowe*, ed. Brian Morris (Mermaid Critical Commentaries), p. 83.
3. John Russell Brown, *Shakespeare and His Comedies*, p. 43.
4. See Kenneth Burke, *Counter Statement,* pp. 157-61.
5. See Herford and Simpson, vol. I, pp. 121-22.
6. See Nevill Coghill, "The Basis of Shakespearian Comedy," *ES* (1950), pp. 3-9.
7. See Madeleine Doran, *Endeavours of Art: A Study of Form in Elizabethan Drama*, p. 149.
8. *Ibid*., p. 168. This type of construction by means of controlling the central design of a play by a satiric conception also appears in Chapman, Marston and Middleton as well as in Congreve and Wycherley.
9. Daniel C. Boughner, "Jonsonian Structure in *The Tempest*," *SQ*, XXI (Winter 1970), p. 6.
10. 'The four-fold structure,' implying a division of the plot into four distinctive movements was invented by Terence in *Andria*. It was further described by Donatus in *Comentum Terente*. It was rediscovered and adopted to the Renaissance stage by Machiavelli in his translation of *Andria* (1500) as well as in his original comedies, *Clazia* (1506) and *La Mandragola* (1518). It ultimately received a more adequate description in the *Poetics* (1501) of J.C. Scaliger. (See T.W. Baldwin, *Shakespeare's Five Act Structure*, esp. pp. 325-41) *Ben Jonson*, rejecting the authority of Terence (Herford and Simpson, vol. VII, p. 436), studied Machiavelli and not only imported the quadripartite structure to England but naturalized it on the English stage.
11. Madeleine Doran, p. 169. Herford and Simpson also so take it. (Vol. I, p. 376; vol. IX, p. 421)
12. Ray L. Heffner, Jr., "Unifying Symbols in the Comedy of Ben Jonson," *Ben Jonson: A Collection of Critical Essays,* p. 146.
13. Madeleine Doran, p. 99.
14. See C.R. Baskervill, *English Elements in Jonson's Early Comedies,* pp. 7, 212-33.
15. See L.C. Knights, *Drama and Society in the Age of Jonson*, p. 188.

16. See Alan Dessen, "*The Alchemist*: Jonson's 'Estates' Play," *Renaissance Drama*, VII, pp. 35-54.
17. M.C. Bradbrook, *The Growth and Structure of Elizabethan Comedy,* p. 110.
18. Ray L. Heffner, pp. 74-97.
19. Edward B. Partridge, "The Allusiveness of *Epicoene*," *ELH*, XXII (1955), pp. 93-107.
20. Dryden, "An Essay on Dramatic Poesy," p. 91.
21. Herford and Simpson, vol. I, pp. 123 and 336.
22. Madeleine Doran, p. 339.
23. Freda L. Townsend, *Apologie for "Bartholomew Fair": The Art of Jonson's Comedies*, p. 96.
24. Ray L. Heffner, p. 134.
25. Edward B. Partridge, *The Broken Compass,* p. 225.
26. T.S. Eliot, *Elizabethan Dramatists,* p. 76.
27. Herfrod and Simpson, vol. I, p. 398.
28. O.J. Campbell, "The Dramatic Construction of *Poetaster*," *HLQ*, IX (1936), p. 37.
29. See John Harrington, "A Brief Apology for Poetry," *Elizabethan Critical Essays*, ed. G.G. Smith, vol. II, p. 203.
30. E.W. Talbert, "The Classical Mythology and the Structure of *Cynthia's Revels*," *PQ*, XXII (July 1943), p. 194.
31. See R.A. Small, *The Stage-Quarrel,* pp. 25-58.
32. Herford and Simpson, vol. I, pp. 437-38.
33. This Jonson himself tells us explicitly (Envy's 'Prologue,' l. 14). *Poetaster* was finished in fifteen weeks owing to circumstances of unusual urgency. "Rumours had reached Jonson that his enemies, stung by the unmistakable references in 'Hedon' and 'Anaides' (in *Cynthia's Revels*) were preparing a single revenge; . . . He resolved to parry this attack by a counterstroke of his own." (Herford and Simpson, vol. I, p. 415)
34. O.J. Campbell, *Comicall Satyre and Shakespeare's "Troilus and Cressida,"* p. 117.
35. E.W. Talbert, "The Purpose and Technique of Jonson's *Poetaster,*" *SP*, XLII (April 1945), p. 251.
36. It is, however, not possible to say whether the critical interest of these plays was determined by "the theatre for which they were written or whether they were presented by the Children of the Revels because they had been so written." (Wallace A. Bacon, p. 134)
37. See Herford and Simpson, vol. II, p. 64.
38. See D.A. Scheve, "Jonson's *Volpone* and Traditional Fox Lore,"

RES, New Ser., I (1950), pp. 242-44.

39. In Jonson's Epigram LXXXV (Herford and Simpson, vol. VIII, p. 55) the hawk is described as a bird sacred to Apollo, since it pursues the truth, strikes at ignorance, and makes the fool its quarry.
40. See Jonas A. Barish, "The Double Plot in *Volpone*," *MP*, LI (1953-54), pp. 83-101.
41. A possible reason for this change in Jonson's artistic strategy could be found in Jonson's disapproval of mere variety. He seems to have felt that mere variety or novelty was a sign of luxurious decadence.
42. L.A. Beaurline, "Ben Jonson and the Illusion of Completeness," *PMLA*, vol. 34. (1969), p. 58.
43. Edward B. Partridge, *The Broken Comapss*, p. 162.
44. L.C. Knights, *Drama and Society in the Age of Jonson*, p. 207.
45. See Hugh Kenner, "Art in a Closed Field," *VQR*, XXXVIII (1962), pp. 597-613.
46. L.A. Beaurline, p. 53.
47. W.A. Bacon, p. 145.
48. Edward B. Partridge attempts a satisfactory explanation of the unity of the last plays, barring *The Devil is an Ass*, in terms of image clusters. See *The Broken Compass*, pp. 178-212.
49. William Archer, *The Old Drama and the New*, p. 81.
50. Edmund Wilson, "Morose Ben Jonson," in Jonas A. Barish, p. 62.
51. See Harold F. Brooks, "The Name of Action in *Komos*."
52. L.J. Potts, *Comedy*, p. 117.

"A New Sufficient Play": *Bartholomew Fair*

If we were to add yet another to Polonius's list of hybrid dramatic forms, we might call *Bartholomew Fair* a holiday play, topical satire, satirical festive comedy, and 'comedy of vapours.' In this lengthy rubric lies the source of the play's richness. In Jonson's own description, however, it is "a new sufficient play" ('The Indvction,' l. 81)

Bartholomew Fair was written when Jonson's mind had reached the peak of its maturity. The play was produced at the Hope on "the one and thirtieth day of *Octob.* 1614." ('The Indvction,' l. 68) But, surprisingly enough, it was not included in the Folio of 1616.[1] It is generally felt that Jonson did not have sufficient time to prepare the play accurately for the press. But *Bartholomew Fair*, we may say, was deliberately omitted from the Folio inasmuch as its implications go far beyond those of the earlier plays. It is clear that Jonson, in the four years since *The Alchemist* (1610), had begun to move into a new comic world wherein he was prone to give more concession to the popular taste than he did before. He creates in *Bartholomew Fair* a world into which he infuses more of sympathy, tolerance and humanity than it is usually acknowledged he ever possessed.

Bartholomew Fair was written three years after *Catiline* (1611) which was an unmistakable failure.[2] Keenly disappointed at its cold reception Jonson "had bitterly resented the rebuff and appealed to the judgement of the reading public, with surly assurances of its incompetence to judge."[3] All the same, the three intervening years seemed to have completely allayed his rancour. Being too self-confident to distrust his art, Jonson quickly changed his estimate of the public. He became aware of the "jig-given times" in which he was living. Besides, there was an assuaging influence on him. His recent masques *Challenge at Tilt* (December 27, 1613) and *Irish Masque* (December 29, 1613) were so well liked that the latter was repeated on January 3, 1614. So he was now in a cheerful mood.

Naturally Jonson was disposed to meet his unruly audience in a pleasant fashion. He was ready to give them as much as they wanted, instead of as much as they ought to want, and also to resent no man's disapproval. 'The Indvction' to the play announces the author's changed disposition. He no longer brands his public, in an armed prologue as ignorant enemies of art if they find his play dull. He no longer swears the play was good "and if you like it you may." Instead, he says "I'le be iudg'd by you, Gentlemen, now," (l. 30) and further categorically declares:

> euery person here, have his or their free-will of censure, to like or dislike at their owne charge, the *Author* hauing now departed with his right: It shall bee lawfull for any man to iudge his six pen'orth . . . to the value of his place; prouided alwaies his place get not aboue his wit. (ll. 85-91)

Nevertheless, lest the character of his art, which on the face of it bears so largely the character of a holiday riot of the comic and satiric Muse, should be misconstrued, Jonson is extremely careful in introducing the play. Despite his strong desire to give his audience what they want, he postulates that they shall not expect from him what they would from a raree-show. Therefore, with any amount of ingenuity and tact he makes the 'stage-keeper' apprise the audience of these limitations on his part:

> But for the whole *Play,* will you ha' the truth on't? . . . Hee has not hit the humors, he do's not know 'hem; hee has not conuers'd with the *Bartholomew*-birds, as they say; hee has ne're a Sword, and Buckler man in his *Fayre*, nor a little *Dauy*, to take toll o' the Bawds there, as in my time, nor a *Kind-heart*, if any bodies teeth should chance to ake in his *Play.* Nor a Iugler with a wel-educated Ape, to come ouer the chaine, for the *King* of *England*, and backe againe for the *Prince*, and sit still on his arse for the *Pope*, and the *King* of *Spaine*! None o' these fine sights! Nor has he the Canuas-cut i' the night, for a Hobby-horseman to creepe in to his she-neighbour, and take his leap, there! Nothing! ('The Indvction,' ll. 6-22)

Thus, *Bartholomew Fair* came to be composed as a sort of compromise in which "it is covenanted and agreed, by and betweene the parties," the 'Spectators' and 'Hearers' on the one party and the author of *Bartholomew Fair* on the other,

> to remaine in the places, their money or friends haue put them in, with patience, for the space of two houres and an halfe, and somewhat more. In which time the *Author* promiseth to present them by vs, with *a new sufficient Play* [my italics] called BARTHOLOMEW FAYRE, merry, and as full of noise, as sport: made to delight all, and to offend none: Prouided they haue either, the wit, or the

honesty to thinke well of themselues.[4] ('The Indvction,' ll. 78- 85)

It is this consciousness that he was attempting something still original, experimental and difficult at this mid-Jacobean time that explains Jonson's insistence that his play was not to be judged by popular Elizabethan criteria, which have "stood still, these fiue and twentie, or thirtie yeeres." ('The Indvction,' ll. 108-9)

It is not for nothing that Jonson called *Bartholomew Fair* "a new sufficient play." It is daringly 'new' in that it is the first of its kind among Jonson's plays. It is purely Jonsonian. Absolutely original in conception[5] and construction alike, it stands a little apart from the other comedies of Jonson. No doubt, there are some clear points of resemblance between this and the earlier comedies in point of the topsy-turvy social world presented. But the presentation of the social world in it is intensified and the terms of its presentation invariably engage new worlds of experience hardly admitted earlier. Although stylistic affinities link this play with the great comedies and with the earlier plays, several important advances open into novel forays.

Bartholomew Fair is 'new' in its fresh subject and novel scheme. The Fair itself is the true subject to which is closely related all the bewildering multiplicity of details. With its multitude of interests and attractions, the fair itself "provides the perfect environment for Jonson's genius."[6] The Fair consists of a noisy and colourful mass of booths for the roast pig and toy sellers, the gingerbread woman and ballad-singers, the quack doctors, freaks and showmen—all with the single ambition of getting as much money as possible out of customers' pockets. There is neither a hero nor a dominant character. But the Fair bringing, as it does, all this motley multitude together provides a real unity and tone as the Forest of Arden does in *As You Like It*. The fair is a kind of Arden, where, in spite of or because of various pieces of knavery and deviousness, the principal characters learn something about themselves and refresh and renew their human resources.

As regards the scheme, Jonson for once seems to approach "the art which conceals art," which is difficult even for the most masterful and self-conscious of artists to practise. Although Jonson's shaping and contriving hand is still active, here it operates less obtrusively if more subtly. However admirable might be the method in the greatest of his plots, it is somewhat too easily described or formulated. But there is no trace of artifice in the artistry of *Bartholomew Fair*. Jonson brings all the resources of his mature mastery to bear on a problem of writing a masterpiece while virtually dispensing with a strong main plot and one or two major protagonists. Again, the lines of cleavage between the tricksters and the dupes, which so largely determine the structure of Jonsonian comedy, are here managed most adroitly. The comic results come about inevitably as natural incidents of the Fair, without the intervention of a professional contriver – Brainworm or Buffone, Mosca or Face.

Bartholomew Fair is also new in that it is more inclusive than any of Jonson's plays. Thoroughly diverse with symbolically infinite scope, the play itself moves steadily toward greater expansiveness and inclusiveness. Characters, actions and interests are all multiplied. Never before such a number of characters has so crowded the stage. Besides being a fair at Smithfield, Bartholomew Fair provides a symbolic locale. As suggested in 'The Indvction' (ll. 113-34), the fair stands for human life as well as the world of comic drama. The people of the Fair are described in such a manner as to give the impression that they were the characters of a play.

Bartholomew Fair is 'new' too in its tone which is more extrovert and happier than that of the foregoing comedies which are closed away almost within doors. In conformity with Jonson's promise in his Induction, the play "has the air of a kind of saturnalia of the comic muse – a true holiday play in keeping with its holiday theme."[7] The satirist in Jonson is not wholly absent even here but he is very much in holiday mood. For all its touches of satire, it presents an affectionate and expansive picture of London at play. The play stretches itself into a vaster background and breathes more of open air than it is common in Jonson. It is the most expansive of his mature comedies and the most English in atmosphere. Conceived in the spirit of rollicking mirth, and executed with lively energy, it is the most high-spirited and hilarious of his comedies. Vibrating with life, the play is full of colour, bubbling with boisterous spirits and the zestful rendering of London low-life. Jonson gives free and wholehearted expression to that extraordinary zest for life which, as with Dickens, is as much part of his comic vision as the satirical moralist's scourging of affectation and excess. A broad Dutch painting of the humours of a London carnival, an air of relaxation blows through it as in *Midsummer Night's Dream.* The play provokes laughter at every point but there comes a time towards the end when one almost sympathises with the characters.

Then, *Bartholomew Fair* is "sufficient" in that it is a perfect fulfilment of Jonson's dramatic art marking the highest development of the 'Comedy of Humours.' It was written at a time when Jonson was in a state of such lively energy that there was no danger of the playwright being overwhelmed by the critic. We may justly consider it to be the most perfect representative of Jonson's characteristic comedy. A finished performance of the 'Comedy of Humours,' *Bartholomew Fair* represents the culmination of Jonson's dramatic art.

The most concretely realistic piece of portraiture Jonson ever did, *Bartholomew Fair* is all 'deedes, and language, such as men do vse.' It shows admirably how Jonson could make the commonplace artistic by furnishing a veritable picture of an actual cloth fair.

The play appears to be a transcript of real life. Jonson seems to have been attracted towards the subject of the Fair as a study in vulgar realism. This is made clear to us in 'The Indvction' where Jonson cajoles the audience through the Stage-keeper, saying that

> the whole *Play* . . . is like to be a very conceited scuruy one, in plaine English. When 't comes to the *Fayre*, once: you were e'en as good goe to *Virginia*, for any thing there is of *Smith-field.* (ll. 6-11)

Bartholomew Fair may justly be regarded as a unique example of Jonson's 'pure realism.' Further removed from his classical models, both incidents and characters in this play are freer from imitation of Plautus or Aristophanes than those in other comedies of Jonson. Most local in atmosphere, the play is a realistic portrayal of the annual Fair[8] held at Smithfield, London, on every twentyfifth day of August. It shows how well was Jonson acquainted with every corner and habit of Smithfield.

Stinking and dirty and populated by rogues and cheats, the Fair provides a typically realistic locale. The Fair is at once the scene and subject of the play. The visitors to the Fair—the clothiers, toysellers, gingerbread and pig women, ballad singers, cut-purses, freaks, quack doctors, Puritans and showmen—still more numerous than the clients of the Alchemist—are closely studied from life, and are representative of the various classes and disposition of the civic world.

It looks as though *Bartholomew Fair* was a dramatisation of 'conny-catching' material of the Elizabethan and Jacobean prose pamphlets by Greene, Nashe and Dekker. Such episodes as the cutting of Bartholomew Cokes' purses, the tobacco taking, the wandering madman's appearances, while also displaying London's low-life, demonstrate the criminal techniques and the depravity of petty criminals, prostitutes and fairground booth holders. Besides, "the densely physical, strongly visual language of the low-life characters gives conviction to episodes which are, plainly enough, absolutely conventional to the 'genre' and had been the stock-in-trade of the pamphleteers before Elizabeth died."[9]

The play furnishes a lively picture, the hurly-burly and rough roaring merriment of the Fair inimitable in its varied realism. The scenes are typical of London low-life compressed and heightened as it naturally would be in the annual merry-making of Bartholomew Fair. For instance, we find Leatherhead, the horse-courser and Joan Trash, the ginger-bread woman, indulging in quarrelling. Leatherhead complains:

> Doe you heare, Sister *Trash*, lady o' the Basket? Sit farther with your ginger-bread-progeny there, and hinder not the prospect of my shop, or I'll ha' it proclaim'd i' the *Fayre*, what stuffe they are made on.

Trash immediately retorts:

> Why, what stuffe are they made on, Brother *Leatherhead*? nothing but what's wholesome, I assure you.

But Leatherhead brags out:

> Yes stale bread, rotten egges, musty ginger, and dead honey, you know. (II, ii, 2-10)

Witnessing this spirited quarrelling we feel as if we were in a busy bustling fair.

The intensely popular nature of the subject of the play seems to have dictated to Jonson that it should be a prose play 'par excellence.' The play is written wholly in prose remarkable for its clearness and flexibility. It is admirably suited to the different speakers and imitative of the manners of the time. It is fully animated, idiomatic and precise. And, what is more, "there is music in Jonson's prose, but it is a music of brusque dissonances and irregular rhythms, which those addicted to the clear, regular, euphonious music of Shakespeare must sensitize themselves in new ways to hear rightly."[10]

Jonson had a first-hand knowledge of the Fair. He had gone to the real Bartholomew Fair a great many times and had taken a vast and critical delight in its goings-on, enjoying its dirt, its noise, its vulgarity and its bounce. Hence he could heartily enter into the characters and talk their very language. He had an intimate knowledge of those characters and of their manner of life as well as of their speech. Naturally enough, the dialogue is a perfect dictionary of technical speech of all sorts, from the slang of the horse-courser and of the ginger-bread-woman to the cant of the Puritan.

The language of each speaker is magnificently alive. The local life of each speech is found in its colloquial rhythm as well as in its imagery. We find Leatherhead, the Hobby-Horse-seller and toy man, make business crying out:

> what do you lacke, Gentlemen, what is 't you lacke? a fine Horse? a Lyon? a Bull? a Beare? a Dog, or a Cat? an excellenct fine *Bartholomew*-bird? or an instrument? what is't you lacke? (II, v, 4-7)

Thus the horse-courser talks so exactly like a horse-courser down to the minute jargon of his trade. Ursula, the pig-woman, enters complaining the hardships of her vocation:

> Fie vpon't: who would weare out their youth, and prime thus, in roasting of pigges, that had any cooler vocation? Hell's a kind of cold cellar to't, a very fine vault, O'my conscience! (II, ii, 42-45)

In Busy's talk the typical puritan cant is vibrating. He reacts to Mrs. Littlewit's visiting the Fair to eat roast pig:

> Verily, for the disease of longing, it is a disease, a carnall disease, or appetite, incident to women; and as it is carnall and incident, it is naturall, very naturall: Now pigge, it is a meat, and a meat that is nourishing, and may be longed for, and so consequently eaten; it may be eaten; very exceeding well eaten; but in the *Fayre*, and as a *Bartholomew*-pig, it cannot be eaten, for the very calling it a *Bartholomew*-pigge and to eat it so, is a spice of Idolatry, and you make the *Fayre*, no better then one of the high *Places*. This I take it, is the state of the question. A high place. (I, vi, 48-57)

In this long set speech the mind of the Puritan is clearly expressed. As in the hands of Racine and the mature Shakespeare, here "the speaker appears to utter his mind directly, so that the speech mirrors the mental process as it develops."[11] Thus, in the words of Jonson himself, "the language" employed in the play "sauours of *Smithfield*, the Booth, and Pigbroth, or prophanenesse." ('The Indvction,' ll. 150-51)

Jonson, in this manner, presents a most vivid picture of contemporary London life, providing an extremely rich field for the study of English social history. Vibrating with the very life of Bartholomew Fair, the play has 'Hogarth-come to life' in it. The author, as it were, takes the reader to the Fair. And "part of the pleasure for the first audience must have been that shock of recognition as they saw their own great fair put vividly and realistically upon the stage of Hope Theatre at Bankside in October 1614, only a couple of months after the Fair itself had been held as usual at Smithfield."[12]

Bartholomew Fair sufficiently answers Jonson's intention 'to sport with humane follies.' Jonson, by now, not only collected a great many more things to be satiric about but knew much better how to achieve the kind of realistic satirical comedy he had been trying to write in 1598. Besides, the Fair itself—with its varied gross appeals to the senses, its wealth of physical detail, its cheats and dupes, its bright shells and hollow centres, its dialects and slang—offers Jonson tremendous scope for his satire. Exasperated by the demands of the groundlings and exhausted by the rivalry of Marston, Dekker and other poetasters and professionals, Jonson, though committed himself 'to sport with humane follies' only, was led to adopt the idiom of the Silver Age, and to address himself in the tone of Martial and Tacitus. And, in *Volpone,* the 'follies' attacked almost border on 'tragedies.'

But the satire in *Bartholomew Fair* is not that found in Jonson's previous work. In the earlier plays he lapsed not infrequently into long descriptions and minute character-analysis as he defined the follies he sought to expose with a scholar's exactness. The satire in the present play does not brag itself. For, the dramatist is now more reticent and of better temper in the standing matters of quarrel with his public. This is evident not only from the indenture between him and the public set forth in 'The Indvction' but also from Justice Overdo's general invitation to supper at the close of the play:

> I inuite you home, with mee to my house, to supper: I will haue none to feare to go along, for my intents are *'Ad correctionem, non ad destructionem; Ad aedificandum non ad diruendum*: so lead on.
> (V, vi, 110-13)

All the same, there is an earnest attempt to correct the extravagant 'humours' and reconcile the contentions natures of men. The play is at once a satire on the Puritans and on the stage trashery they condemned. Jonson had dealt with their financial and political aspirations in *The Alchemist.* Now he fastens his attention upon the simpler unpolitical ambitions of the Puritan brethren. In the figures and actions of Win-the-Fight, Dame Purecraft, and Zeal-of-the-land Busy are forcefully represented, hypocrisy, gluttony, superstitiousness, and contempt for classical antiquity, or for any learning other than that of scriptural revelation.

Win-the-Fight is hypocritical, vain and frivolous. She is so well-versed in hypocrisy that she tells her husband that she has no need to cut her laces in order to play the hypocrite. She says:

> No I'll not make me vnready for it. I can be *Hypocrite* enough, though I were neuer so straight lac'd. (I, v, 160-61)

At the Fair she turns her thoughts even in the direction of lechery. She easily adapts herself to the idea of taking twenty lovers "and be honest still, that were fine sport." (IV, v, 44)

Dame Purecraft, the sanctified widow, is superstitious, hypocritical and avaricious. When she discovers Quarlous, disguised as a madman, she thinks in terms of marrying him because she has been told by the 'cunning-men' that she must marry a madman or run mad herself. But unable to secure the madman through her hypocritical piety, she tells him about the wealth she has amassed through her dexterous practice as a "wilfull holy widow" (V, ii, 48-74)

Busy is made to display himself as the most arrant hypocrite of them all. The gentleman who considers eating pig in the Fair to be 'a carnall disease' immediately changes his mind, himself smitten with the savoury temptation of pig at the Fair. He says that the pig

> may be eaten, and in the *Fayre* . . . in a Booth, the tents of the wicked, the place is not much, not very much, we may be religious in midst of the prophane, so it be eaten with a reformed mouth, with *sobriety*, and humblenesse. (I, vi, 70-74)

We find Busy in the Fair in pompous orations against every frivolity. To him long hair is 'an Ensine of pride, a banner'; a bottle of ale is a 'drinke of Satan's, a diet-drinke of Satan's' and tobacco is a smoke used to keep people "in mist and error." He reaches the peak of his oratory in his blatant denunciation of the puppet play. To him Leatherhead, the puppetmaster, is "the proud Nebuchadnezzar of Faire" because he sets up idols for the "children to fall downe to, and worship." (III, vi, 56-59) Thus, Jonson's satiric lash descends with full force upon Busy.

The plot of *Bartholomew Fair* is so organised as to expose implicitly not merely the hypocrisy, gluttony and avarice of the Puritans, the folly of the obviously foolish Cokes, and Littlewits, but the more harmful folly of the lawgivers – Wasp, Busy and Overdo. Wasp is exposed as a master without self-mastery, Busy as a preacher without sense or sincerity, and Overdo as a judge without judiciousness or tolerance. The play ends with every one chastened by experience but not otherwise punished.

Then, *Bartholomew Fair* presents precisely such 'persons' as Jonson's typical '*Comoedie* would chuse.' The characters "are not mere warped or eccentric individuals, like the 'Humours,' more or less at odds with their *milieu,* but the very growth of the soil."[13] What supplants 'Humours' approximately is 'vapours' which is used sixty-nine times in the play.[14] Jonson himself suggests this in a marginal note:

> Here they continue their game of *vapours,* which is *non sense.* Euery man to oppose the last man that spoke: whethe(r) it concern'd him, or no. (IV, iv, 27-28)

First of all, the characters in *Bartholomew Fair* are remarkable for their very unusual great number. It contains a greater number of characters than have before or after been brought together within the compass of one single piece.[15] Nevertheless, all the personages are drawn with painstaking exactness as well as with unflagging animation. Almost every character is worked out with elaborate detail. They are admirably studied and grouped together with consummate insight into dramatic effect.

Closely studied from life, most of the characters surpass in keenness of observation, and wealth and precision of detail any previous creation of Jonson's. The portraits in the previous plays are incisive, but in *Bartholomew Fair* they are made more vivid and animating through careful attention to individual frailties. Naturally they are richer in characteristic traits and more intimately true to their place and time than the characters in the earlier plays. To take but a few examples, Bartholomew Cokes is a better country gull than Stephen who is almost a caricature. Busy is a finished picture whereas Ananias is a lively sketch. Surly, the honest man, cannot be compared in significance with the equally luckless detector of 'enormities,' Overdo. The women characters are no less real. The puritanical Dame Purecraft and the bestial Ursula stand out clearly and there is plenty of humour in the drawing of both Win-the-fight and Alice.

Regarding the 'profit and delight' that the 'Comedy of Humours' should provide, *Bartholomew Fair* reveals a new maturity in the playwright. Jonson's primary purpose here is not, as Gregory Smith thinks, "to convey the impression of a fair with its bustling confused humanity."[16] Jonson certainly has a more significant purpose. With the maturity of mind now attained, he appears to be interested in projecting, of course, quite implicitly, his own view of life. Towards this end the setting of the Fair seems particularly to be a happy choice. For, it provides an exquisite image which dramatizes the feeling Jonson had about life.

He projects a profound view of life through Troubleall's perpetual question – "Have you a warrant?" He goes on asking others:

> I question nothing, pardon me. I do only hope you haue warrant, for what you doe. . . . (IV, i, 14-15)

To witness one or two encounters of Troubleall, a former clerk who has been dismissed from his post by Adam Overdo and has run mad upon the conceit, first with Edgeworth:

> TRO: Whither goe you? Where's your warrant?
> EDG: Warrant for what, Sir?
> TRO: For what you goe about. . . . (IV, ii, 2-4)

Then with Quarlous and Winwife:

> TRO: Haue you any warrant for this, Gentlemen?
> QVAR: WIN – w. Ha!
> TRO: There must be a warrant had, beleeue it.
> WIN – w: For what?
> TRO: For whatsoeuer it is, any thing indeede, no matter what.
> (IV, iii, 71-76)

What is more, Troubleall insists that the warrant has to be signed by none other than Overdo:

> If you haue Iustice Overdoo's warrant 'tis well: you are safe; that is the warrant of warrants. I 'le not giue this button, for any mans warrant else. (IV, i, 19-21)

Jonson, then, through Troubleall is asking a most devastating question "where is your warrant?" That is, by whose warrant, whose permission you do what you do? In other words, Jonson is questioning as to who is responsible for the folly and evil we see around us? He gives the answer too. Since the warrant has got to be signed by Overdo, who symbolises a well-intentioned man, we ourselves are responsible for the folly and evil in the world. And we must search our hearts and minds for the warrant.

Besides, through the characterisation of Justice Overdo, Jonson seems to warn us that even the best of warrants is not in itself sufficient to insure right action in the world. When, at last, Justice Overdo discovers and prepares to judge the 'enormities' he has observed, he is simply dumbfounded and humbled to discover the respectable Mrs. Littlewit to be a bawd, his favourite Edgeworth a cutpurse and, to cap it all, his own wife a drunken, incipient whore. Caught up in the vicious circle he himself is beaten. Thus, the discoverer and chastiser of enormities is brought to a realization that what he calls 'enormities' are what other people call life. As Anne Barton rightly observes, Overdo "appears as a refugee from another kind of contemporary comedy, one in which the disguised hero acts as a surrogate for the dramatist himself, guiding the action cunningly towards a last scene in which confusion will be reduced to order, vices punished, goodness rewarded and society left purged and regenerate."[17] Overdo, therefore, capitulates not to the logic of a puppet but to the good sense of Quarlous:

> . . . remember you are but *Adam,* Flesh, and blood! You haue your frailty, forget your other name of *Ouerdoo*, . . . (V, vi, 96-98)

Thus, Jonson leaves us with the reflection that we are 'but Adam, Flesh, and blood.' "We have entered, in the Fair, an underworld of amoral human energies, and brought back the sense that, in a strict count, none does offend, none, more than another, and that the recognition of that fact is a more secure basis for an un-self-righteous morality than those moral schemes which working 'a priori,' fail to come to terms with flesh and blood."[18]

Jonson himself who had travelled through the carnival of life was no less persuaded than Overdo that the world was full of folly and self-deception and knavery. But by the time he came to write *Bartholomew Fair* his own self-righteousness seemed to have begun to weaken. Consequent on this phenomenon Jonson arrives at a philosophical tolerance in *Bartholomew Fair*. He seems to have realized that life is full of irony and the good-natured get into as much trouble as the rascals. He, however, achieves a kind of moral health through making Overdo emerge triumphant in good-natured humility. He is, as Quarlous says "*Adam*, Flesh, and blood" (V, vi, 97) and this truth is brought home to him in the Fair. No doubt, Overdo will certainly stick to his guns but his vision will be clearer. Jonson's ultimate message is that compassion may, after all, become 'a justice.' Humiliated Adam Overdo confesses:

> I will be more tender hereafter. I see compassion may become a *Iustice*, though it be a weaknesse, I confesse; and neerer a vice, then vertue. (IV, i, 83-84)

Thus the speciality of *Bartholomew Fair* is that, unlike other plays of Jonson, it not merely ridicules man's eccentricities and castigates him for his follies, but also celebrates man's humanity and reconciles him to his limitations. At the end, each of us could join all the fallen in saying 'I too am *Adam*, Flesh and blood.'

Further, a celebration of a rite of summer on a large scale, *Bartholomew Fair* has an infinite scope for mirth. Jonson is here in the best of humours. His 'whip of steel' is laid aside for gusts of Rabelaisian laughter. The play largely bears the character of a holiday riot of the comic muse. It gives us a conception of the Elizabethan forerunner of a present London bank-holiday.

A festive comedy, the play has infinite deal of humour. The humour of incident and action is as delicious as the humour of characterisation. The very sight of the laden Numps brings roars of laughter to the audience. The perpetual punishing of the innocent Justice is excessively mirth-making. The constant coming and going of the afflicted Troubleall with his perpetual question, 'where is your warrant?,' is amusing on the stage. The overthrow of Busy by the argumentative puppet is delightfully effective. Then, Ursula, who is "all fire and fat," watering the ground with her sweat as she goes about "like a garden pot," causes much amusement.

Again, for the most part, the play is given over to natural and rollicking fun – spontaneous and varied. This varies from the rough horse-play of Wasp's beating the Justice and the tragical destruction of Mrs. Overdo's French hood, to the highly respectable wooing of Grace Wellborn. The action moves from one side-splitting situation to another. The project of making a wealthy match devised by Winwife and Quarlous in pursuit of which they are friendly rivals is highly comical. The very visit of Cokes and his party and of Busy and his party to the Fair provokes laughter. Overdo himself, seeing to discover the 'enormities' of the Fair, offers any amount of pleasure. The puppet show at the close contributes much to the comic effect of the play. We may even take Bartholomew Fair as we would take Bunyan's Vanity Fair as a miscellany of entertaining rogues and strange toys for afternoon pastime. Thus, the moving panorama of the Fair with its entertainments and its 'enormities,' the bustling action and the crowd of first-rate character parts, all combine to make it good theatre.

Even from the point of view of its plot-structure, *Bartholomew Fair* strikes a new note. We find in its structure an interesting variation on the quickening and lengthening plot which we find in *The Alchemist* and in much of *Volpone*. Jonson begins in *Bartholomew Fair* with what are to be components in the action, but are not at first combined in a discernible plot. Jonson then sets going a whirlpool of action which they are more and more drawn into until they are all grouped round in it. What Jonson, as Chaucer in the arrangement of the portraits in the 'Prologue,' does in the construction of *Bartholomew Fair* "is to get away from 'mathematic form,' from the simply logical and systematic, so as to create original form, living and in the full sense artistic."[19]

Bartholomew Fair is a panoramic structure. It is looser but more comprehensive than Jonson's other great comedies. Structurally, it "sustains the most delicate balance between order and chaos, between form and a seemingly undisciplined flow which sets out to imitate the random, haphazard nature of life itself, while maintaining an artistic control so tight that no episode, no character, however minor, can be removed without causing irreparable damage to the whole."[20] It is interesting to note that the sheer abundance which was characteristic of much popular Elizabethan comedy is combined in *Bartholomew Fair* with an extraordinary discipline. Though there are three separable intrigues in motion in *Epicoene,* they all have a similar pattern of development and are under the control of three intiguers. But, five or six actions seem always to be ripening simultaneously in *Bartholomew Fair.* There are more than a dozen intriguers and no single pattern of development will fit all the kinds of action which the fair breeds. The play's principal virtue lies in its controlled complexity, in the truly remarkable variety and richness of character and incident that Jonson has managed to shape into a unified work of art.

Notwithstanding the diversity, the looseness of structure and the complexity, there are evidences of careful workmanship in *Bartholomew Fair.* It is often repeated that the play is practically or entirely without a plot.[21] If plot is to be conceived of in a broader sense as "the organising principle that accounts for and connects the separate parts of the play in the actual form in which they appear,"[22] then, we have a plot in *Bartholomew Fair.* The people who make up the fair and, consequently, the special dramatic world in which the action takes place, and the outsiders who visit this world constitute the plot of the play.

Also, it is not as though the play wanted 'nothing but a plan.' It does have a definite plan. The structure of the play appears to be casual but the underlying design is always clear. It is slow to reveal itself—the pieces appear at first without relation to a structure and then as more and more they are set in motion, their vicissitudes build up into a plot of design.

The first Act is essentially expository. It is almost a prologue to the four acts that follow. It introduces one segment of the large cast of characters—the uxorious Littlewit with his harmless wife and her hypocrite mother, the cynics, Quarlous and Winwife, and the two law-givers, Wasp, the tutor, and Zeal-of-the-land Busy, the hypocritical Puritan. Though these are already united through kinship, friendship, business, or Puritanical religious zeal, they are really linked by one thing—their strong desire to go to the Fair. They are presented in ones and twos. The act culminates in the entrance of Busy.

Justice Overdo, who enters at the beginning of the second Act, provides a link between the first and second Acts. In the second Act we move to the Fair. The characters of Act I enter the microcosm of the Fair which represents a different moral world or level of reality. The people of the Fair, though poor, dishonest, ill-educated, and less restrained than the visitors, are more frank about their physical needs and their dishonest way of life. At the centre of the Fair and of the comedy stands Ursula, the pig woman. As the comedy progresses, the people of Act I meet and mingle with the folk of the Fair. As the action develops, frank animal appetite reveals the true nature of the visitors' spiritual and intellectual shortcomings of hypocrisy, folly, and pride.

The puppet play, "Hero and Leander," in Act V forms the climax of the continuously developing action. The basic function of this play-within-the-play is to bring all the characters together. As J.J. Enck has pointed out, "the puppet performance has a logical, almost inevitable, place in the progression of *Bartholomew Fair*," and "rounds out the play in exhibiting what the Smithfield men and women are not."[23] The dramatic function of the puppet play is to present a further level of reality which reflects, and distorts, the preceding one. The distorting mirror of the puppet play reduces life to miniature size, as the 'reality' of the play-world opens out to a further level of illusion that makes no claim at all to being human. "The audience is made to identify with the actors who are watching the puppet play because they share the experience of being spectators and because the puppets, speaking doggerel verse and like bad actors offering no illusion of life, make the world around them on a stage appear more real."[24]

The play ends genially. The two authoritarian figures, the Puritan and the Justice are discomfited. With his prodigious rhetorical tirade against the theatre, Busy is outmanoeuvred in debate by Lantern's puppet, and 'retires crestfallen.' Overdo is silenced when one of the unmasked 'prostitutes' in the Fair turns out to be his own wife. The play comes to a close as Overdo invites all the characters back to his house for supper. The end of the play is good-humoured and forgiving, prolonging the recurring holiday-spirit of the piece. Thus, an analysis of the structure shows Jonson's mastery of dramatic design in which one plane of reality is ingeniously enclosed within another.

Both on the linear and the thematic levels the play has a unity of its own kind. Ursula's booth, characterised by large congregation of people, bawdry and thievery, huge consumption of roast pigs and ale, vapours, enormity, justice, folly, pissing and the burning of the pig-women, is the linear centre of the play. Once the rogues and gulls enter the Fair all virtually converge in Ursula's booth before they appear anywhere else. The booth is headquarters for Edgeworth, the cutpurse, and Whit and his associate pimps. Also, it is the sole object of Mrs. Littlewit's desires as well as the longings of Busy, although he will not admit it. In this manner, the action becomes all of a piece in Ursula's booth.

The thematic centre of the play, however, is the 'warrant' which the madman, Troubleall, demands of almost all the characters. Troubleall's main function is to trouble everybody with his embarrassing question, 'Have you a warrant for what you doe?' He is obsessed with the necessity of documentary sanction for even the slightest action so much so he

> . . . will not eate a crust nor drinke a little, nor make him in his apparell, ready. His wife, Sirreuerence, cannot get him make his water, or shift his shirt, without his warrant. (IV, i, 59- 61)

In the absurd 'humour' of Troubleall we have a grand, extravagant comic conceit which serves as the most significant unifying device in the play. Troubleall intervenes crucially in several of the threads of plot, settling the dispute between Grace's lovers, freeing Overdo and Busy from the stock, and enabling Quarlous to cheat Overdo and marry the rich widow Purecraft.

The greatest achievement of the 'Comedy of Humours,' *Bartholomew Fair* thus represents the culmination of Jonson's dramatic art. The play is undoubtedly a supreme effort of Jonson's dramatic genius, a masterpiece where the richest humour and most vivid realism combine with brilliant satire and profound view of life. Furthermore, the vitality and the exuberance native to the fair itself combined with tolerance, sympathy and humanity that lie at the heart of the play make it unique among Jonson's comedies. In *The Alchemist* we see the finished artist in comedy emerging, and with *Bartholomew Fair* his mastery is complete.

Bartholomew Fair may yield its fruits slowly but the longer one dwells on it the more richly one is rewarded. The wealth of incident and character makes the play rather difficult to read and follow, but once the play is put on the stage the difficulty disappears. The whole play is full of colour, movement and excitement and it comes wonderfully alive on the stage. Perhaps, it would be even more successful as a film. However, through its sensuous diction, the individual syntax and rhythm of its speech, and the action which is rendered at once naturalistic in detail and extravagant in effect, the world of the Fair comes pungently alive to us over these three hundred and fifty years. The play, thus, remains the most signal triumph of Jonson's difficult and original dramatic art.

NOTES

1. In 1616, the first volume of Jonson's 'Works' (he himself called them so) was published, an admiraby printed edition containing the best of his plays and masks, his epigrams, and his poems, *The Forest.*
2. *Catiline* failed chiefly because Jonson worked out the play on the

assumption that like himself the public was deeply interested in classical archaeology. He had conceived the masses to be hearers and readers "extraordinary." But they proved themselves very "ordinary."

3. Herford and Simpson, vol. II, p. 132.
4. The manner of this genial compact and generous appeal must have gone a long way in conciliating the goodwill of the audience, besides exciting their curiosity.
5. C.R. Baskervill questioning the play's originality ("Some Parallels to *Bartholomew Fair*," *MP*, VI (July 1908) pp. 109-27), traces the main motive and situation of *Bartholomew Fair* in the old play, *Sir Thomas More*. But, since *Sir Thomas More* was not published till 1844, it is not likely that Jonson knew the play. However, for the cutpurse scenes in the play Jonson may have been indebted to Shakespeare's *The Winter's Tale*. Shakespeare's Autolycus belongs to the same general class of rogues like Lanthom Leatherhead of *Bartholomew Fair*. Behind both Autolycus and Leatherhead are Greene's 'conny-catching' pamphlets.
6. Wallace Bacon, "The Magnetic Field: The Structure of Jonson's Comedies," *HLQ*, XIX (1956), p. 145.
7. Herford and Simpson, vol. II, p. 133.
8. The Fair, a chartered resort for all the gross pleasures of the capital, was founded in the 12th century and its decay and final dissolution took place 730 years later. Morley's *Memorials of Bartholomew Fair* and Walfords *Fairs Past and Present* are useful to get at the history of the Bartholomew Fair
9. Brian Gibbons, *Jacobean City Comedy,* p. 184.
10. Jonas A. Barish, "Baroque Prose in the Theatre: Ben Jonson," *PMLA*, LXXIII (1958), p. 195.
11. Harold F. Brooks, "Marlowe and Early Shakespeare," *Christopher Marlowe,* ed. Brian Morris (Mermaid Critical Commentaries), p. 85.
12. Michael Jamieson, ed., *Three Comedies* (A Penguin International Edition), 'Introduction,' p. 25.
13. Herford and Simpson, vol. II, p. 139.
14. See James Robinson, "*Bartholomew Fair*: Comedy of Vapors," *SEL*, I (1961), pp. 65-80.
15. There are thirty speaking characters besides many supernumeraries. The large number of characters in *Bartholomew Fair* has often been adversely commented on. But the popular London Fair could have hardly been presented with less. The reduction of characters, then, would be at the cost of the verisimilitude of the

play.

16. Gregory Smith, *Ben Jonson*, p. 94.
17. Anne Barton, p. 104.
18. E.A. Horsman, ed., *Bartholomew Fair* (The Revels Plays), 'Introduction,' p. xxviii.
19. Harold F. Brooks, *Chaucer's Pilgrims: The Artistic Order of the Portraits in the Prologue,* p. 57.
20. Anne Barton, p. 197.
21. See Henry Wells, *Elizabethan and Jacobean Playwrights*, pp. 55-66. T.M. Parrott and Robert Ball, *A Short View of Elizabethan Drama,* p. 143.
    Freda L. Townsend, *Apologie for "Bartholomew Fayre": The Art of Jonson's Comedies,* p. 73.
22. Richard Levin, "The Structure of *Bartholomew Fair,*" *PMLA*, LXXX (1965), p. 173.
23. J.J. Enck, *Ben Jonson and the Comic Truth*, p. 199.
24. J.E.M. Latham, "Form in *Bartholomew Fair,*" *English*, XXI (Spring 1972), p. 9.

Conclusion

A perfect expositor of the movement of the 'Angry Young Men' towards satirical and realistic portrayal of life in drama, Ben Jonson rebelled against the romantic excesses of the age. In the midst of that luxuriant romanticism he emerged essentially as a native classicist with the definite purpose of effecting a reform of theatrical taste and convention both by his precept and example on the lines of what he assimilated from the ancients. With his many-sided acquirements, embracing all that was best in the classical as well as in the contemporary writers, he was eminently fitted for the self-appointed task of reforming and regenerating the Elizabethan drama.

Strongly disapproving of the conventional notion of considering comedy and tragedy as fundamentally opposed to each other, Jonson came forward with his 'Comedy of Humours' which is a combination of the classical and native traditions in the theatre. Here the point to bear in mind is that Jonson chose to exploit the theory of 'humours,' ready to hand and familiar to his audience, in order to express his own theories of drama, and as he developed as a dramatist, the achievement of his plays transcended theoretical considerations more and more frequently.

Jonson's chief merit lies in drawing comedy from the improbable realms of romantic flights to the levels of ordinary existence—"deedes, and language such as men doe vse." He breathes an air of realism into his comedy by making the setting, incident, character, and dialogue contemporary with the times. Nonetheless, Jonson is not a literal-minded transcriber of mere fact. In his plays there is an interplay between realism and fantasy which gives them the unity and the universality of great art.

More than any contemporary playwright Jonson brilliantly succeeds in projecting 'an image of the times'—the theatrical world, the non-dramatic poetry, the court life, the scholarship and the spirit of the Renaissance, besides the variegated aspects of daily life—in his comedies. Yet, his vigorous intellectual grasp of the pageant of life combined with a trenchancy of language and control of dramatic form make his comedies appeal to all times. His plays, with all their powerful symbolic suggestions, come alive, or gain new life once they are experienced aesthetically.

Jonson also succeeds admirably well in his endeavour to make his comedy convey serious thought intermingled with an intelligent type of laughter, if not completely in his early plays but almost perfectly in his mature comedies. Achieving a harmonious fusion of 'profit and delight,' comedy in his hands becomes a perfect communication between the author and the audience. However, Jonson is neither a doughty champion of didacticism nor a conventional moralist, but essentially a comic dramatist using didactic theory for literary and dramatic purposes.

In keeping with his didactic attitude, Jonson is determined to "sport with humane follies" in his comedy. With his conception of satire as a medium for the essential dramatic art, Jonson stands apart from the formal satirists. Satire in his early plays is levelled mostly against individual vices and affectations. But, broadened in scope and increased in intensity, the satire in the middle and later plays is employed mainly against social vices—avarice, lechery, witchcraft and hypocritical puritanism—that were eating into the vitals of society of the day. Though all these vices are more vigorously and thoroughly satirised by Jonson than by others, he is unmistakably a comic artist. He works his satire into the character and the character into the plot so ingeniously that to remove satire is to remove plot and character. Jonson's relentlessness is, therefore, born of his intellectual uprightness as well as of his artistic integrity.

It is not Jonson's intention to body forth such full-blooded and lifelike personages as step out of the pages of Shakespeare, but "persons, such as (his characteristic) *Comoedie* would chuse" to depict, namely, fools, gallants, knaves, dupes and dupers, sharpers and schemers and loose women, in which attempt he astonishingly succeeds. In the study of Jonson's art of comic characterisation, however, the theory of 'humours' should not be over-worked so as to mean that all his characters are of 'humours' type. Even in the early plays the 'humour' is not simply a type, and in the middle and later plays the 'humour' definition fails to account for the total effect produced. Jonson is also not incapable of producing immortal, individualistic characters like Bobadill and Busy when the occasion demands. In their own way, Jonson's characters are as effective as of any other great dramatists.

In his endeavour to find a proper structure for his comedy, Jonson effects some experiments in his early plays, and ultimately achieves an organic form which has at its base a concern with physical as well as symbolic situations. However indebted is Jonson to the classical and Morality traditions, the form he finally achieves is distinctly his own—'a particular kind by it selfe.' Critics often question whether Jonsonian structure is linear or thematic. But Jonsonian structure can be said to be at once linear and thematic—two levels of meaning being carried on a single action, each complementing the other.

In its constant evolution, Jonson's 'Comedy of Humours' reaches its perfection in *Bartholomew Fair*, 'a new sufficient play.' The play is "new" in its fresh subject-matter, in its scheme as well as in its very tone. The play is "sufficient" in that it is a perfect fulfilment of the "Comedy of Humours." However perfect the other masterpieces are in and by themselves, it is certainly in *Bartholomew Fair* that Jonson's dramatic art reaches its culmination, attaining as it does the acme of perfection.

It is no easy matter to pass an impartial final judgement on the dramatic achievement of Jonson. However, we may say that Jonson, on the whole, did what he had set out to do. He succeeded well in his attempt to make English comedy realistic and purposeful. In each of his plays, he shows a clear understanding of the aims and methods of classical comedy and professedly follows them. In his masterpieces he rather transcends those aims and methods to create a unique and unforgettable comic universe. This is because Jonson's critical theory could not always dictate successful literary practice. Led by his artistic sense, he made departures from his critical tenets now and then. But this does not necessarily mean that his critical utterances were insincere. It only means that his theory was not complete enough to cover all his practices.

There is no point in condemning Jonson for what he never set out to do. He deliberately imposed, though not always bound by them, a great many limitations on his art as a dramatist by his insistence on the preservation of the three classical Unities as well as the Unity of tone, by his advocacy of realism in setting, character, and speech, by his acceptance of the theory of 'humours' as the basis of characterisation, and by his purpose of moral elevation through satire. Hence his so-called deficiencies – exotic locations, a taste for young love, absence of charm and colourful portrayal of characters, the lack of appeal to sentiment or emotion, responsiveness to nature and the vicissitudes of the human lot, as critics generally point out – are not in truth deficiencies at all, but the outcome of a principle of deliberate exclusion.

Nevertheless, the frequent comparison of Jonson with Shakespeare has got in the way of a full appreciation of his success as a practitioner of the 'Comedy of Humours.' He has been, more often than not, compared with Shakespeare invariably to his entire disadvantage. For instance, Hazlitt's famous distinction between the 'natural spring' of Shakespeare's wit and the 'leaden cistern' in which Jonson's is confined and Shakespeare's living men and Jonson's machines 'governed by mere routine, or by the convenience of the poet,' has come to possess an authority which it does not merit at all. This method is essentially unwholesome inasmuch as the schools of art which Shakespeare and Jonson represent are so thoroughly incompatible, although each is master of his chosen type. Though the accident of history placed Jonson in the same period as Shakespeare, Jonson's mode of drama is properly and intentionally different from Shakespeare's. Jonson helps put Shakespeare's achievement into perspective, while Shakespeare's example makes Jonson's work difficult to judge or even to see clearly. One must necessarily grasp this point to begin enjoying Jonson.

It is, therefore, not with Shakespeare that Jonson must be compared, but with Aristophanes, Menander and Terence among the ancients, and among the moderns with Moliére. With his highly stylised and disciplined writing, Jonson is not in the tradition of Chaucer, Shakespeare, Browning and Dylan Thomas, but in the more critical and satirical one of Congreve, Pope, Oscar Wilde, Bernard Shaw, T.S. Eliot, John Osborne and Harold Pinter.

A just appreciation of Jonson's achievement demands from the reader a good knowledge of the age in which he lived and wrote. We must see him as a contemporary unbiased by time. Jonson also requires a careful and close study, and a certain intellectual activity, rather 'intelligent saturation in his work as a whole.' Jonson's greatness as a writer of comedy can be seen only when his dramatic output is considered as a whole. Above all, one requires some notion of the underlying principles of the playwright's art for a full appreciation of his achievement. For, Jonson, the conscious artist, seems to build his theory always a little in advance of his experience, so that the experience is moulded by the theory rather than the other way. The theory, on the whole, was probably beneficial to his practice.

If Shakespeare marked the height to which the drama of the age attained, Jonson exercised the more potent influence on what came after. He was the first to endeavour to relate practice to principle. Naturally enough, he was not only the arbiter of his own age but gave laws which afforded sanction and precedent to generations of successors. The point, however, to be noted is that he enforced rules only after he had convinced himself of their contemporary relevance. Again, his influence was rather intensively provocative than absolute. Furthermore, it was general rather than direct or personal.

The first poet Laureate, a writer of verse, prose, satire and criticism besides being a brilliant playwright, Jonson had much more influence than Shakespeare on the subsequent course of English literature. This is partly due to the fact that Shakespeare's genius, so much in a class of its own, is not amenable to imitation. It is also because Jonson, unlike Shakespeare, was both a theorist and a creative artist. He had clear and definite ideas about the way plays should be written which the both expounded at some length and observed practically.

The influence of Jonson on his age was clearly an influence of restraint. He invited the attention of his age to classical tradition, as its discipline provided for the immediate necessities of the English drama. By his own example he enforced a respect for more orderly and precise craftsmanship. He first showed his age how the rich abundance and variety of incident and character could be secured even under conditions of an art which excluded all aid from legend and romance and from the prodigal use of space and time. He also showed how the jest of comedy could be had without any stirring or sensational plot. Jonson thus set a standard of literary excellence not recognized before his time.

Jonson's comedies were imitated as soon as they appeared. For instance, his *Every Man in His Humour* (1568) was followed by the anonymous play, *Every Woman in Her Humour* (acted by 1600). Beaumont and Fletcher studied in his school as testified by the latter's *The Woman Hater*. In its sinew and restraint Beaumont's blank verse seems to bear an impress of Jonson's. Then, Chapman, Marston and Middleton profited from Jonson's ideal of restraint, of considerate workmanship, and of his constructive originality. Massinger and Shirley owed something to Jonson especially in their shrewd penetrating observation of manners. Of later dramatists, Nathaniel Field, Richard Brome, Randolph, Nabbes, and May appear to have employed Jonson's methods and written plays in his manner. As a matter of fact, all realistic comedy that followed Jonson can be said to owe itself to him in some repsect or other.

Jonson's influence on the non-dramatic literature of his day was, perhaps, even greater. Jonson, who survived Shakespeare for over twenty years, drew about him a school of young poets and playwrights who were 'sealed' of the 'Tribe of Ben.' They affectionately called him 'Father,' and liked to call themselves 'Sons of Ben.' They attempted the drama as well as the lyric, and the occasional verse of their dear master.

It was, however, reserved for the age of Dryden to realise to the full the assimilated classical ideals Jonson had championed. Jonson's 'Comedy of Humours' extended itself into the 'Comedy of Manners.' His satirically heightened picture of contemporary life handled with a restraint and finish survived on the stage after the Restoration in the comedies of Davenant, Dryden, Etherege and Vanbrugh.

Jonson's influence as a dramatist has been felt in the novel as well. Constantly read, his plays seem to have encouraged, in the field of fiction, a study of the absurdities of character and the incongruities of manners. Fielding and Smollett can be said to be conscious of the incentive of Jonson's plays. There is a perceptible trace of Jonson in Dickens, who knew his plays and himself acted Bodadill, not only in the subject-matter but in method of creating character. There are specific resemblances between Zeal-of-the-land Busy and Stiggins. Further, his comic invention is often strikingly Jonsonian in method and effect.

The satirical comedy of Jonson is recreated by Sheridan and Oscar Wilde. Especially characters like Sir Anthony Absolute, Lydia Languish and Sir Lucius O'Trigger of *The Rivals*, Joseph Surface and Charles Surface of *The School for Scandal* very much remind us of Jonsonian types of 'humour' characters.

But the successor who most resembles Jonson is George Bernard Shaw. Jonson's influence is discernible not only in Shaw's preference for lively intellectualized talk over action, or the portrayal of emotion, but in such things as the method of creating characters with an emphasis on the external detail and the phrases of colloquial speech. Besides being most self-conscious artists, both give a full canvas of boldly-drawn images in rapid and interesting movement. Again, both, within definite limitations, have the same certainty of touch and the knack of setting their characters moving with a brilliant liveliness that seldom fails.

Jonson seems to be inseparable from his critical heritage. The student of his works in the late twentieth century, as D.H. Craig, a specialist in Renaissance literary theory, rightly suggests, must still begin with questions which Jonson himself raised and which his contemporaries and his immediate posterity were compelled to answer.

In so far as Jonson is a realist and the motive and interest of his plays social, he may be claimed to be the founder of modern English Comedy. His fine sense of form and love of solid construction, combined with a great vitality and creative vigour give his plays a unique position. The discipline that a thorough assimilation of Jonson's work invariably imposes, is, perhaps, a special need of all times in the realm of drama. What Jonson said of Shakespeare we may as well say of Jonson himself that

> He is not of an age, but for all time.

[illegible] in the subject [illegible]

[illegible]

But the success of the most [illegible]

[illegible]

In [illegible]

[illegible]

Bibliography

Collation of the Ben Jonson Folios. H.L. Ford. London, 1932.
A Concise Bibliography. S.A. Tannenbaum. New York, 1938.
A Bibliography of the English Printed Drama to the Restoration. W.W. Greg. 4 vols. London, 1940-1959.

Collected Plays

Works. Ed. P. Whalley. 7 vols. London, 1756.
The Works of Ben Jonson. Ed. W. Gifford. 9 vols. London, 1816.
The Works of Ben Jonson. (With W. Gifford notes and Memoir). Ed. F. Cunningham. 9 vols. London: Bickers and Son, 1875.
Complete Plays. Ed. F.E. Schelling. 2 vols. London, 1910.
Ben Jonson. Ed. C.H. Herford, Percy and Evelyn Simpson. 11 vols. Oxford, Clarendon Press, 1925-1952.

Selected Plays

Ben Jonson. Ed. B. Nicholson. 3 vols. (The Mermaid Series). London, 1893-1894.
Selected Works. Ed. H. Levin. New York, 1938.
Five Plays. In the World's Classics. London, 1953.
Three Comedies. Ed. Michael Jamieson. (Penguin Books) England, 1966.

Separate Plays

The Case is Altered. Ed. W.E. Selin. New Haven, 1919.
Every Man in His Humour. (The quarto edition) Ed. H.H. Carter. New Haven, 1921.
Every Man in His Humour. Ed. R.S. Knox. London, 1923.
Every Man Out of His Humour. Ed. W.W. Greg and F.P. Wilson. London, 1920.
Cynthia's Revels. Ed. W. Bang and L. Krebs. London, 1908.
Poetaster. Ed. H. De Vocht. London, 1934.
Sejanus. Ed. W.D. Briggs. Boston and London. D.C. Health, 1911.

Volpone. Ed. J.D. Rea. (Yale Studies in English) New Haven, 1919.
Volpone. Ed. David Cook. (A University Paperback Text) London, 1967.
Epicoene. Ed. L.A. Beaurline. London, 1967.
The Alchemist. Ed. F.E. Schelling. London, 1905.
Bartholomew Fair. Ed. E.A. Horsman. London, 1960.
Bartholomew Fair. Ed. Edward B. Partridge. London, 1964.
The Staple of News. Ed. De Winter. (Yale Studies in English) New York, 1905.
The New Inn. Ed. George Tennant. (Yale Studies in English) New York, 1908.
The Magnetic Lady. Ed. Harvey W. Peck. (Yale Studies in English) New York, 1914.
The Sad Shepherd. Ed. W.W. Greg. Louvain, A. Uystpruyst, 1905.

Other Works Consulted

Ascham, R. *The Whole Works*. Ed. J.A. Giles. 4 vols. London, 1865.
Bacon, F. *Essays.* Ed. W.P. Ker. 2 vols. Oxford, 1900.
Beaumont, F. and Fletcher, J. *Works.* Ed. Arnold Glover and A.R. Waller. 10 vols. Cambridge University Press, 1095-12.
Chapman, G. *The Plays and Poems*. Ed. T.M. Parrott. 2 vols. London: Routledge, and New York: Dutton, 1910.
Dekker, T. *Dramatic Works*. Ed. R.H. Shepherd. (Pearson's Reprint) 4 vols. London, 1873.
______. *Non-Dramatic Works of Thomas Dekker*. Ed. A.B. Grosart. 5 vols. London, 1884-86.
______. *Satiromastix.* Ed. J.H. Penniman. Boston, 1913.
Donne, J. *Works*. Ed. H. Alford. 6 vols. London, 1839.
Ford, J. *Works.* Ed. William Gifford. 3 vols. London, 1869.
Gayley, C.M. Ed. *Representative English Comedies*. 3 vols. Macmillan, 1912.
Greene, R. *Life and Complete Works of Robert Greene. Ed. A.B. Grosart. 15 vols. London, 1881-86.*
______. *A Notable Discovery of Coosnage*. Ed. G.B. Harrison. London, 1923.
______. *The Third and Last Part of Cony-Catching*. Ed. G.B. Harrison. London, 1923.
______. *Greene's Groats-Worth of Witte.* Ed. G.B. Harrison. London, 1923.
Hazlitt, W.C. Ed. Dodsley's *Select Collection of Old English Plays*. London, 1874.
Heywood, T. *Dramatic Works.* (Pearson's Reprint) 6 vols. London, 1874.

Kyd, T. *Works.* Ed. F.S. Boas. Oxford, 1901.

Lodge, T. *The Complete Works.* Ed. Edmund Goose. 4 vols. Glasgow, 1883.

Lyly, J. *The Complete Works of John Lyly.* Ed. R. Warwick Bond. 3 vols. Oxford, 1902.

Marlowe, C. *Works.* Ed. R.H. Case. 6 vols. London, 1930-33.

Marston. J. *The Plays.* Ed. H. Harvey Wood. 3 vols. Edinburgh, 1934-39.

Massinger, P. *Plays.* Ed. Gifford. 4 vols. 1805.

Middleton, T. *The Works.* Ed. A.H. Bullen. 8 vols. London, 1885.

Nashe, T. *The Works of Thomas Nashe.* Ed. McKerrow Corr. F.P. Wilson. 5 vols. Oxford, 1958.

______. *The Unfortunate Traveller.* Ed. M. Ayrton. London, 1948.

Plautus, T.M. Trans. Paul Nixon. 5 vols. Cambridge, 1947-53.

Pollard, A.W. Ed. *English Miracle Plays, Moralities, and Interludes.* Oxford, 1954.

Schwickert, H.C. Ed. *Early English Plays.* New York, 1928.

Shakespeare, W. *The Complete Works of Shakespeare.* Ed. Peter Alexander. 1964 edition.

Shaw, G.B. *The Collected Works of Bernard Shaw.* Ed. Ayot St. Lawrence. New York, 1930.

Spenser, E. *Works.* Eds. E.A. Greenlaw, C.G. Osgood, and F.M. Padelford. Baltimore, 1932.

Terentius, A.P. *Comedies.* Trans. J. Sargeaunt. 2 vols. Cambridge, 1947-53.

Tourneur, C. *Works.* Ed. Allardyce Nicoll. London, 1930.

Webster, J. *Complete Works.* Ed. F.L. Lucas. 4 vols. London, 1928.

Reference Works

Abercrombie, L. *The Theory of Poetry.* New York, 1926.

______. "The Function of Poetry in the Drama," *English Critical Essays.* Ed. P.M. Jones. Oxford, 1933.

Alden, R.M. *The Rise of Formal Satire in England under Classical Influence.* Philadelphia, 1899.

Alexander, Margaret. *Shakespeare and His Contemporaries.* London, 1979.

Allen, D.C. "Science and Invention in Greene's Prose," *PMLA*, LIII (1938), 1007-18.

Archer, W. *The Old Drama and the New.* London, 1923.

Armstrong, W.A. "The Audiences of the Elizabethan Private Theatres," *RES*, X (1959), 234-40.

Ashton, J.W. *Types of English Drama.* New York, 1940.

Atkins, J.W.H. *Literary Criticism in Antiquity.* 2 vols. Cambridge, England, 1934.

_____. *English Literary Criticism, The Renascence.* London, 1947.

Baldwin, C.S. *Renaissance Literary Theory and Practice*. New York, 1939.

Baldwin, T.W. *Shakespeare's Five Act Structure.* Urbana, 1944.

Barber, C.L. *Shakespeare's Festive Comedy, A Study of Dramatic Form and its Relation to Social Custom.* Princeton, 1959.

Barker, R. *Thomas Middleton.* London, O.U.P., 1958.

Baskervill, C.R. *The Elizabethan Jig.* New York, 1965.

Battenhouse, R. "Recent Studies in Elizabethan and Jacobean Drama," *SSL*, XII (1972), 392-428.

Bentley, G.E. *Shakespeare and Jonson, Their Reputations in the 17th Century Compared.* 2 vols. Chicago, 1945.

______. *The Development of English Drama*. New York, 1950.

______. *The Jacobean and Caroline Stage*. 7 vols. Oxford, 1941-56.

______. Ed. *The Seventeenth Century Stage, A Collection of Critical Essays.* Chicago and London, 1968.

Bergson, H.L. *An Essay on the Meaning of the Comic.* London, 1911.

Boas, F.S. *An Introduction to Tudor Drama*. Oxford, 1933.

______. *An Introdcution to Stuart Drama.* London, 1946.

______. *Shakespeare and His Predecessors.* London, 1902.

Boughner, D.C. "The Braggart in Italian Renaissance Comedy," *PMLA*, LVIII (1943), 42-83.

Boulton, M. *The Anatomy of Drama*. London, 1960.

Bradbrook, M.C. *Themes and Conventions of Elizabethan Tragedy.* Cambridge, England, 1935.

______. *The Growth and Structure of Elizabethan Comedy.* Chatto and Windus, 1955.

______. *Elizabethan Stage Conditions.* Cambridge, 1962.

Bradely, J.F. and Admas, J.Q. *The Jonson Allusion-Book.* New Haven, 1922.

Brooke, C.F.T. *Tudor Drama.* Boston, 1911.

Brooks, H.F. *Chaucer's Pilgrims, The Artistic Order of the Portraits in the Prologue.* London, 1962.

______. "Marlowe and Early Shakespeare," *Christopher Marlowe* (Mermaid Critical Commentaries). London, 1968.

______. "The Name of Action in *Komos.*"

Brown, J.R. *Shakespeare and his Comedies.* London, 1957.

______. *Shakespeare's Plays in Performance.* London, 1966.

______. *Effective Theatre. London,* 1969.

______. *Shakespeare's Dramatic Style.* London, 1970.

Bush, D. *English Literature in the Early Seventeenth Century* (1600-1660).

Oxford, 1952.

Butcher, S.A. *Aristotle's Theory of Poetry and Fine Art.* (4th Ed.) New York, 1951.

Buxton, J. *Elizabethan Taste.* London, 1963.

Caputi, A. *John Marston, Satirist.* Cornell, 1961.

Cartwright, R. *Shakespeare and Ben Jonson*. London, 1864.

Chambers, E.K. *The Elizabethan Stage.* 4 vols. Oxford, England, 1923.

______. *The Medieval Stage*. 2 vols. Oxford, 1903.

Chambers, R.W. *Man's Unconquerable Mind*. London, 1939.

Chandler, F.W. *The Literature of Roguery.* London, 1909.

Chatterji, R. "Theme, Imagery and Unity in *A Chaste Maid in Cheapside*," *Renaissance Drama,* VIII (1965), 105-26.

Coghill, N. "The Basis of Shakespearian Comedy," *ES* (1950), 1-28.

Coleridge, S.T. *Literary Remains.* London, 1886.

Craig, H. *English Religious Drama.* Oxford, 1955.

Crane, M. *Shakespeare's Prose.* Chicago, 1951.

Cruickshank, A.H. *Philip Massinger.* Oxford, Blackwell, 1920.

Curry, W.C. *Chaucer and the Mediaeval Science.* New York, 1926.

Daiches, D. *Critical Approaches to Literature*. London, 1956.

Dudden, F.H. *Henry Fielding*, 2 vols. Oxford, 1952.

Dunn, T.A. *Philip Massinger, The Man and the Playwright*. Edinburgh, 1957.

Eliot. T.S. *Selected Essays.* London, 1953.

______. *Elizabethan Dramatists.* London, 1962.

Ellis-Fermor, U. *The Jacobean Drama*. London, 1936.

______. *The Frontiers of Drama*. London, 1948.

Enright, D.J. and Chickera, E.D. *English Critical Texts*. London, 1962.

Evans, B.I. *The Language of Shakespeare's Plays.* London, 1952.

Fleay, F.G. *A Biographical Chronicle of The English Drama* 1559-1642. London, 1891.

Foakes, R.A. and Ricket, R.T. Ed. *Henslowe's Diary.* Cambridge, 1961.

Ford, B. Ed. *The Age of Shakespeare.* (The Pelican Guide to English Literature) Vol. 2. London, 1964.

Freytag, G. *Technique of the Drama*. Trans. Elias MacEwan. Chicago, 1894.

Frye. N. *The Anatomy of Criticism.* Princeton, 1957.

Gibbons, B. *Jacobean City Comedy, A Study of Satiric Plays by Jonson, Marston and Middleton.* London, 1968.

Gilbert, A.H. Ed. *Literary Criticism, Plato to Dryden.* New York, 1940.

Gosson, S. *The School of Abuse.* Ed. Edward Arber. London, 1869.

Granville-Barker, H. *On Dramatic Method.* London, 1931.

Gregg, K.L. *Thomas Dekker, A Study in Economic and Social Backgrounds*. Seattle, 1924.

Greig, J.Y.T. *The Psychology of Laughter and Comedy.* London, N.Y, 1923.

Grierson, J.C.H. *Cross Currents in English Literature of the 17th Century.* London, 1951.

Jacquot, J. *George Chapman.* Paris, 1951.

Jonas, L. *The Divine Science.* New York, 1940.

Jordan, J.C. *Robert Greene.* New York, 1915.

Judges, A.V. *The Elizabethan Underworld.* London, 1930.

Jung, C.G. *Modern Man in Search of a Soul*. London, 1933.

Haller, W. *The Rise of Puritanism.* New York, 1937.

Harrison, G.B. *Elizabethan Journals.* 1591-1603. 3 vols. 1928.

Hazlitt, W. *Lectures on the English Comic Writers.* London, 1819.

Herford, C.H. *Studies in the Literary Relationships of England and Germany in the Sixteenth Century.* Cambridge, 1886.

Hunt, M.L. *Thomas Dekker.* New York, 1911.

Kaufmann, R.J. Ed. *Elizabethan Drama, Modern Essays in Criticism.* New York, 1961.

Kelley, F. *The Jacobeans at Home.* London, 1962.

Kenner, H. "Art in a Closed Field," *VQR*, XXXVIII (1962), 597-613.

Kernan, A. *The Cankered Muse.* New Haven, 1959.

Kittredge, G.L. *Witchcraft in Old and New England.* Cambridge, 1929.

Klein, D. *Literary Criticism from the Elizabethan Dramatists*. New York, 1910.

Knappen, M.M. *Tudor Puritanism, A Chapter in the History of Idealism.* Chicago, 1939.

Knights, L.C. *Drama and Society in the Age of Jonson.* London, 1937.

Knight, W.G. *The Golden Labyrinth*. London, 1962.

Lorand, S. *Psychoanalysis Today.* London, 1948.

Lynch, K.M. *The Social Mode of Restoration Comedy.* New York and London, 1926.

Madden, D.H. *The Diary of Master William Silence, A Study of Shakespeare and of Elizabethan Sport.* Green Wood Press, 1969.

McCarthy, D. *Humanities.* London, 1953.

Merchant, W.M. "Marlowe the Orthodox," *Christopher Marlowe* (Mermaid Critical Commentaries). London, 1968.

Meredith, G. *An Essay on Comedy.* New York, 1897.

Muncaster, M. "The Use of Prose in Elizabethan Drama," *MLR*, XIV (1919), 10-15.

Neilson, W.A. *The Chief Elizabethan Dramatists.* Boston, 1911.

Nicoll, A. *The Theory of Drama.* London, 1931.

______. *World Drama*. New York, 1950.

______. *British Drama*. Harrap, 1961.

Ornstein, R. *The Moral Vision of Jacobean Tragedy*. Madison, 1960.

Parrott, T.M. and Ball, R. *A Short View of Elizabethan Drama*. New York, 1943.

Penniman, J.H. *The War of the Theatres*. Boston, 1897.

Peter, J. *Complaint and Satire in Early English Literature*. Oxford, 1956.

Potts, L.J. *Comedy*. London, 1949.

Raleigh, W. *Shakespeare*. London, 1907.

Rama Sarma, M.V. *Heywood, A Prose Shakespeare*. Glasgow and London, 1962.

Riviere, J. Trans. *Collected Papers*. London, 1950.

Rossiter, A.P. *English Drama from Early Times to the Elizabethans*. London, 1950.

Rowse, A.L. *The England of Elizabeth*. London, 1951.

Rulfs, D.J. "Reception of the Elizabethan Playwrights on the London Stage 1776-1883," *SP*, XLVI (1949), 54-69.

Saintsbury, G. *History of Criticism*. 3 vols. 1900-1904.

______. Ed. *Elizabethan and Jacobean Pamphlets*. London, 1892.

Schelling, F.E. *Elizabethan Drama*, 2 vols. Coultable, 1908.

______. *Foreign Influences in Elizabethan Plays*. New York, London, 1923.

Schlegel, A.W. *A Course of Lectures on Dramatic Art and Literature*. London, 1871.

Schoenbaum, S. *Internal Evidence and Elizabethan Dramatic Authorship*. London, 1966.

Scott-James, R.A. *The Making of English Literature*. London, 1928.

Simpson, P. *Studies in Elizabethan Drama*. Oxford, 1955.

Sisson, C.J. *Thomas Lodge and Other Elizabethans*. Harvard, 1933.

Smith, G. Ed. *Elizabethan Critical Essays*. 2 vols. Oxford, 1904.

Spingarn, J.E. *History of Literary Criticism in the Renascence*. New York, 1899.

Stoll, E.E. *Poets and Playwrights*. Minneapolis, 1930.

Stonex, A.B. "The Usurer in Elizabethan Drama," *PMLA* (1916), 190-210.

Stubbes, P. *Anatomy of the Abuses in England in Shakespeare's Youth* (1583). London, 1882.

Styan, J.L. *The Elements of Drama*. Cambridge, England, 1960.

Thorndike, A. *English Comedy*. New York, 1929.

Thorp, W. *The Triumph of Realism in Elizabethan Drama* 1558-1642. Princeton Studies in English, III, 1928.

Tillyard, E.M.W. *Elizabethan World Picture*. Chatto and Windus, 1943.

______. *The English Renaissance, Fact or Fiction*. London, 1952.

Trevelyan, G.M. *England Under the Stuarts.* Mehuen, 1904.

______. *English Social History.* London, N.Y., Tornoto, 1942.

Van Dam, B.A.P. *The Authority of Ben Jonson Folio of* 1616. (Anglia 26), 1903.

Vandiver, Jr. E.P. "The Elizabethan Dramatic Parasite," *SP*, XXXII (1935), 411-27.

Velte, M. *The Bourgeois Elements in the Dramas of Thomas Heywood.* Princeton, 1922.

Walker, H. *English Satire and Satirists*. London, 1928.

Ward, A.W. *A History of English Dramatic Literature*. 3 vols. London, 1899.

Wells, H.W. *Elizabethan and Jacobean Playwrights.* New York, 1939.

Willey, B. *The Seventeenth Century Background.* Oxford, 1946.

Wilson, F.P. *Elizabethan and Jacobean.* Oxford, 1975.

Wilson, J.D. *Life in Shakespeare's England*. (Pelican Books) 1944.

Wilson, M. *Sir Philip Sidney.* London, 1931.

Wilson, T. *Discourses Upon Usury*. London, 1934.

Wimsatt, Jr., W.K. and Brooks, C. *Literary Criticism, A Short History.* Indian Ed. 1964.

Wright, C.T. "Some Conventions Regarding the Usurer in Elizabethan Literature," *SP*, XXXI (1934), 176-97.

______. "The Usurer's Sin in Elizabethan Literature," *SP*, XXV (1938), 178-94.

Wright, L.B. *Middle-Class Culture in Elizabethan England.* Folger Shakespeare Library, 1958.

Biographical and Critical Studies on Ben Jonson

Books

Bamborough, J.B. *Ben Jonson.* London, 1959.

______. *Ben Jonson*. London, 1970.

Barish, J.A. *Ben Jonson and the Language of Prose Comedy.* Cambridge: Harvard University Press, 1960.

______. Ed. *Ben Jonson, A Collection of Critical Essays.* (Twentieth Century Views) NJ: Prentice Hall, 1963.

Barton, Anne. *Ben Jonson, Dramatist.* New York: Cambridge University Press, 1984.

Baskervill, C.R. *English Elements in Jonson's Early Comedy.* Austin: University of Texas Press, 1911.

Baum, H.W. *The Satiric and the Didactic in Ben Jonson's Comedy.* Chapel Hill, University of North Carolina Press, 1947.

Baurline, L.A. *Jonson and Elizabethan Comedy*. San Marino, 1978.
Blissett, W., Patrick J. and Van Fossen, R. Eds. *A Celebration of Ben Jonson*. Toronto, 1973.
Brock, D.H. *A Ben Jonson Companion*. Harvester Press, 1983.
Bryant, J.A. *Ben Jonson: The Compassionate Satirist*. Athens: Georgia, 1972.
Boughner, D.C. *The Devil's Disciple*. New York, 1968.
Campbell, O.J. *Comicall Satyre and Shakespeare's "Trolilus and Cressida."* San Marino, The Huntington Library, 1938.
Castelain, M. *Ben Jonson,* L'Homme et l'oeuvre. Paris: Librarie Hachette et cie, 1907.
Cave, Richard Allen. *Ben Jonson*. London, Macmillan, 1991.
Champion, L. *Ben Jonson's Dotages*. Lexington: Mass., 1967.
Chan Mary E. *Music in the Theatre of Ben Jonson*. Oxford: Clarendon Press, 1980.
Chute, M. *Ben Jonson of Westminster*. New York: Dutton, 1953.
Craig, D.H. Ed. *Ben Jonson, The Critical Heritage*. London and New York: Routledge, 1990.
Dessen, A.C. *Jonson's Moral Comedy*. Evanston, 1971.
Donaldson, Ian *The World Upside Down*, Oxford: Clarendon Press, 1970.
Doran, M. *Endeavors of Art*. Madison, University of Wisconsin Press, 1954.
Duncan, D. *Ben Jonson and the Lucianic Tradition*. Cambridge, 1979.
Dunn, E.C. *Ben Jonson's Art*. Northampton, Mass.: Smith College, 1925.
Eliot, T.S. "*Ben Jonson*" in *Selected Essays*. London: Faber, 1932.
Enck, J.J. *Jonson and the Comic Truth*. Madison: University of Wisconsin Press, 1979.
Evans, W.M. *Ben Jonson and the Elizabethan Music*. New York, 1965.
Farley-Hills, David "Ben Jonson," *Jacobean Drama*. London: Macmillan Press, 1988.
Gibbons, B. *Jacobean City Comedy, A Study of Satiric Plays by Jonson, Marston and Middleton*. London, 1968.
Gilbert, A.H. *The Symbolic Persons in the Mosques of Ben Jonson*. New York, 1965.
Grene, Nicholas. *Shakespeare, Jonson and Moliere: The Comic Truth*. London: Macmillan, 1980.
Gun, Coburn. *The Aritstophanic Comedies of Ben Jonson*. The Hague, Mouton, 1969.
Jackson, G.B. *Vision and Judgment in Ben Jonson's Drama*. New Haven and London, 1968.
Johnston, G.B. *Ben Jonson, Poet*. 1945.
Kerr, M. *Influence of Ben Jonson on English Comedy*. Philadelphia, 1912.

Knights, L.C. *Drama and Society in the Age of Jonson.* London: Chatto and Windus, 1937.

Knoll, R.E. *Ben Jonson's Plays, An Introduction.* Lincoln, Nebr. , 1964.

Leggatt, A. *Ben Jonson: His Vision and His Art.* London and New York: Methuen, 1981.

Le Luna, B.N. *Jonsonian Romish Plot.* Oxford, 1967.

Linklater, E. *Ben Jonson and King James.* London, 1931.

Mc Euen, K. *Classical Influence Upon the Tribe of Ben.*

Miles, Rosalind. *Ben Jonson, His Craft and Art.* London and New York: Routledge, 1990.

Nichols, J.G. *The Poetry of Ben Jonson.* London, 1969.

Noyes, R.G. *Ben Jonson on the English Stage 1660-1776.* Harvard University Press, 1935.

Orgel, S. *The Jonsonian Masque.* Cambridge, Mass., 1968.

Palmer, J. *Ben Jonson.* New York: The Viking Press, 1934.

Parfitt, George. *Ben Jonson, Public Poet and Private Man.* London: J.M. Dent, 1976.

Partridge, A.C. *The Accidence of Jonson's Plays, Masques and Entertainments.* Cambridge, 1953.

Partridge, E.B. *The Broken Compass.* London: Chatto and Windus, 1958.

Peterson, R.S. *Imitation and Praise in the Poems of Ben Jonson.* New Haven and London, 1981.

______. *Studies in the Syntax of Jonson's Plays.* Cambridge, 1953.

Sackton, A.H. *Rhetoric as a Dramatic Language in Ben Jonson.* New York: Columbia University Press, 1948.

Savage, J.E. *Ben Jonson's Basic Characters.* Mississippi, 1973.

Small, R.A. *The Stage Quarrel between Ben Jonson and the Socalled Poetasters.* Breslau, M. and H. Marcus, 1899.

Smith, G. *Ben Jonson.* London: Macmillan, 1919.

Summers, Claude J. and Ted-Larry Pebworth. *Ben Jonson.* Boston: Twayne, 1979.

Swinburne, A.C. *A Study of Ben Jonson.* London: Chatto and Windus, 1889.

Symonds, J.A. *Ben Jonson.* London: Longmans Green, 1986.

Thayer, C.G. *Ben Jonson, Studies in the Plays.* University of Oklahoma, Norman, 1963.

Townsend, F.L. *Apologie for "Bartholomew Fayre," The Art of Jonson's Comedies.* New York, 1947.

Trimpi, W. *Ben Jonson's Poems, A Study of the Plain Style.* 1962.

Wheeler, W.C. *Classical Mythology in the Plays, Masques, and Poems of Ben Jonson.* Princeton University Press, 1938.

Womack, Peter. *Ben Jonson.* Oxford: Basil Blackwell, 1986.

Woodbridge, E. *Studies in Jonson's Comedy.* (Yale Studies in English, vol. V) Boston and New York: Lamson, Wolffe, 1898.

Articles

Adams, Jr., J.Q. "The Source of Jonson's *Volpone,*" *MP*, II (1904-05), 289-300.

Bacon, W.A. "The Magnetic Field, The Structure of Jonson's Comedies," *HLQ*, XIX (1955), 121-53.

Barish, J.A. "*Bartholomew Fair* and its Puppets," *MLQ*, XX (1959), 3-17.

______. "The Double Plot of *Volpone*," *MP*, LI (1953), 83-92.

______. "Baroque Prose in the Theatre, Ben Jonson," *PMLA*, LXXIII (1958), 184-95.

______. "Ovid, Juvenal, and *The Silent Woman*," *PMLA*, LXXI (1956), 213-24.

Baskervill C.R. "Some Parallels to *Bartholomew Fair*," *MP*, VI (1908-09), 109-28.

Beaurline, L.A. "Ben Jonson and the Illusion of Completeness," *PMLA*, 84 (January 1969), 51-59.

Berringer, R.W. "Jonson's *Cynthia's Revels* and the War of the Theatres," *PQ*, XXII (1943), 1-22.

Boughner, D.C. "Jonsonian Structure in *The Tempest*," *SQ*, XXI (Winter 1970), 3-10.

Bowers, F.T. "Dekker and Jonson," *TLS* (12 Sept. 1936).

Brown, H.B. "Jonson and Rabelais," *MLN*, XLIV (1929), 6-12.

Bryant, J.A. "*Catiline* and the Nature of Jonson's Tragic Fable," *PMLA*, LXIX (1954), 265-77.

______. "The Significance of Ben Jonson's First Requirement for Tragedy: Truth of Argument," *SP*, XLIX (1952), 195-212.

______. "Jonson's Revision of *Every Man in His Humour,*" *SP*, LIX (1962).

Cubeta, P.M. "A Celebration of Charis: An Evaluation of Jonsonian Poetic Strategy," *ELH*, XXV (Sept. 1958).

Dessen, A.C, "*Volpone* and the Late Morality Tradition," *MLQ*, XXV (1964), 383-99.

Ducean, H.D. "*The Alchemist* and the Literature of Alchemy," *PMLA*, LXI (1946), 699-710.

Duffy, E.M.T. "Ben Jonson's Debt to Renaissance Scholarship in *Sejanus* and *Catiline,*" *MLR*, XLII (1947), 24-30.

Duncan, D. "A Guide to *The New Inn,*" *EC*, XX (July 1970), 311-26.

Freehafer, J. "Loenard Digges, Ben Jonson and Beginning of Shakespeare Worship," *SQ*, XXI (Winter 1970), 63-76.

Gilbert, A.H. "The Eavesdroppers in Jonson's *Sejanus*," *MLN*, LXIX (1954), 164-66.

______. "The Poet's Morals in Jonson's *Poetaster*," *MLQ*, XII (1951), 13-19.

______. "The Function of the Masques in *Cynthia's Revels*," *PQ*, XXII (1943), 211-30.

______. "The Italian Names in *Every Man Out of His Humour*," *SP*, XLIV (1947), 195-208.

Goldberg, S.L. "Folly into Crime, The Catastrophe of *Volpone*," *MLQ*, XX (1959), 233-42.

Goodman, P. *The Structure of Literature.* Chicago: University Press, 1954. (On the Structure of *The Alchemist*, 82-100).

Gray, H.D. "The Chamberlain's Men and the *Poetaster*," *MLR*, XLLII (1947), 173-79.

Greg, S.W.W. "Shakespeare and Jonson," *RES*, XXII (1946).

Hallet, C.A. "The Satanic Nature of *Volpone*," *PQ*, XLIX (Jan. 1970), 41-55.

Hayes, H.R "Satire and Identification: An Introduction to Ben Jonson," *Kenyan Review*, XIX (1957), 267-83.

Heffner, Jr., R.L. "Unifying Symbols in the Comedy of Ben Jonson." *Ben Jonson: A Collection of Critical Essays.* Ed. J.A. Barish.

Hill, W.S. "Biography, Autobiography, and *Volpone*," *SEL*, XII (1972), 310-28.

Holt, L.H. "Notes on Ben Jonson's *Volpone*," *MLN*, XX (1905).

Honing, E. "*Sejanus* and *Coriolanus:* A Study in Alienation," *MLQ*, XII (1951), 407-21.

Huxley, A. "Ben Jonson," *On the Margin.* London, 1923.

Kay, W.D. "The Shaping of Ben Jonson's Career: A Reexamination of Facts and Problems," *MP*, 67 (Feb. 1970), 224-37.

Kernan, A. *The Cankered Muse.* New Haven: Yale University Press, 1959.

Kifer, D.R. "*The Staple of News,* Jonson's Festive Comedy," *SEL*, XII (1972), 329-44.

King, A.H. "The Language of Satirized Characters in *Poetaster:* A Socio-Stylistic Analysis, 1597-1602." ("Lund Studies in English," vol. X) Lund, C.W.K. Gleerup, 1941.

Knowlton, E.C. "The Plots of Ben Jonson," *MLN,* XLIV (1929), 86-92.

Leavis, F.R. "English Poetry in the Seventeenth Century," *Scrutiny*, IV (1935), 236-56.

Levin, B.R. "The Structure of *Bartholomew Fair,*" *PMLA*, 80 (1965), 172-79.

Levin, H. "Jonson's Metempsychosis," *PQ*, XLIV (1965), 445-53.

Levin, L.L. "Clement Justice in *Every Man in His Humour,*" *SEL*, XII

(1972), 292-307.
Marotti, A.F. "All About Jonson's Poetry," *ELH,* 39 (1972), 208-37.
Mc Cullen, K.A. "Jonson and Juvenal," *RES*, XXI (1945), 92-104.
Mc Galliard, J.C. "Chaucerian Comedy: *The Merchant's Tale,* Jonson and Moliere," *PQ*, XXV (1946), 343-70.
Nash, R. "Ben Jonson's Tragic Poems," *SP*, LV (1947), 26-40.
______. "The Parting Scene in Jonson's *Poetaster*," *PQ*, XXI (1952), 54-62.
Parfitt, G.A.E. "The Poetry of Ben Jonson," *EC*, XVIII (1968).
Partridge, E.B. "The Allusiveness of *Epicoene*," *ELH*, XXII (1955), 93-107.
______. "The Symbolism of Clothes in Jonson's Last Plays," *JEGR*, LVI (1957), 396-409.
Perkinson, R.H. "*Volpone* and the Reputation of Venetian Justice," *MLR*, XXXV (1940), 11-18.
Perry, W. "Influence of Ben Jonson on Nathaniel Field," *SP*, XLIII (1946), 482-95.
Potts, A.F. "*Cynthia's Revels*, *Poetaster*, and *Troilus and Cressida*," *SP*, V (1954), 297-302.
Putney, R. "Jonson's Poetic Comedy," *PQ*, XLI (1962), 188-204.
Redwine, Jr., J.D. "Beyond Psychology: The Moral Basis of Jonson's Theory of Humour Characterization," *ELH*, XXVIII (1961), 316-24.
Rickes, C. "*Sejanus* and Dismemberment," *MLN*, LXXVI (1961), 301-8.
Robinson, J. "*Bartholomew Fair*: Comedy of Vapors," *SEL*, I (1961), 65-80.
Schelling, F.E. "Ben Jonson and the Classical School," *PMLA*, XII (1898), 221-49.
Schere, D.A. "Jonson's *Volpone* and Traditional Fox Lore," *RES* (1950), 242-44.
Simpson, P. "The Art of Ben Jonson," *ES*, XXX (1944), 35-49.
Slights, W.W.E. "*Epicoene* and the Prose Paradox," *PQ*, XLIX (April 1970), 178-87.
Snuggs, H.L. "The Comic Humours, A New Interpretation" *PMLA*, LXII (1947), 114-22.
______. "The Source of Jonson's Definition of Comedy," *MLN,* LXX (1950), 543-44.
Spingarn, J.E. "The Source of Jonson's *Discoveries*," *MP*, II (1905), 451-60.
Stoll, E.E. "Review of *The Old Drama and the New,*" *MLR*, XX (1925), 147-57.
Stonex, A.B. "The Source of Jonson's *The Staple of News*," *PMLA*, XXX (1915), 821-30.

Talbert, E.B. "The Classical Mythology and the Structure of *Cynthia's Revels*," *PQ*, XXII (1943), 193-210.

______. "New Light on Ben Jonson's Workmanship," *SP*, XL (1943), 154-85.

______. "The Purpose and Technique of Jonson's *Poetaster*," *SP*, XLII (1945), 225-52.

Waith, E.M. "The Poet's Morals in Jonson's *Poetaster,*" *MLQ*, XII (1951), 13-19.

______. "The Staging of *Bartholomew Fair*," *SEL*, II (1962), 181-95.

Weld, J.S. "Christian Comedy: *Volpone,*" *SP*, LI (1954), 172-93.

Index